OXFORD
SLAVONIC PAPERS

Edited by

ROBERT AUTY   J. L. I. FENNELL

and

I. P. FOOTE

General Editor

NEW SERIES

VOLUME XI

OXFORD

AT THE CLARENDON PRESS

1978

Oxford University Press, Walton Street, Oxford OX2 6DP

OXFORD LONDON GLASGOW
NEW YORK TORONTO MELBOURNE WELLINGTON
KUALA LUMPUR SINGAPORE JAKARTA HONG KONG TOKYO
DELHI BOMBAY CALCUTTA MADRAS KARACHI
IBADAN NAIROBI DAR ES SALAAM CAPE TOWN

ISBN 0 19 815653 7

© *Oxford University Press 1978*

*Printed in Great Britain
at the University Press, Oxford
by Vivian Ridler
Printer to the University*

THE editorial policy of the New Series of *Oxford Slavonic Papers* in general follows that of the original series, thirteen volumes of which appeared between the years 1950 and 1967 under the editorship of Professor S. Konovalov (volumes 11–13 edited jointly with Mr. J. S. G. Simmons, who also acted as General Editor of the New Series, volumes 1 to 4). It is devoted to the publication of original contributions and documents relating to the languages, literatures, culture, and history of Russia and the other Slavonic countries, and appears annually towards the end of the year. Reviews of individual books are not normally included, but bibliographical and review articles are published from time to time.

The British System of Cyrillic transliteration (British Standard 2979: 1958) has been adopted, omitting diacritics and using -y to express -й, -ий, -ий, and -ый at the end of proper names, e.g. Sergey, Dostoevsky, Bely, Grozny. For philological work the International System (ISO R/9) is used.

ROBERT AUTY
J. L. I. FENNELL
I. P. FOOTE

The Queen's College, Oxford

WITH deep regret we record the death of Robert Auty on 18 August 1978.

J. L. I. F.
I. P. F.

CONTENTS

REMARQUES SUR LA VALEUR DU TERME 'TSAR'
APPLIQUÉ AUX PRINCES RUSSES AVANT LE MILIEU
DU XVᵉ SIÈCLE   1

By WLADIMIR VODOFF, *Directeur d'études à l'École pratique des Hautes Études, Paris*

OSIP NEPEA AND THE OPENING OF ANGLO-RUSSIAN
COMMERCIAL RELATIONS   42

By SAMUEL H. BARON, *Professor of History, University of North Carolina, Chapel Hill*

MUSIC IN SIXTEENTH-CENTURY MOLDAVIA: NEW
EVIDENCE   64

By A. E. PENNINGTON, *Fellow of Lady Margaret Hall, Oxford*
Plates I–II

N. I. KOSTOMAROV AND THE ORIGINS OF THE
VESTNIK EVROPY CIRCLE   84

By ALEXIS E. POGORELSKIN, *Rhodes Visiting Fellow, St. Hilda's College, Oxford*

THE TREE-STUMP AND THE HORSE: THE POETRY
OF ALEXANDER KUSIKOV   101

By GORDON MCVAY, *School of European Studies, University of East Anglia*

SIXTEENTH-CENTURY CROATIAN GLAGOLITIC
BOOKS IN THE BODLEIAN LIBRARY   132

By ROBERT AUTY, *Professor of Comparative Slavonic Philology, University of Oxford*
Plates I–II

Remarques sur la valeur du terme 'tsar' appliqué aux princes russes avant le milieu du xve siècle

By WLADIMIR VODOFF

LA valeur du substantif 'tsar' (*car'* ou *cěsar'* en translittération) est bien connue dans l'histoire médiévale des Slaves méridionaux, Bulgares et Serbes, grâce à de nombreux travaux, en particulier ceux de K. Jireček, G. Ostrogorsky, Fr. Dölger et des historiens bulgares contemporains.[1] On ne peut en dire autant pour l'histoire des Slaves orientaux du xie au milieu du xve siècle: la rareté de l'emploi du mot *car'*, dans les sources médiévales, pour désigner un prince russe rend délicate la définition de sa valeur exacte et explique la variété des conclusions auxquelles ont abouti différents savants.

Il y a déjà plus d'un siècle, I. I. Sreznevskij, commentant le colophon de l'Évangéliaire du prince de Kiev Mstislav (1125-32), où celui-ci est qualifié de *car'*, estimait que ce vocable ne pouvait désigner qu' 'un souverain indépendant' (*vlastelin nezavisimyj*) et lui attribuait ainsi une valeur politique indéniable.[2] Cette valeur a été vigoureusement soulignée, beaucoup plus récemment, par B. A. Rybakov qui, en se fondant sur une inscription de la cathédrale Sainte-Sophie de Kiev où Jaroslav le Sage (†1054) est appelé *car'* et sur plusieurs passages de la Chronique hypatienne où ce même titre est décerné à des princes de Kiev du xiie siècle, a conclu que Jaroslav 'étant devenu, après la mort de Mstislav de Černigov, "autocrate dans tout le pays russe" (1036), prit le titre impérial exprimé non plus seulement par le terme oriental *kagan*, mais également par le mot *car'* qui plaçait le grand-prince de la Russie au même rang que l'empereur de Byzance.'[3] Cette thèse trouve

---

[1] K. Jireček, 'Staat und Gesellschaft im mittelalterlichen Serbien', *Denkschriften der Kaiserlichen Akademie der Wissenschaften in Wien, Philosophisch-historische Klasse*, lvi (2) (1912), 1-23; G. Ostrogorsky, 'Avtokrator i Samodržac: Prilog za istoriju vladalačke titulature u Vizantiji i u južnih Slovena', *Glas Srpske Kraljevske Akademije*, clxiv, drugi razred, 84 (1935), 121-60; Fr. Dölger, 'Bulgarisches Zartum und byzantinisches Kaisertum', in Fr. Dölger, *Byzanz und die europäische Staatenwelt* (Ettal, 1953), 140-58; et V. Tăpkova-Zaimova, 'L'idée impériale à Byzance et la tradition étatique bulgare', *Byzantina*, iii (1971), 287-95. Voir également une mise au point de G. Stökl, 'Die Begriffe Reich, Herrschaft und Staat bei den orthodoxen Slawen', *Saeculum*, v (1954), 109-10.

[2] I. I. Sreznevskij, *Drevnie pamjatniki russkogo pis'ma i jazyka (X–XIV vv.)*, 2ème éd. (Spb., 1882), col. 52.

[3] B. A. Rybakov, *Russkie datirovannye nadpisi XI–XIV vv.* (Archeologija SSSR, Svod istoričeskich istočnikov, E 1-44) (M., 1964), 14-16; il faut remarquer ici que M. D. Priselkov, dans *Istorija russkogo letopisanija* (L., 1940), auquel renvoie B. A. Rybakov (op. cit., 14, n. 4) pour étayer sa thèse, parle certes de 'l'instauration en Russie du pouvoir impérial en 1037'

un écho, un peu affaibli il est vrai, dans une étude de T. Wasilewski, pour lequel les deux principaux témoignages qui viennent d'être mentionnés (l'Évangéliaire de Mstislav et l'inscription de Sainte-Sophie) signifient que 'les souverains de Kiev... étaient appelés empereurs par les Russes persuadés de leur souveraineté, ainsi que du fait que seul un empereur était entièrement souverain'.[4] Le point de vue de B. A. Rybakov est également repris dans l'étude lexicologique d'A. S. L'vov;[5] on le retrouve, enfin, sous la plume de Ja. N. Ščapov qui, toutefois, en citant l'exemple d'un prince de Smolensk qualifié de *car'*, a fait remarquer que ce titre ne semblait pas avoir été exclusivement réservé aux souverains de Kiev.[6]

A l'inverse, M. A. D'jakonov, dans son livre bien connu sur le pouvoir des princes de Moscou, ne faisait partir l'usage du terme *car'* appliqué à des princes russes que du règne de Vasilij II l'Aveugle (1425–62).[7] Ce point de vue fut critiqué par A. I. Sobolevskij qui releva plusieurs exemples nouveaux dans le Dit (*Skazanie*) sur le martyre des princes Boris et Gleb, dans le colophon d'un manuscrit copié au XIIIᵉ siècle en Volhynie et dans le Panégyrique d'Ivan Kalita de Moscou (†1340); il en a conclu que l'attribution du titre de *car'* à des princes russes était attestée avant le XVᵉ siècle, mais restait exceptionnelle, sans avoir cherché à préciser les conditions dans lesquelles ce terme pouvait être employé.[8] Une opinion très voisine avait été formulée par V. O. Ključevskij dans son cours de terminologie historique russe professé en 1884–5, mais publié seulement en 1959: 'on appelait, dans l'ancienne Russie, parfois notre prince *car'*, mais ce n'était qu'un insigne honorifique particulier; tel n'était pas le titre officiel de tous les princes de Kiev.'[9] De nos jours, H. Schaeder dénie au terme *car'* dans la Russie médiévale 'toute signification véritablement institutionnelle' (*keine strengere staatsrechtliche Bedeutung*).[10]

(p. 81), mais il fait allusion là au pouvoir de l'empereur byzantin, qui, selon la thèse erronée d'A. A. Šachmatov (voir ibid. 26), se serait étendu à la Russie de Kiev à la suite de la nomination du premier métropolite grec, et non pas à la création d'un quelconque pouvoir impérial autochtone.

[4] T. Wasilewski, 'La place de l'État russe dans le monde byzantin pendant le haut Moyen Âge', *Acta Poloniae historica*, xxii (1970), 47.

[5] A. S. L'vov, *Leksika 'Povesti vremennych let'* (M., 1975), 200.

[6] Ja. N. Ščapov, 'Pochvala knjazju Rostislavu Mstislaviču kak pamjatnik literatury Smolenska XII v.', *Trudy Otdela drevnerusskoj literatury* (abr. *TODRL*), xxviii (1974), 53, n. 21 (signalons que le texte sur David Rostislavič se trouve dans la Chronique hypatienne, cf. n. 65, et non dans la Laurentienne, comme un lapsus l'a fait écrire à l'Auteur).

[7] M. A. D'jakonov, *Vlast' moskovskich gosudarej: očerki iz istorii političeskich idej Drevnej Rusi* (Spb., 1889), 58. De nos jours, l'emploi du terme *car'* en Russie avant le début de l'époque moderne est également passé sous silence par G. Stökl, op. cit. (n. 1).

[8] A. I. Sobolevskij, 'Archeologičeskie zametki, 6, Car'', *Čtenija v Istoričeskom obščestve Nestora letopisca*, vi (1892), otdel II, 7–9.

[9] V. O. Ključevskij, 'Terminologija russkoj istorii', dans V. O. Ključevskij, *Sočinenija*, vi (M., 1959), 138.

[10] H. Schaeder, *Moskau das Dritte Rom*, 2ᵉᵐᵉ éd. (Darmstadt, 1957), 45, n. 3.

Un point de vue original avait été exprimé par V. S. Ikonnikov qui situait l'usage du terme *car'* à partir du règne, à Kiev, de Vladimir Monomaque (1113-25) et le liait à l'envoi d'une couronne au prince russe par l'empereur Alexis I Comnène; il attribuait, de plus, aux milieux ecclésiastiques l'initiative d'avoir appliqué ce terme aux princes russes.[11]

Une position extrêmement prudente a été adoptée récemment par A. Poppe qui dénie toute valeur institutionnelle à l'inscription de Sainte-Sophie et écrit, à propos de ce témoignage et de celui qu'apporte l'Évangéliaire de Mstislav : 'c'est une contribution intéressante qui met en lumière l'idée que la cour et les milieux ecclésiastiques se faisaient du pouvoir du prince'; quant à l'usage ultérieur, de plus en plus fréquent, du titre de *car'*, l'historien polonais se contente de dire qu'il n'apparaît que dans 'des circonstances particulières'.[12]

Pour l'époque suivante (XIIIe siècle), on trouve exprimé avec insistance le point de vue selon lequel le terme *car'* aurait connu une faveur particulière dans les régions du sud-ouest de l'ancien État kiévien et aurait été, par conséquent, fréquemment attribué aux princes de Volhynie et de Galicie. Formulée par A. A. Šachmatov, cette thèse a été reprise par A. S. Orlov, D. S. Lichačev et, tout récemment, par Ja. D. Isajevyč.[13]

Enfin, l'attribution du titre de *car'* au grand-prince de Vladimir, Michail Jaroslavič de Tver', par le moine Akindin ('Seigneur prince, tu es *empereur* dans ton pays') n'a pas manqué de susciter des rapprochements avec la célèbre formule des juristes occidentaux *Rex est imperator in regno suo*, ce qui conférerait au prince russe, au moins dans l'esprit de l'auteur de cette formule, un pouvoir absolu et souverain à l'intérieur de son pays (*zemlja*).[14]

---

[11] V. S. Ikonnikov, *Opyt issledovanija o kul'turnom značenii Vizantii v russkoj istorii* (Kiev, 1869), 313-14. Cette thèse est, en grande partie, annihilée par l'interprétation que donne l'historiographie moderne de l'envoi de la couronne par l'empereur au prince de Kiev, cf. n. 101. Quant à la référence que fait l'auteur au texte de Daniel le Reclus (Daniil Zatočnik), il s'agit d'une leçon tardive où le terme *car'* a été probablement interpolé, cf. H. Schaeder, op. cit. (n. 10), 53-4, n. 6.

[12] A. Poppe, 'Le prince et l'Église en Russie de Kiev depuis la fin du Xe siècle et jusqu'au début du XIIe siècle', *Acta Poloniae historica*, xx (1969), 110, n. 38.

[13] A A. Šachmatov, 'Issledovanie o Radzivilovskoj ili Kenigsbergskoj letopisi', dans *Radzivilovskaja ili Kenigsbergskaja letopis'* (Izdanie Obščestva ljubitelej drevnej pis'mennosti, cxviii) (Spb., 1902), 32; A. S. Orlov, 'O galicko-volynskom letopisanii', *TODRL*, v (1947), 33; D. S. Lichačev, 'Galickaja literaturnaja tradicija v žitii Aleksandra Nevskogo', ibid. 54; et Ja. D. Isaevič (Isajevyč), 'Iz istorii kul'turnych svjazej Galicko-Volynskoj Rusi s zapadnymi Slavjanami v XII–XIV vv.', dans *Pol'ša i Rus'* (M., 1974), 263.

[14] Ce rapprochement a été fait, entre autres, par A. V. Soloviev, ' "Reges" et "regnum Russiae" au Moyen Âge', *Byzantion*, xxxvi (1966), 169, et tout récemment, par C. J. Halperin, '*Tsar' russkoi zemli*: The *Vita* of Dmitrii Donskoi and Early Muscovite Political Thought', communication faite à la *Muscovite History Conference* (Oxford, 1975), texte dactylographié, 6-7. Sur la valeur juridique et politique de cette formule en Occident, cf. A. Bossuat, 'La formule "Le roi est empereur en son royaume" et son emploi devant le Parlement de Paris',

Pour la plupart, ces travaux se fondent chacun sur un ou plusieurs exemples pris isolément. C'est pourquoi il nous a paru utile de re-grouper ici, dans l'ordre chronologique, un nombre aussi important que possible de citations — sans prétendre toutefois à l'exhaustivité que seul un traitement des sources par ordinateur permettrait d'at-teindre — pour essayer de comparer les différents contextes, littéraires et historiques, où le terme *car'* est employé.

Dans notre étude, nous ne nous sommes pas limité au substantif *car'* ou *cěsar'* lui-même; nous avons inclus ses dérivés, tels que l'adjectif *car'skyi*, le verbe *carstvovati* et le substantif *carstvie* (*carstv'e*) ou *carstvo*. En dehors des exemples précis, nous utilisons dans notre exposé, pour des raisons de commodité, les formes contractes du type *car-*, celles-ci ne présentant, du point de vue sémantique, aucune différence avec les formes originelles du type *cěsar-*;[15] les deux formes sont d'ailleurs fréquemment confondues dans les manuscrits où le terme est presque toujours abrégé et, le plus souvent, dans le domaine russe, dès les textes slavons du XIᵉ siècle, sous la forme ц҃рь sans c suscrit.[16]

La limite chronologique de cette étude a été fixée au milieu du XVᵉ siècle, date où apparaissent, dans la Russie du nord-est, des textes témoignant, à la différence de ceux des époques antérieures, d'un usage fréquent, sinon systématique, du terme *car'* pour désigner un prince russe. Ces textes sont: le Panégyrique du grand-prince de Tver' Boris Aleksandrovič attribué au moine Thomas (*Inoka Fomy Slovo pochval'noe o blagovernom velikom knjaze Borise Aleksandroviče*) rédigé entre 1446 et 1453,[17] le Discours contre les Latins (*Slovo na latynju*) qui daterait de 1461–2,[18] enfin l'Éloge funèbre de Dmitrij Donskoj (*Slovo o žitii i prestavlenii velikogo knjazja Dmitrija Ivanoviča, carja russkogo*)[19] dont

Revue historique de droit français et étranger, xxxix (1961), 371–81, G. Post, *Studies in Medieval Legal Thought: Public Law and the State, 1100–1322* (Princeton, 1964), 453–82, et J.-F. Lemari-gnier, *La France médiévale, institutions et sociétés* (Paris, 1970), 264–5.

[15] Cf. D. I. Prozorovskij, 'O značenii carskogo titula do prinjatija russkimi gosudarjami titula imperatorskogo', *Izvestija Imp. russkogo archeologičeskogo obščestva*, viii (3) (1875), 211. En particulier, nous n'avons pas pu trouver confirmation dans les sources de la distinction qu'a proposée entre *car'* ('the khan of Chingizide blood') et *cěsar'* ('the caesar, or junior emperor') M. Cherniavsky, dans '*Khan or Basileus*: an Aspect of Russian Medieval Political Theory', *Journal of the History of Ideas*, xx (1959), 464.

[16] Cf. U. Sill, *Nomina sacra im Altkirchenslavischen* (München, 1972), 136–7, tableau 19.

[17] Texte publié par N. P. Lichačev (Spb., 1908) *Pamjatniki drevnej pis'mennosti i iskusstva*, clxviii. Sur l'auteur présumé de cette œuvre, cf. W. Philipp, 'Ein Anonymus der Tverer Publizistik im 15. Jh.', *Veröffentlichungen der Abteilung für slavische Sprachen und Literaturen des Osteuropa-Instituts der F. U. Berlin*, vi [*Festschrift für D. Čyževskyj*] (1954), 230–7. Sur l'emploi du terme *car'* dans ce texte, cf. Ja. S. Lur'e, 'Rol' Tveri v sozdanii russkogo nacional'nogo gosudarstva', *Učenye zapiski Leningradskogo gosudarstvennogo universiteta*, xxxvi, Serija istoriče-skich nauk, nᵒ 3 (1939), 89.

[18] Texte publié par A. N. Popov, *Istoriko-literaturnyj obzor drevnerusskich polemičeskich sočinenij protiv latinjan XI–XV vv.* (M., 1875), 360–95. Sur sa date, cf. Ja. S. Lur'e, *Ideologičeskaja bor'ba v russkoj publicistike XV — načala XVI v.* (M.-L., 1960), 371.

[19] Texte publié dans *Polnoe sobranie russkich letopisej* (abr. *PSRL*), iv (1–2) (L., 1925), 351–66.

la date est controversée : face à la thèse d'A. V. Soloviev, reprise récemment par C. J. Halperin, selon laquelle cette œuvre aurait été écrite peu après la mort de Dmitrij (1389),[20] l'école philologique soviétique situe sa composition au XVe siècle, dans les années quarante d'après M. D. Salmina; pour notre part, nous nous rallions tout à fait à ce dernier point de vue.[21]

Le terme *car'*, ou originellement *căsarĭ*, du latin *caesar* par l'intermédiaire du gothique *kaisar*, appartient au fonds slave commun. Il est attesté, tout comme ses dérivés, chez les Slaves orientaux dès le XIe siècle : dans les textes scripturaires ou patristiques, il traduit généralement le grec βασιλεύς là où la Vulgate utilise *rex*, c'est-à-dire pour désigner Dieu, 'le Roi des cieux', les 'rois' d'Israël ou différents autres monarques de la Bible, même païens (à l'exception, dans le Nouveau Testament, de l'empereur romain, 'césar', appelé *kesarĭ*, du grec tardif καῖσαρ), ou bien le souverain en général. Concurrencé, dans ce dernier sens, comme nous le verrons, par *knjaz'* (originellement *kŭnjazĭ*, graphie rarement attestée dans nos sources), le terme *car'* apparaît aussi bien dans les traductions[22] que dans une œuvre originale telle que le Sermon sur la Loi et la Grâce (*Slovo o zakone i blagodati*) du métropolite Hilarion.[23]

Dans le domaine politique, le terme *car'* désigne systématiquement l'empereur ou les empereurs (en cas d'association au trône) de Byzance : cet usage, attesté dès les traités byzantino-russes du Xe siècle conservés dans 'le Récit des temps passés' (*Povest' vremennych let*),[24] a subsisté jusqu'à la fin de l'Empire grec : en effet, l'autorité 'universelle' de l'empereur, notamment en matière ecclésiastique, ne fut guère contestée, à quelques exceptions près,[25] par les princes russes, sans que,

[20] A. V. Solov'ev (Soloviev), 'Epifanij Premudryj kak avtor "Slova o žitii i prestavlenii velikago knjazja Dmitrija Ivanoviča, carja rus'skago"', *TODRL*, xvii (1961), 85–106. Ce point de vue a été repris par W. Philipp, dans 'Die gedankliche Begründung der Moskauer Autokratie bei ihrer Entstehung, 1458–1522', *Forschungen zur osteuropäischen Geschichte*, xv (1970), 89 et par C. J. Halperin, op. cit. (n. 14), 8–9.

[21] Cf. Ja. S. Lur'e, *Ideologičeskaja bor'ba* (n. 18), 359–60, M. D. Salmina, 'Slovo o žitii i o prestavlenii velikogo knjazja Dmitrija Ivanoviča, carja Rus'skago', *TODRL*, xxv (1970), 81–104; nous nous proposons de traiter de cette question dans une étude particulière.

[22] Cf. D. I. Prozorovskij, op. cit. (n. 15), 207–8, et A. I. Sobolevskij, op. cit. (n. 8), 7–8. Sur l'emploi de *knjaz'* pour rendre le grec βασιλεύς, cf. *infra*, pp. 22–4.

[23] *Des Metropoliten Ilarion Lobrede auf Vladimir den Heiligen und Glaubensbekenntnis*, éd. par L. Müller (Wiesbaden, 1962), 97–8, 110–12, etc.

[24] *Povest' vremennych let* (abr. *PVL*), i (M.–L., 1950), 23 sqq.

[25] En dehors des initiatives des princes de Kiev, Jaroslav Vladimirovič et Izjaslav Mstislavič (cf. nn. 175, 176) l' 'exception' la plus connue est constituée par l'interdiction qu'aurait faite le grand-prince Vasilij I au métropolite de commémorer le nom de l'empereur dans la liturgie; il fut, pour cela, sévèrement blâmé dans une épître du patriarche Antoine IV (1394–7), *Russkaja istoričeskaja biblioteka* (abr. *RIB*), vi, 2ème éd. (Spb., 1906), addendum, col. 265–76; voir également D. Obolensky, *The Byzantine Commonwealth: Eastern Europe 500–1453* (1971), 264–8.

d'ailleurs, cette reconnaissance du pouvoir du *basileus* altère en quoi que ce soit l'indépendance politique du pays vis-à-vis de Byzance.[26]

Une valeur politique très différente fut attribuée au terme *car'*, lorsque celui-ci, à partir du XIIIᵉ siècle, fut appliqué, dans les chroniques principalement,[27] au souverain suprême de l'Empire mongol ou à différents membres de la dynastie chingisside et surtout, à partir du règne de Möngka Temur (1267–80), au khan de la Horde d'Or.[28] Comme l'a montré M. Cherniavsky, le titre impérial était décerné par les Russes au souverain tatar avec sa pleine valeur politique, son usage étant, au XIVᵉ siècle lors des dissensions internes à la Horde, strictement réservé au khan légitime.[29] Il est, d'ailleurs, intéressant de souligner que les textes témoignent parfaitement du parallélisme qui existait apparemment dans la mentalité des Russes du Moyen Âge entre, d'une part, le patriarche et l'empereur détenteurs des pouvoirs suprêmes dans l'Empire (confondu en théorie avec l'*oikouménè*) et, d'autre part, le métropolite et le khan tatar détenteurs des mêmes pouvoirs en Russie. Citons, par exemple, un passage de la Compilation moscovite de la fin du XVᵉ siècle (*Moskovskij letopisnyj svod konca XV veka*):

Тое же зимы прииде Фегностъ епископъ Сараиски из Грекъ, посыланъ бо бѣ митрополитомъ к патриарху и *царемъ* Менгутемерем ко *царю* Греческому Палеологу.[30]

Au XVᵉ siècle, l'usage du terme *car'* fut étendu au sultan turc, ainsi qu'aux khans de Crimée et de Kazan'.[31]

Enfin, comme nous le verrons dans l'un des exemples cités dans cet article (n° 44), l'empereur germanique était également désigné par le même terme.

A côté de ces emplois du titre de *car'*, dont le caractère systématique prouve incontestablement la valeur institutionnelle, l'application du même terme aux princes russes revêt, de prime abord, un aspect pour le moins épisodique.

Même avant le milieu du XIIIᵉ siècle, à une époque où les princes russes ne devaient leur pouvoir à aucune autorité politique étrangère,

---

[26] Cf. D. Obolensky, op. cit. (n. 25), 223–4, A. Poppe, op. cit. (n. 12), 109 et 'La dernière expédition russe contre Constantinople', *Byzantinoslavica*, xxxii (1971), 233, n. 85.

[27] L'usage du terme *car'* pour désigner le khan semble plus rare dans les documents diplomatiques. On le trouve cependant dans la traduction russe des *jarlyki* accordés par les khans aux métropolites, cf. *Pamjatniki russkogo prava*, iii (M., 1955), 465 sqq.; on relève également le terme *car'* dans quelques traités conclus entre les princes russes, cf. *Duchovnye i dogovornye gramoty velikich i udel'nych knjazej XIV–XVI vv.* (M.-L., 1950), 41, 106, mais, le plus souvent, le khan n'est guère mentionné personnellement, seule figure 'la Horde' en tant qu'institution, pour ainsi dire, impersonnelle, cf. ibid. 20, 31, 36, 38, etc.

[28] Cf. A. N. Nasonov, *Mongoly i Rus'* (M.-L., 1940), 30, n. 2.

[29] M. Cherniavsky, op. cit. (n. 15), 464–8.

[30] *PSRL*, xxv (M.-L., 1949), 152. Pour chaque citation, nous reproduisons le texte en graphie cyrillique moderne à partir des différentes éditions, en donnant entre parenthèses les lettres que nous restituons, entre crochets celles que nous croyons devoir supprimer. Les lettres suscrites sont reproduites en italique. [31] Cf. A. I. Sobolevskij, op. cit. (n. 8), 8.

ceux-ci ne sont jamais désignés par le terme *car'* dans les documents diplomatiques, très rares, il est vrai, pour l'époque prémongole.[32] Il en va de même, *a fortiori*, pour la période ultérieure, si l'on excepte l'attribution du titre impérial à saint Vladimir (†1015) dans des chartes galiciennes tardives ou dans une épître de Vasilij II (1441). Le mot *car'* n'apparaît pas davantage dans les sceaux des différents princes russes où ceux-ci sont qualifiés de (μέγας) ἄρχων ou de *knjaz' (velikyi)*.[33]

Dans les relations des Russes avec les peuples et les États voisins, le terme *car'*, ou ses équivalents dans d'autres langues, est quasiment inexistant avant le dernier quart du XVe siècle où il apparaît, de façon d'ailleurs très irrégulière, dans les rapports entre la cour d'Ivan III et le monde germanique.[34] Pour la période que nous étudions, on ne peut citer qu'un passage du texte allemand d'un traité conclu en 1417 entre Pskov et l'Ordre livonien, où le grand-prince de Moscou Vasilij I aurait été appelé par les ambassadeurs de la cité russe *unse here de Rusche* keiser *Wassile Dymittrius*, mais nous ignorons le terme russe que recouvre l'allemand *keiser*, et les éditeurs de la charte ont prudemment traduit наш господин, русский государь Василий Дмитриевич.[35] Un autre témoignage, grec cette fois, permettrait, si l'on en croit A. V. Soloviev, de supposer que le grand-prince de Vladimir, Michail Jaroslavič de Tver' (†1318), aurait fait un usage officiel, au début du XIVe siècle, du titre impérial.[36] Cette hypothèse se fonde sur un fragment de Maxime Planude d'après lequel l'ambassadeur du prince russe aurait déclaré à l'empereur Andronic II Paléologue:

... ὁ αὐθέντης μου ὁ βασιλεὺς τῶν 'Ρὼς ὁ ἐπὶ τῆς τραπέζης τῆς ἁγίας βασιλείας σου προσκυνεῖ δουλικῶς τὴν ἁγίαν βασιλείαν σου.[37]

Ce témoignage isolé, dont on ignore encore une fois la forme originale et qui n'a fait l'objet d'aucune étude critique, peut difficilement être pris à la lettre, comme le voulait A. V. Soloviev. D'ailleurs, un peu plus haut, dans le même fragment, le prince russe est appelé ἄρχων τῶν 'Ρώς, conformément à l'usage byzantin tel qu'il est attesté depuis

[32] En dehors des traités byzantino-russes (cf. n. 24), on ne connaît que quelques chartes novgorodiennes, le plus souvent dans des copies, rédigées au nom du prince de Kiev, ainsi qu'un traité avec le Gotland, cf. *Gramoty Velikogo Novgoroda i Pskova* (M.-L., 1949), 139-41, 56, ou bien les 'statuts ecclésiastiques' des princes dont les refontes successives rendent difficile la reconstitution du formulaire original, cf. Ja. N. Ščapov, *Knjažeskie ustavy i cerkov' v Drevnej Rusi XI-XIV vv.* (M., 1972) et *Drevnerusskie knjažeskie ustavy XI-XV vv.* (M., 1976). Sur la diplomatique russe de l'époque prémongole, cf. S. M. Kaštanov, 'Russkie knjažeskie akty X-XIV vv., do 1380 g.', *Archeografičeskij ežegodnik*, 1975 (M., 1976), 106-9.

[33] Cf. V. L. Janin, *Aktovye pečati Drevnej Rusi X-XV vv.*, i (M., 1970), 16 sqq., et E. I. Kamenceva et N. V. Ustjugov, *Russkaja sfragistika i geral'dika*, 2ème éd. (M., 1974), 62-8, 76-90.

[34] Cf. H. Schaeder, op. cit. (n. 10), 54.   [35] *Gramoty Velikogo Novgoroda* (n. 32), 319.

[36] A. V. Soloviev, op. cit. (n. 14), 169 (la référence au texte de Maxime Planude est erronée, cf. n. 37).

[37] H. Haupt, 'Beiträge zu den Fragmenten des Dio Cassius', *Hermes, Zeitschrift für klassische Philologie*, xiv (1879), 445; le texte a été reproduit par A. S. Pavlov, *RIB*, vi, addendum, col. 273-4.

Constantin Porphyrogénète.[38] Il est possible que l'usage du terme
βασιλεύς s'explique, dans le passage cité, par le désir de souligner la
position 'servile' du βασιλεὺς τῶν 'Ρώς devant la 'Sainte majesté impériale'
(ἡ ἁγία βασιλεία), position encore accentuée par l'allusion à une fonction
subalterne auprès de la Table de l'empereur qu'aurait exercée le
prince russe.[39] Compte tenu de ces remarques, il nous semble impossible
de voir derrière le témoignage isolé de Maxime Planude une quelconque réalité institutionnelle ou politique. Cette conclusion trouve,
enfin, sa confirmation dans les autres exemples relevés par A. V.
Soloviev: nulle part, à l'exception du traité de 1417 cité plus haut, on
ne trouve trace d'une utilisation de la titulature impériale par les
princes russes; ceux-ci sont désignés, le plus souvent, par le terme latin
rex (ou son équivalent dans les langues vulgaires) ou par sa transposition
en grec, ῥήξ, voire μέγας ῥήξ, expression où l'épithète *megas* semble avoir
été empruntée au titre russe *knjaz' velikyi*.[40]

Ainsi, le fait que les princes russes n'aient quasiment jamais été
qualifiés d' 'empereurs' dans les sources étrangères confirme notre
première constatation sur l'absence, pour les princes contemporains
tout au moins, de toute titulature impériale dans les sources diplomatiques et sigillographiques russes.

Essayons maintenant de voir si le témoignage des sources narratives
et littéraires russes et celui de quelques documents diplomatiques
tardifs (pour saint Vladimir) peuvent infirmer cette première conclusion négative.

Aucun témoignage n'a pu être recueilli pour le Xᵉ et le début du
XIᵉ siècle. Certes, des hypothèses ont été émises, d'après des sources
fragmentaires, sur l'attribution du titre impérial à saint Vladimir.
Elles ont été regroupées et présentées, il y a une vingtaine d'années,
par D. Obolensky; mais, dans un ouvrage récent, le même Auteur
admet que ces hypothèses ne peuvent être tenues pour certaines.[41]
Nous reparlerons plus loin des textes des XIVᵉ et XVᵉ siècles dans lesquels Vladimir Svjatoslavič est qualifié de *car'*.

Le plus ancien témoignage de l'emploi du terme *car'* pour désigner
un prince russe est sans conteste fourni par l'inscription conservée dans
la cathédrale Sainte-Sophie de Kiev et rédigée, comme l'ont indubi-
tablement prouvé ses éditeurs, à l'occasion de la mort de Jaroslav le
Sage (1054):

---

[38] Cf. D. Obolensky, *The Byzantine Commonwealth* (n. 25), 200.
[39] Obolensky traduit cette fonction par 'chambellan', dans 'Byzance et la Russie de Kiev',
Messager de l'Exarchat du Patriarche de Moscou en Europe occidentale, xxix (1959), 28 (reproduit
dans D. Obolensky, *Byzantium and the Slavs* (1971)). Sur l'attribution de cette fonction au prince
russe, cf. M. A. D'jakonov, op. cit. (n. 7), 14–15.
[40] A. V. Soloviev, op. cit. (n. 14), 150–9, 169–71.
[41] D. Obolensky, 'Byzance et la Russie...' (n. 39), 28–33, et *The Byzantine Commonwealth*
(n. 25), 200–1.

Enfin, dans le Récit sur l'assassinat d'Andrej Bogoljubskij (1174),[55] on trouve appliqués pour la première fois à un prince russe, non seulement le célèbre passage de saint Paul (*Romains*, xiii, 1) sur la soumission aux autorités, mais aussi la définition du pouvoir *impérial* formulée au VIe siècle par Agapet.[56]

n° 15 ...пишеть ап(о)с(то)лъ Павелъ: всяка д(у)ша властемь повинуется, власти бо *от* Б(ог)а учинены суть. Естествомь бо ц(е)с(а)рь земнымъ подобенъ есть всякому чл(о)в(ѣ)ку, властью же сана вышши яко Б(ог)ъ.[57]

Toujours dans la seconde moitié du XIIe siècle, le terme *car'* et ses dérivés sont utilisés avec une relative fréquence dans la Chronique de Kiev, compilée en 1198 par l'abbé du monastère Saint-Michel de Vydubič, Moïse, souvent à partir de biographies ou de nécrologies princières, et conservée dans la Chronique hypatienne.[58]

Le premier exemple relevé dans ce texte concerne, une fois de plus, les saints princes martyrs Boris et Gleb; le prince Rostislav Mstislavič, déjà mentionné, évoque, en effet, leur mémoire dans un discours qu'il aurait tenu, peu avant sa propre mort, à Polycarpe, abbé du monastère des Grottes:

n° 16 ...хотѣлъ быхъ поревновати, якоже и вси правовѣрнии ц(а)ри пострадаша и прияша възмъздие *от* Г(оспод)а Б(ог)а своего, якоже с(вя)тии м(у)ч(е)н(и)ци кровь свою прольяша.[59]

Ce texte semble avoir été directement inspiré par celui de la prière d'Igor' Ol'govič (n° 10).[60]

Trois autres exemples concernent le prince de Kiev Izjaslav Mstislavič († 1154). Le premier se rapporte à l'année 1149, lorsque, d'après le texte de la Chronique, Jurij Dolgorukij, prince de Suzdal', aurait fait tenir à son neveu ces propos:

n° 17 Даи ми Переяславль, ать посажю с(ы)на своего у Переяславли, а ты сѣди ц(е)с(а)р(с)твуя в Киевѣ.[61]

Dans le passage suivant, le prince, blessé dans une bataille en 1151, se fait reconnaître de ses hommes en disant:

n° 18 Азъ Изяславъ есмь, кн(я)зь вашь, и сня съ себе шеломъ, и позна(ша) и, и то слышавше мнози и въсхытиша и руками своими с радостью, яко ц(а)ря и кн(я)зя своег(о).[62]

[55] Sur ce texte et sur sa tradition manuscrite, cf. N. N. Voronin, 'Povest' ob ubijstve Andreja Bogoljubskogo i ee avtor', *Istorija SSSR*, 1963, n° 3, 80–97, et B. A. Rybakov, *Russkie letopiscy* (n. 48), 80.

[56] Sur la diffusion du texte d'Agapet en Russie, cf. I. Ševčenko, 'A Neglected Byzantine Source of Muscovite Political Ideology', *Harvard Slavic Studies*, ii (1954), 142–50.

[57] *PSRL*, ii, col. 592; *PSRL*, i (2), col. 370.

[58] Cf. M. D. Priselkov, op. cit. (n. 3), 47–54, et B. A. Rybakov, *Russkie letopiscy* (n. 48), 182–3.

[59] *PSRL*, ii, col. 530–1.

[61] *PSRL*, ii, col. 380.

[60] Cf. I. P. Eremin, op. cit. (n. 48), 89.

[62] Ibid. col. 439.

Въ 6562, м(ѣся)ца феврарі 20, жсъпене ц(а)ря наш(е)го...[42]

n° 1

Un autre exemple concernant également Jaroslav provient d'un texte un peu plus tardif, la Vie (*Čtenie*) des princes martyrs Boris et Gleb rédigée par le moine Nestor vers 1078–9. D'après ce texte, le métropolite Jean aurait consulté le prince sur la canonisation éventuelle de ses frères en ces termes:

Лѣпо ли бы намъ, благовѣрныи царю, церковь имя ею възградити и n° 2 уставити день, воньже празновати има.[43]

Les exemples suivants concernent Boris et Gleb eux-mêmes et sont empruntés au Dit sur la passion de ces princes (*Skazanie i strast' i pochvala svjatuju mučeniku Borisa i Gleba*). La date exacte de ce texte est controversée. D'après A. Poppe, il aurait été écrit avant la canonisation de Boris et Gleb située en 1072. Mais si l'on s'en tient, comme semble le faire J. Fennell, à l'opinion de N. N. Voronin, le Dit sur la passion serait contemporain du Dit sur les miracles opérés par les reliques des deux saints (*Skazanie o čudesech*) et les deux œuvres dateraient de 1115–17.[44] Dans la conclusion du Dit sur la passion, on lit ce passage:

...ц(е)с(а)ря ли, князя ли ва проглаголю, нъ паче чл(о)в(ѣ)ка убо проста n° 3 и съмѣрена, съмѣрение бо сътяжала еста, имьже высокая мѣста и жилища въселиста ся. По истинѣ вы цесаря ц(е)с(а)ремь и князя княземь. n° 4

L'expression цесаря ц(е)с(а)ремъ est très probablement une réminiscence biblique, *Esdras*, vii, 12. Un peu plus loin, le même texte, en donnant le portrait de l'un des saints frères dans sa jeunesse, précise:

...съ убо бл(а)говѣрный Борисъ... свѣтя ся ц(е)с(а)рьскы...[45] n° 5

Nous ne disposons, ainsi, pour le XIe siècle que de deux témoignages certains de l'attribution du terme *car'* à des princes russes. Leur nombre augmente nettement au siècle suivant, à partir du règne à Kiev de Vladimir Monomaque (1113–25). Certes, le premier des exemples que nous citerons n'est pas très probant. Dans une épître à Vladimir, le métropolite Nicéphore (1104–21) s'adresse ainsi aux princes russes:

Подобаеть бо княземъ, яко отъ Бога избраномъ и призваномъ на правовѣрную вѣру его, Христова словеса разумѣти извѣст(н)о и основание церковное тврьдое, да[н]и ти будуть основание, якоже есть святыя

[42] B. A. Rybakov, op. cit. (n. 3), 14–15, planche xvii (3–4); et S. A. Vysockij (Vysoc'kyj), *Drevnerusskie nadpisi Sofii Kievskoj XI–XIV vv.*, i (Kiev, 1966), 39–41, tableaux ix (1), x (1).

[43] *Die altrussischen hagiographischen Erzählungen und liturgischen Dichtungen über die heiligen Boris und Gleb*, éd. par D. I. Abramovič, rééd. par L. Müller (München, 1967), 18; sur la date de cette œuvre, cf. J. Fennell et A. Stokes, *Early Russian Literature* (1974), 18.

[44] A. Poppe, 'Opowieść o męczeństwie i cudach Borysa i Gleba, okoliczności i czas powstania utworu', *Slavia orientalis*, xviii (1969), 267–92, 359–82; N. N. Voronin, '"Anonimnoe" skazanie o Borise i Glebe, ego vremja, stil' i avtor', *TODRL*, xiii (1957), 11–56; et J. Fennell et A. Stokes, op. cit. (n. 43), 20.

[45] *Die altrussischen hagiographischen Erzählungen* (n. 43), 49, 51; et *Uspenskij sbornik XII–XIII vv.* (M., 1971), 56, 58, f. 17a, 18a (n° 3, 4).

Церкве, на свѣтъ и наставленіе порученымъ имъ людемъ отъ Бога.
n° 6 Единъ бо Богъ *царствуетъ* небесными, вамъ же, съ его помощію, *царьст-*
вовати земными, долѣшнимъ симъ въ роды и роды.[46]

L'emploi, dans ce texte, du verbe *carstvovati* pour parler du règne
des princes russes (qualifiés par ailleurs de *knjazi*) peut s'expliquer
par le parallèle, très fréquent dans la littérature byzantino-slave, entre
le règne de Dieu dans les cieux, exprimé normalement par βασιλεῖν en
grec et *carstvovati* en slave, et celui des princes ici-bas.

Un témoignage beaucoup plus explicite date du successeur de
Vladimir Monomaque à Kiev, son fils Mstislav (1125–32). Dans le
colophon d'un Évangéliaire, copié pour ce prince, un familier de
celui-ci, Naslav, racontant comment il fut chargé par son souverain de
porter le volume à Constantinople pour le faire relier et orner, utilise
deux fois le terme *car'* et une fois celui de *cesarstvie* pour parler de son
prince :

n° 7 Азъ рабъ Б(о)жии недостоиныи... съпьсахъ памяти дѣля *ц(а)рю*
нашему и людемъ о съконьчаньи ев(а)г(гелі)а, иже бяшеть казалъ
Мьстиславъ кънязь... и возивъ Ц(а)рюгороду и учинихъ химипетъ,
Б(о)жею же волею възвратихъся исъ Ц(а)рягорода и съправихъ вьсе
злато и сребро и драгыи камень, пришедъ Кыеву и съконьчася вьсе
дѣло м(ѣ)с(я)ца августа въ 2... Азъ же худыи Наславъ много труда
подъяхъ и печали, нъ Б(ог)ъ утѣши мя добрааго кънязя м(о)л(и)твою. И
тако даи Б(ог)ъ вьсѣмъ людемъ угодня ему творити, слышащемъ его
n° 8 *ц(е)с(а)рствие* пребывающе въ радости и въ веселии и въ любъви и даи
Б(ог)ъ его м(о)л(и)твою вьсѣмъ хрьстияномъ и мънѣ худому Наславу...
n° 9 обрѣсти честь и милость *от* Б(ог)а и *от* своего *ц(а)ря* и *от* братие...[47]

Un peu plus tard, nous retrouvons le terme *car'* dans le récit sur
l'assassinat par la populace de Kiev d'un prince de Černigov, entré
dans les ordres, Igor' Ol'govič (1147). Ce récit, conservé dans la
Chronique hypatienne, a pu être rédigé à Černigov peu après les
événements sanglants de Kiev; il fut, en tout cas, repris, quelques
années plus tard, par Polycarpe, abbé du monastère des Grottes, et
intégré dans la Chronique kiévienne. Du point de vue littéraire, ce
texte est, sans nul doute, inspiré par le Dit sur la passion de Boris et
Gleb.[48] Dans la prière qu'il aurait prononcée avant son assassinat,
Igor' évoque la mémoire des princes martyrs en les désignant par le
terme *cari* :

n° 10 ...како с(вя)тии правовѣрнии *ц(а)ри* прольяша крови своя, стражюще
за люди своя...

[46] K. F. Kalajdovič, *Pamjatniki russkoj slovesnosti* (M., 1821), 163.
[47] F. I. Buslaev, *Istoričeskaja christomatija cerkovno-slavjanskogo i russkogo jazykov* (M., 1861), col. 35–6; et I. I. Sreznevskij, op. cit (n. 2), col. 52–3.
[48] Cf. D. S. Lichačev, *Russkie letopisi i ich kul'turno-istoričeskoe značenie* (M.–L., 1947), 221–2, et B. A. Rybakov, *Russkie letopiscy i avtor 'Slova o polku Igoreve'* (M., 1972), 335; sur les sources littéraires de ce texte, cf. I. P. Eremin, 'Kievskaja letopis' kak pamjatnik literatury', *TODRL*, vii (1949), 85–6.

Plus loin, au moment de la mort du prince, l'épithète 'impérial' est
appliquée directement à Igor' :

...безаконнии же нем(и)л(о)стивии побивше... ѣще живу сущу ему,
ругающеся *ц(а)рьскому* и с(вя)щеному тѣлу и волокоша и... на кн(я)жь n° 11
дворъ и ту прикончаша и.[49]

A peu près à la même époque, nous trouvons un autre exemple dans
le Panégyrique de Rostislav Mstislavič, prince de Smolensk (1127),
puis de Kiev (1154), rédigé, peu après sa mort (1167), auprès de la
cathédrale de Smolensk. Dès le début du texte, Rostislav est qualifié
de требл(а)ж(е)нныи и с(вя)тыи княз(ь), puis, l'auteur, après avoir
rappelé les mérites du défunt (essentiellement la création de la chaire
épiscopale de Smolensk), ajoute :

А Б(о)гъ ему дас(ть) за доброту его сторицею и *ц(а)рствовати* в всеи n° 12
Рускои земли, а на ономъ свѣте — ц(а)рство н(е)б(е)сное.[50]

Comme dans le passage n° 6, l'emploi du verbe *carstvovati* peut
s'expliquer, en partie au moins, par le parallélisme entre le règne des
princes sur la terre et celui de Dieu dans les cieux. C'est pourquoi
l'exemple suivant nous semble plus probant; il est extrait de la chronique princière consacrée à Andrej Bogoljubskij par un de ses contemporains, autour de 1170, et reprise dans les compilations ultérieures.[51]
Le passage cité appartient à un texte autonome, le Récit sur la déposition de l'évêque Théodore, véritable acte d'accusation, rédigé dans
l'entourage du métropolite, où l'expulsion de l'évêque de Suzdal'-
Vladimir par le prince Andrej[52] est commentée en ces termes :

(Бог)... сп(а)се рабы своя рукою крѣпкою и мышцею высокою, рукою
бл(а)гоч(ес)тивою, *ц(а)рскою* правдиваго и бл(а)говѣрнаго князя Андрѣя.[53] n° 13

A cet exemple on peut ajouter un autre concernant le même
prince de Vladimir; il est emprunté à la quatrième rédaction de la
Vie de saint Léonce, évêque de Rostov du XIe siècle, où, à propos d'un
pèlerinage à la tombe du saint, le prince est qualifié ainsi :

...благочестивыи *царь* и князь нашь... n° 14

D'après N. N. Voronin, ce texte daterait de la dernière décennie du
XIIe siècle, mais l'emploi du terme *car'* placé en apposition à *knjaz'* peut
être dû à une interpolation plus tardive, le texte étant conservé dans
un manuscrit du XVIe siècle.[54]

[49] *PSRL*, ii (Spb., 1908), col. 350, 352.
[50] Ja. N. Ščapov, op. cit. (n. 6), 59; l'édition du texte est précédée d'une étude substantielle, en particulier sur les circonstances de sa composition, 47–59.
[51] Cf. B. A. Rybakov, *Russkie letopiscy* (n. 48), 72–6.
[52] Sur cet épisode, cf. W. Vodoff, 'Un "parti théocratique" dans la Russie médiévale?' *Cahiers de civilisation médiévale*, xvii (1974), 197–8, 203–4; sur l'origine du texte, cf. N. N. Voronin, 'Andrej Bogoljubskij i Luka Chrizoberg', *Vizantijskij vremennik*, xxi (1962), 44.
[53] *PSRL*, i (2) (L., 1927), col. 357; *PSRL*, ii, col. 554.
[54] Cf. N. N. Voronin, 'Žitie Leontija Rostovskogo i russko-vizantijskie vzaimootnošenija vo vtoroj polovine XII v.', *Vizantijskij vremennik*, xxiii (1963), 25, 42–3.

Enfin, la mort d'Izjaslav est rapportée en ces termes:

...разболѣся великии кн(я)зь Киевьскии Изяславъ, и ч(е)стныи б(лаг)о-
вѣрныи и Х(ри)с(т)олюбивыи, славн(ы)и Изяславъ Мьстиславечь, вънукъ
Володимерь, и плакася по нем вся Руская земля и вси Чернии Клобуци
[и] яко по ц(а)ри и г(осподи)нѣ своемъ, наипаче же яко по отци...[63]   n° 19

A la mort du prince de Smolensk Roman Rostislavič (1180), sa
veuve se serait lamentée ainsi, en évoquant, une fois de plus, la mémoire
de saint Boris, désigné pour la circonstance par son prénom chrétien,
Roman:

Ц(е)с(а)рю мои, бл(а)гыи, кроткыи, смиреныи, правдивыи, во истину   n° 20
тебе нар(е)чено имя Романъ, всею добродѣте(лию) сыи подобенъ ему,
многия досады прия от Смолнянъ и не видѣ тя, г(о)с(поди)не, николи же
противу ихъ злу никотораго зла въздающа, но на Б(о)зѣ вся покладывая,
пров(о)жаше.[64]

La mémoire d'un autre prince de Smolensk, David Rostislavič
(†1197), est célébrée en ces termes:

...бѣ бо любя дружину, а злыя кажня, якоже подобаеть ц(е)с(а)р(е)мь   n° 21
творити.[65]

Les trois derniers extraits de la Chronique de Kiev concernent un
seul prince, Rjurik Rostislavič (†1215), et se rapportent au même
événement : l'inauguration d'un nouveau mur au monastère Saint-
Michel de Vydubič, à Kiev. Cet événement est décrit avec beaucoup
de solennité par le chroniqueur, Moïse, abbé du monastère; la description des festivités se termine par un discours que ce dernier aurait
adressé au grand-prince de Kiev. C'est ce texte, rédigé dans le style
artificiel et ampoulé des προσφωνητικοὶ λόγοι byzantins,[66] qui clôt la
Compilation de 1198, due à la plume du même ecclésiastique. Dans la
description de la fête, on relève le passage suivant:

...великыи кн(я)зь Рюрикъ кюръ Василии... возвеселися д(у)х(о)вно о
пришедши(х) в дѣло таково ц(е)с(а)рьскои мысли его.   n° 22

Dans le discours lui-même, l'abbé Moïse, évoquant la dévotion
future des Kiéviens pour saint Michel, précise que celle-ci sera due, en
partie au moins, au 'miracle' qui s'est produit pendant le règne de
Rjurik:

...новаго ради чюдеси, иже во д(ь)ни ц(е)с(а)р(с)тва твоего свѣршися.   n° 23

---

[63] Ibid. col. 469.
[64] Ibid. col. 617.
[65] Ibid. col. 703.
[66] Sur ce texte, cf. Ju. K. Begunov, 'Reč' Moiseja Vydubickogo kak pamjatnik toržest-
vennogo krasnorečija XII v.', *TODRL*, xxviii (1974), 60–76. L'article se termine par une
édition critique du texte.

Enfin, dans la péroraison, l'orateur s'adresse en ces termes au prince:

n° 24 …и Б(ог)ъ м(и)л(о)сти и о(те)цъ щедротамъ и любы единочад(н)аго с(ы)на его и причастье с(вя)т(а)го Духа да будеть съ ц(е)с(а)р(с)твомъ твоимъ…[67]

Au XIIIe siècle, les exemples deviennent moins nombreux et apparaissent uniquement dans des textes d'origine galicienne ou volhynienne. Le premier est emprunté à la Chronique ou plutôt à la 'Geste' de Daniil Romanovič (†1264), rédigée vers 1256–7 à la cour de ce dernier et conservée, à la suite de la Chronique de Kiev, dans l'Hypatienne.[68] Le titre de *car'* y est attribué au père de Daniil, Roman Mstislavič, prince de Volhynie et de Galicie, qui réussit à imposer son autorité, directement ou indirectement, à toute la *Rus'* méridionale. Le passage cité appartient au récit de l'humiliation que Daniil eut à subir devant le khan tatar:

…Данилови Романовичю, князю бывшу велику, обладавшу Рускою землею, Кыевомъ и Володимеромъ и Галичемъ со братомъ си, (и) инѣми странами, н(ы)нѣ сѣдить на колѣну и холопмъ называеться(я), и дани хотять, живота не чаеть, и грозы приходять; о злая ч(е)сть татарьская! n° 25 Его ж о(те)цъ бѣ ц(е)с(а)рь в Рускои земли, иже покори Половецькую землю и воева на иные страны всѣ. С(ы)нъ того не прия ч(е)сти, то иныи кто можеть прияти?[69]

Ce passage, dont le caractère littéraire est évident, reprend le thème de la toute-puissance de Roman dans 'le pays russe' annoncé dès le début de l'œuvre. Pour l'exprimer ici, l'auteur s'est inspiré, comme l'a montré A. S. Orlov, d'un passage du Roman d'Alexandre (*Aleksandrija*) où, après la défaite de Darius, sa toute-puissance passée est rappelée en ces termes: …толикыи царь Дарїи, толико языкъ побѣдивъ и вся грады поработивъ…[70]

L'exemple suivant est d'origine volhynienne et remonte au règne de Vladimir Vasil'kovič, prince de Vladimir en Volhynie (1269–88). Il est extrait du colophon d'un manuscrit des œuvres de saint Éphrem le Syrien, copié pour un membre de l'entourage du prince:

n° 26 Въ лѣто семое тысящѣ написашася книгы сия при ц(е)с(арс)твѣ n° 27 бл(а)говѣрнаго ц(е)с(а)ря Володимѣра, с(ы)на Василкова, унука Романова, бог(о)любивому тивуну его Петрови…[71]

---

[67] *PSRL*, ii, col. 711–12, 714, 715 (n° 22–4); et Ju. K. Begunov, op. cit. (n. 66), 75, 76 (n° 23, 24).

[68] Sur cette œuvre, cf. L. V. Čerepnin, 'Letopisec Daniila Galickogo', *Istoričeskie zapiski*, xii (1941), 228–53, et la bibliographie très complète donnée par G. A. Perfecky, *The Hypatian Codex, part two: the Galician-Volynian Chronicle, an annotated translation* (München, 1973), 143–6.

[69] *PSRL*, ii, col. 807–8.

[70] A. S. Orlov, 'K voprosu ob Ipat'evskoj letopisi', *Izvestija Otdelenija russkogo jazyka i slovesnosti Rossijskoj Akademii nauk*, xxxi (1926), 116; et G. A. Perfecky, op. cit. (n. 68), 137, n. 94.

[71] I. I. Sreznevskij, op. cit. (n. 2), col. 149.

Le même prince est qualifié deux fois de *car'*, au moment de sa mort, dans la Chronique volhynienne.

Cette œuvre, conservée, elle aussi, dans l'Hypatienne, et que l'on pourrait appeler 'la Geste' de Vladimir Vasil'kovič, fut entreprise du vivant de ce prince et achevée peu après sa mort (1288).[72] Le premier passage décrit les moments qui suivirent le décès du prince survenu hors de sa capitale :

…княгини же его (с слу)гами дворьными омывше его и увиша и оксами- n° 28
томъ со круживомъ, якоже достоить ц(е)с(а)ремь, и возложиша и на
сани и повезоша до Володимѣря…

Un peu plus loin, la veuve de Vladimir Vasil'kovič se lamente en ces termes :

Ц(е)с(а)рю мои бл(а)гыи, кроткыи, смиреныи, правдивыи, во истину n° 29
нареч(е)но быс(ть) тобѣ имя во кр(е)щеньи Иван, всею добродѣтелью
подобенъ есь ему, многыа досады приимъ *от* своихъ сродникъ, не
видѣхъ тя, г(о)с(поди)не мои, николи же противу ихъ злу никоторого
же зла воздающа, но на Б(о)зѣ вся покладывая, провожаше.[73]

Ce passage est un emprunt quasiment littéral au récit sur la mort de Roman Rostislavič de Smolensk (cf. n° 20) tel qu'il a été conservé dans la Chronique de Kiev;[74] l'évocation du prénom chrétien de Vladimir Vasil'kovič, Jean, prive ce texte d'une partie de son sens: on est en peine de savoir à quel saint Jean (Baptiste?) le prince Vladimir Vasil'kovič s'est rendu 'semblable par ses vertus'. Il est possible, de plus, que l'emprunt de ce passage à la Chronique de Kiev ait inspiré à l'auteur du récit sur la mort du prince de Vladimir en Volhynie la comparaison entre la toilette mortuaire de celui-ci et celle des empereurs (n° 28).

En dehors de ces cinq emplois du terme *car'* appliqué, plus ou moins directement, à des princes de Volhynie ou de Galicie, on relève plusieurs fois le substantif *car'* ou le verbe *carstvovati* dans la version galicienne de la *Povest' vremennych let* conservée au début du manuscrit de la Chronique de Perejaslavl'-Zaleskij.[75] Ce texte est précédé du titre suivant:

Лѣтописець Рускихъ царѣи   n° 30

Plus loin, dans le récit du célèbre 'appel aux Varègues' (862), on lit la phrase suivante:

Поищемъ собѣ князя [и] поставить надъ собою царствовати.   n° 31

[72] Cf. I. P. Eremin, 'Volynskaja letopis' 1289–1290 gg. kak pamjatnik literatury', *TODRL*, xiii (1957), 102–3.
[73] *PSRL*, ii, col. 918, 919–20 (n° 27, 28). Cette fois, G. A. Perfecky, op. cit. (n. 68), 108, emploie, pour traduire *car'*, le terme plus général 'king'.
[74] Cf. I. P. Eremin, 'Volynskaja letopis'' (n. 72), 113.
[75] Cf. A. S. Orlov, op. cit. (n. 13), 32–3.

De même, l'installation d'Oleg à Kiev (882) est rapportée en ces termes:

nº 32   …и сѣдѣ Олегъ, княжа и *царствуа* въ Киевѣ…

On trouve même un usage assez inattendu de *carstvovati* — que nous ne prendrons pas pour cette raison en considération — au lieu de ся прозывати dans la proposition: …нача *царствовати* Русская земля…[76]

Au xivᵉ siècle, des cas d'emploi du terme *car'* pour désigner différents princes ont été relevés dans la Russie du nord-est. Le plus ancien exemple appartient à l'épître que le moine Akindin adressa, en 1312–15, à son prince, Michail Jaroslavič de Tver', qui exerçait alors les fonctions de grand-prince de Vladimir, pour l'exhorter à intervenir contre le métropolite Pierre (1308–26) accusé de simonie.[77] Entre autres arguments, Akindin avance celui-ci:

nº 33   *Царь* еси, господине княже, въ своеи земли; ты истязанъ имаши быти на страшнѣмъ и нелицемѣрнемъ судищи Христовѣ, аже смолчиши митрополиту.[78]

Dans le Récit sur l'exécution, à la Horde d'Or en 1318, du même prince — texte rédigé probablement peu après cette date par un ecclésiastique de Tver' —, on relève le passage suivant où l'auteur s'adresse ainsi à son prince humilié avant d'être mis à mort:

nº 34   Господине князь! Видиши ли, селико множество народа стоятъ, видящи тя в таковои укоризне, а прежя тя слышахом *царствующаго* во своеи земли? Абы еси, господине, во свою землю шелъ![79]

Parmi les grands-princes de Vladimir appartenant à la dynastie moscovite, le seul à avoir été qualifié de *car'* dans les sources antérieures au xvᵉ siècle est Ivan Kalita. Dans le Panégyrique rédigé au moment de sa mort (1340) et conservé dans un Évangéliaire, l'auteur applique au prince de Moscou un texte qu'il présente comme une citation d'Ézéchiel:

nº 35   …о семь бо князи великомь Иванѣ пр͠ор(о)къ Езекии гл(аголе)ть: в послѣднее время в апустѣвшии земли, на западъ, въстанеть *ц(е)с(а)рь* правду любя и судъ…

[76] 'Letopisec Perejaslavlja Suzdal'skogo, sostavlennyj v načale XII v.', éd. par M. A. Obolenskij, *Vremennik Imp. Moskovskogo obščestva istorii i drevnostej rossijskich*, ix (1851), 1, 5 (nº 30–2), 6.

[77] Sur ce texte, cf. V. A. Kučkin, 'Istočniki "napisanija" mnicha Akindina', *Archeografičeskij ežegodnik*, 1962 (M., 1963), 60–8, où l'on trouvera l'essentiel de la bibliographie.

[78] *RIB*, vi, col. 158.

[79] Bibliothèque Lénine (Moscou), fonds Undol'skij, nº 1254, f. 44, cité d'après V. A. Kučkin, *Povesti o Michaile Tverskom: istoriko-tekstologičeskoe issledovanie* (M., 1974), 259; on trouvera dans ce volume une étude très complète sur la genèse de ce Récit et sur sa tradition manuscrite.

Une autre citation biblique, plus fidèle (*Psaume* lxxii, 1), est appliquée à Ivan Kalita un peu plus loin:

Б(ож)е, судъ ц(е)с(а)р(е)ві даи же, правду с(ы)н(о)ви ц(е)с(а)р(е)ву, n° 36
сии бо князь великои Iоа(н) имѣвше правыи суд...

Deux fois, pour parler du règne d'Ivan I, l'auteur du Panégyrique emploie le terme *carstvo*:

...будеть тишина велья в Рускои земли, и въсияеть въ д(ь)ни его правда,
якоже и быс(ть) при его ц(а)рствѣ...   n° 37
...всеи Рускои земли поминая велегласно державу его ц(а)рства...[80]   n° 38

Environ un demi-siècle plus tard, en Galicie de nouveau, le titre de *car'* est attribué à saint Vladimir dans trois chartes rédigées au nom du prince Lev Danilovič (†1301), fils de Daniil Romanovič. Ces documents, dont l'authenticité avait déjà été mise en doute par N. M. Karamzin,[81] ont été probablement confectionnés à la fin du xive ou au début du xve siècle, comme le laisse supposer la mention du métropolite Cyprien,[82] pour mieux assurer, dans le cadre du royaume polonais, l'intangibilité du temporel de l'Église orthodoxe.[83] Dans les trois documents, l'auteur présumé de la charte se réfère ainsi à l'initiative qu'aurait prise son lointain aïeul:

...яко прадѣдъ нашъ царь великыи Володимиръ... придалъ митро- n° 39,
политомъ...[84]   [40, 41

A peu près à la même époque, au début du xve siècle, le prince Vladimir Svjatoslavič est appelé *car'* dans une œuvre littéraire, cette fois de la Russie du nord, la *Zadonščina* (1406–7):

Се князь великыи Дмитрiи Иванович и братъ его князь Володимеръ
Ондрѣевич поостриша сердца свои мужеству, ставше своею крѣпостью,
помянувше прадѣда князя Володимера Кiевьскаго, царя русскаго.[85]   n° 42

A la même date, approximativement, le terme *carstvo* a été utilisé, pour parler du règne du grand-prince de Tver' Michail Aleksandrovič, dans un texte écrit, peu après la mort de celui-ci (1399), vraisemblablement sous l'influence directe de l'évêque de Tver' Arsène (†1409):[86]

...бысть яко же исходящу лѣту тридесят(ь) четвертому дръжавныя

---

[80] N. A. Meščerskij, 'K izučeniju rannej moskovskoj pis'mennosti', *Izučenie russkogo jazyka i istočnikovedenie* (M., 1969), 95–6 (n° 34–7); on trouvera dans cet article une étude sur ce texte, 93–4, 97–103, cf. en particulier, p. 100, sur la 'citation' d'Ézéchiel; ajoutons que l'image du roi exerçant 'le droit et la justice' a pu être empruntée à d'autres textes de l'Ancien Testament, le 1er *Livre des rois*, x, 9, ou le 2ème *Livre des chroniques*, ix, 8.

[81] N. M. Karamzin, *Istorija gosudarstva rossijskogo*, 2ème éd., i (4) (Spb., 1842), col. 103–4, n. 203, col. 85.   [82] Cf. *Hramoty XIV st.* (Kiev, 1974), 14.

[83] Ja. N. Ščapov, *knjazeskie ustavy* (n. 32), 55.   [84] *Hramoty XIV st.* (n. 82), 9, 13, 19.

[85] A. Vaillant, *La* Zadonščina, *épopée russe du XVe s.* (Paris, 1967), 3; dans sa traduction, l'Auteur rend *car'* par 'roi', 23. Sur la date du texte, voir p. ix.

[86] Sur les différentes rédactions du Panégyrique de Michail Aleksandrovič, cf. B. I. Dubencov, 'K voprosu o tak nazyvaemom "Letopisce knjaženija Tverskogo"', *TODRL*, xiii (1957), 118–57.

nº 43 области Тфѣрьскаго настолованіа и миръпаго *царства* Михаила, досто-
славнаго великаго князя...[87]

Un peu plus tard, nous trouvons le titre de *car'* décerné au grand-
prince Vitovt de Lituanie (Alexandre de son nom de baptême) dans
le Panégyrique rédigé peu après la mort du prince (1430) et conservé
dans la Chronique lituanienne, où sont évoquées, entre autres, les
réunions de souverains destinées à préparer le couronnement royal —
qui n'eut jamais lieu — de Vitovt.[88] Pour souligner la puissance de son
souverain, l'auteur du texte insiste sur le fait que l'empereur lui-même,
Sigismond de Luxembourg, s'est déplacé jusqu'à Luc'k pour répondre
à l'invitation du grand-prince de Lituanie et commente ainsi cet
événement:

...иж есть царь надо всею землею, и тои пришедъ, поклонися славному
nº 44 *царю*, великому князю Александру.[89]

Tout à fait à la fin de la période que nous étudions, on relève encore
l'épithète *carskyi*, utilisée pour caractériser les activités du jeune Michail
Aleksandrovič de Tver', dans une rédaction tardive du Panégyrique
de ce prince commandée, au milieu du XVᵉ siècle, par le grand-prince
de Tver' Boris Aleksandrovič:[90]

...игоръ же и безчинія ненавидяще и нелѣпаа глаголющихъ уклоня-
nº 45 шеся, но и дружину благоумну съвъкупляше собѣ и съ тѣми *царскыми*
утѣшенми благочиннѣ веселящеся...[91]

Il est à remarquer que, dans ce texte quasiment contemporain du
Panégyrique consacré à Boris Aleksandrovič, l'emploi du terme *car'*
reste exceptionnel, alors qu'il est fréquent dans l'œuvre du 'moine
Thomas'.[92]

Le dernier exemple que nous retiendrons concerne encore une fois
saint Vladimir de Kiev que son très lointain descendant Vasilij II
l'Aveugle qualifie de *car'* dans l'épître qu'il adressa en 1441 au patriarche Mitrophane pour lui demander l'autorisation de procéder à
l'élection d'un métropolite en Russie même, sans l'intervention de
Constantinople; dans un long développement sur l'origine du chris-
tianisme en Russie, le souverain de Moscou rappelle les circonstances
dans lesquelles le fondateur de l'État kiévien aurait installé la première
hiérarchie ecclésiastique dans son pays:

Взимаетъ же къ себѣ, онъ великіи новыи Костяньтинъ, а реку благо-
nº 46 честивыи *царь* Русскіа земля Владимиръ, на свое отечьство..., отъ святыя

---

[87] *PSRL*, xv (1), 2ᵉᵐᵉ éd. (Petrograd, 1922), col. 168.
[88] Sur ce texte, cf. M. Hruševs'kyj, 'Pochvala velikomu knjazju Vitovtu: kil'ka uvah pro
sklad najdavnijšoji rus'ko-lytovs'koji litopysy', *Zapysky Naukovoho tovarystva imeni Ševčenka*,
viii (1895), 1–16.
[89] *PSRL*, xvii (Spb., 1907), col. 102–3; et M. Hruševs'kyj, op. cit. (n. 88), 7.
[90] Cf. n. 86.
[91] *PSRL*, xv (2) (Spb., 1863), col. 467. [92] Cf. n. 17.

великіа, съборныа и апостольскіа Церкве Царьствующаго града, Премудрости Божіа... на Русскую землю митрополита.[93]

Malgré leur caractère probablement incomplet, les dépouillements auxquels nous avons procédé permettent de formuler quelques constatations qui peuvent être acceptées comme hypothèses de travail.

La première est d'ordre quantitatif: l'attribution du terme *car'* et de ses dérivés à un prince russe reste exceptionnelle jusqu'au milieu du xvᵉ siècle: les 46 exemples relevés appartiennent à une trentaine de textes seulement. Dans 22 passages, un ou plusieurs princes russes se voient attribuer explicitement le titre de *car'* (n° 1, 2, 3, 7, 9, 10, 14?, 16, 18–20, 25, 27, 29, 30, 33, 39–42, 44, 46); dans 2 cas, un prince est comparé à un 'empereur' (n° 21, 28), dans 3 autres citations, un texte biblique ou patristique contenant le terme *car'* (grec βασιλεύς) est appliqué à un prince russe (n° 4, 15, 35, 36); le mot *carstvie* ou *carstvo* a été relevé 7 fois (n° 8, 23, 24, 26, 37, 38, 43), le verbe *carstvovati* 6 fois (n° 6, 12, 17, 31, 32, 34), enfin l'adjectif *carskyi* (ou la forme adverbiale *carsky*) apparaît 5 fois (n° 5, 11, 13, 22, 45).

Du point de vue chronologique, les exemples du xiᵉ siècle sont rares: en dehors des deux textes concernant Jaroslav (n° 1, 2), on ne relève que les trois emplois de *car'* dans le Dit sur la passion de Boris et Gleb (n° 3–5), œuvre dont l'appartenance au xiᵉ siècle est possible, mais non certaine. En revanche, l'usage du vocable *car'* semble avoir connu une certaine faveur au xiiᵉ siècle où l'on note au moins 19 exemples (n° 6–24), peut-être 22 si on situe le *Skazanie* vers 1115 (exemples n° 3–5).

A l'époque mongole, l'usage du terme *car'* pour désigner des princes russes redevient plus rare, puisque, même en additionnant des témoignages dispersés (Galicie–Volhynie, Russie du nord-est, Lituanie), on ne relève, pour deux siècles, que 22 exemples (n° 25–46), auxquels on pourrait, peut-être, ajouter les deux témoignages étrangers, celui de Maxime Planude et celui du traité de 1417, ce qui porterait le total à 24.

La seconde constatation est d'ordre linguistique: généralement le mot *car'* ne s'emploie guère avec d'autres déterminants que les adjectifs possessifs (*moi, tvoi, naš', vaš'*). Les exceptions à cette règle sont rares: si on laisse de côté les sources étrangères — où l'emploi d'un déterminant précis était inévitable —, on ne peut citer que le passage où Roman Mstislavič de Volhynie est qualifié de ц(е)с(а)рь в Рускои земли(n° 25)[94] et, surtout, ceux dans lesquels sont évoqués saint Vladimir

[93] *RIB*, vi, col. 527–8.
[94] Sur la valeur politique et non institutionnelle de l'expression *cesar' v Ruskoi zemli* appliquée au prince de Volhynie Roman Mstislavič (n° 25), cf. *infra*, pp. 25–6. L'expression *carstvovati v vsei Ruskoi zemli*, relevée dans le Panégyrique de Rostislav Mstislavič (n° 12), n'a pas davantage de valeur institutionnelle, cf. *supra*, p. 11; de plus, l'usage du verbe *carstvovati* était, dans une certaine mesure, favorisé par l'expansion tardive et limitée du verbe *knjažiti*, cf. *infra*, p. 28.

ou ses prédécesseurs, sans qu'il y ait d'ailleurs uniformité dans cette titulature posthume, puisqu'on trouve, tantôt царь русскии (n° 30, 42), tantôt царь Русскиа земля (n° 46). D'autre part, jamais le titre de *car'* n'est suivi de celui de *samod'rž'c'* (attesté le plus souvent sous la forme *samodr'ž'c'* ou *samoderž'c'*) ou de celui de *samovlast'c'* (ou *samovlastec'*).[95] Or, lorsque les souverains bulgares ou serbes s'arrogèrent le titre impérial, celui-ci était presque toujours suivi d'un déterminant ('Empereur des Bulgares et des Romains' ou 'Empereur des Serbes et des Grecs') et, aux XIIIe et XIVe siècles tout au moins, reprenait la formule byzantine Βασιλεὺς καὶ αὐτοκράτωρ.[96] Il est vraisemblable que si les souverains russes, même sans revendiquer la moindre souveraineté sur 'les Romains' — ce qu'ils ne firent jamais —,[97] avaient pris le titre d' 'Empereur des Russes' ou 'de la Russie', ce titre complet aurait trouvé un écho, même dans les sources narratives. Il semble, par conséquent, que le titre de *car'*, lorsqu'il est attribué à un prince russe, n'est nullement lié à la fonction de souverain suprême de la Russie, sauf pour saint Vladimir et les princes de Kiev du Xe siècle dans l'image que s'en faisaient les lettrés galiciens au XIIIe siècle ou moscovites au XVe.

Cette affirmation trouve sa confirmation dans une troisième constatation: contrairement à l'opinion de B. A. Rybakov,[98] le titre de *car'* n'était pas exclusivement attaché, à l'époque prémongole, au trône 'aîné' (столъ старьшыи) de Kiev. En effet, si l'on procède à une répartition géographique des exemples cités pour les XIe et XIIe siècles, on obtient les résultats suivants:

— principauté de Kiev: n° 1, 2, 7–9, 12, 17–19, 22–4, soit 12 exemples,

— principautés de Rostov et de Murom (détenues, d'après certaines sources, en 1015 par Boris et Gleb): n° 3–5, 10, 16, soit 5 exemples,

— principauté de Vladimir-Suzdal': n° 13–15, soit 3 exemples,

— principauté de Smolensk: n° 20, 21, soit 2 exemples,

— principauté de Černigov: n° 11 (cet unique exemple concerne, rappelons-le, un prince entré dans les ordres et qui avait, de ce fait, abdiqué ses droits politiques),

— un exemple (n° 6) s'applique à l'ensemble des princes russes.

---

[95] Sur l'emploi de ce terme dans les sources russes, cf. *infra*, pp. 26–7.

[96] *Basileus Boulgarias* ou *Basileus Boulgarôn kai Rômaiôn*, pour le premier Empire bulgare; *c(a)r Blgarom i Gr''kom* ou *v'' Ch(rist)a B(og)a věren' c(a)r i sam(o)dr'žec' vsěm''* Blgarom, pour le second Empire bulgare; *v' Christa Boga blagověrni car' Sr'bliem' i Gr'kom'* pour l'Empire de Stefan Dušan, pour lequel on relève, cependant, quelques exemples où les deux derniers mots manquent, cf. G. Ostrogorsky, op. cit. (n. 1), 129–41, 154–7.

[97] Cf. A. Poppe, 'Le prince et l'Église' (n. 12), 109–10.

[98] Cf. n. 3.

Il apparaît ainsi que, sur 24 emplois du terme *car′* ou de ses dérivés, la moitié seulement concerne les princes de Kiev.

Le fait que ces princes n'aient pas eu le monopole de l'usage du titre de *car′* explique que celui-ci ait pu être utilisé épisodiquement, au XIIIᵉ siècle, en Galicie et en Volhynie. Toutefois, sa diffusion dans ces régions ne semble pas avoir eu l'importance que l'on s'accorde à lui attribuer généralement:[99] en effet, exception faite des cas où le titre de *car′* est décerné à Vladimir Svjatoslavič ou à d'autres princes de Kiev du Xᵉ siècle (n° 30–2, 39–41), il ne reste que 5 emplois du terme *car′* ou de celui de *cesarstvo*, dont 4 concernent le même prince, Vladimir Vasil′kovič de Vladimir en Volhynie (n° 26–9), et deux ou trois de ces passages (n° 25, 28?, 29) sont des emprunts littéraires.

En revanche, dans la Russie du nord-est, aux XIVᵉ et XVᵉ siècles, autant que les sources permettent d'en juger, le terme *car′* et ses dérivés, employés au demeurant très rarement jusqu'au milieu du XVᵉ siècle, semblent avoir été réservés à ceux des princes qui exerçaient ou revendiquaient un pouvoir politique sur l'ensemble de cette région, c'est-à-dire les grands-princes de Tver′ (n° 33, 34, 43, 45) et ceux de Moscou (n° 35–8).

Attesté de façon sporadique, attribué à des princes très différents, le titre de *car′* n'était lié, dans la Russie médiévale, à aucun sacre impérial (ce rite ne fut introduit qu'en 1498, à Moscou, pour Dmitrij Ivanovič, petit-fils d'Ivan III) comparable, par exemple, à celui de Stefan Dušan (1346), ni même à aucune cérémonie religieuse susceptible d'être assimilée à un sacre, comme celle que célébra en 913 le patriarche Nicolas le Mystique pour Siméon de Bulgarie.[100] Notamment, l'envoi d'une couronne par Alexis I Comnène à Vladimir Monomaque — événement connu uniquement d'après des sources du XIIIᵉ siècle — ne saurait être interprété comme tel: ce geste symbolique ne faisait que marquer la reconnaissance, par le prince qui recevait cette couronne, de la primauté d'honneur de l'empereur.[101] Certes, l'étude chronologique des sources à laquelle nous avons procédé a montré que le titre de *car′* est devenu d'un usage relativement fréquent à Kiev précisément à partir du début du XIIᵉ siècle, c'est-à-dire après le règne de Monomaque (1113–25), mais nous avons également vu quelques exemples antérieurs à cette date et, surtout, de nombreux cas où le titre de *car′* était porté par des princes autres que ceux de Kiev. De plus, si cet usage avait été la conséquence d'une cérémonie célébrée en faveur de Vladimir Monomaque[102] ou d'un

[99] Cf. n. 13.
[100] Cf. D. Obolensky, *The Byzantine Commonwealth* (n. 25), 254, 107–9; sur le sens de la cérémonie de 913, on trouvera un point de vue récent dans V. Tăpkova-Zaimova, op. cit. (n. 1), 291–2.
[101] Cf. T. Wasilewski, op. cit. (n. 4), 48.
[102] Telle était, rappelons-le, la thèse de V. S. Ikonnikov, cf. n. 11.

autre prince, il aurait été beaucoup plus systématique. Il suffit, pour s'en convaincre, de constater que, à la suite du sacre royal de Daniil Romanovič (1253), la Chronique de Galicie substitue le plus souvent le nouveau titre de *korol'* à celui de *knjaz'*, non seulement pour l'intéressé, mais même pour ses fils que l'on trouve appelés, parfois, королевъ сынъ.[103] Rien de semblable ne peut être noté pour le titre de *car'* dans les sources avant... 1547, ce qui, s'il en était besoin, exclurait toute hypothèse de sacre impérial. Bien au contraire, le terme *car'* et ses dérivés sont fréquemment employés dans la même phrase conjointement avec le terme *knjaz'*, qu'il s'agisse de Boris et Gleb (n° 3, 4), de Vladimir Monomaque et des autres princes russes contemporains (n° 6), de Mstislav Vladimirovič (n° 7), d'Andrej Bogoljubskij (n° 13, 14), d'Izjaslav Mstislavič (n° 18, 19) et de Rjurik Rostislavič (n° 22) de Kiev, de Michail Jaroslavič (n° 33, 34) et de Michail Aleksandrovič (n° 43) de Tver', d'Ivan Kalita (n° 35, 36), ou bien des princes de Kiev du xᵉ siècle dans les sources tardives (n° 31, 32, 42).

Une remarque analogue pourrait être faite à la suite de l'étude du lexique politique des œuvres du milieu du xvᵉ siècle (les Panégyriques de Boris Aleksandrovič de Tver' et de Dmitrij Donskoj, ainsi que le Discours contre les Latins). Il semble donc qu'il n'y ait eu, pour les lettrés russes du xiᵉ au xvᵉ siècle, aucune opposition fondamentale entre les termes *car'* et *knjaz'*, lorsque ceux-ci étaient appliqués à des princes russes. Une étude de ces deux termes employés avec une valeur générale, dans des textes à caractère religieux le plus souvent, permet, semble-t-il, de confirmer cette constatation.

En effet, si, comme nous l'avons dit plus haut, le terme βασιλεύς est, le plus souvent, traduit par *car'*,[104] il est, cependant, parfois rendu par *knjaz'*,[105] notamment lorsqu'il s'agit de désigner le détenteur du pouvoir monarchique en général, *in abstracto*, et non pas un souverain déterminé (un roi d'Israël, par exemple). Ainsi, Luc Židjata, évêque de Novgorod (1036–61), transposait le célèbre passage de la 1ᵉʳᵉ *Épître de saint Pierre* (ii, 17) en ces termes: ...Бога боитесь, князя чтите[106] (grec: ...τὸν θεὸν φοβεῖσθε, τὸν βασιλέα τιμᾶτε).

Un tel usage du terme *knjaz'* est largement attesté, comme l'a fait remarquer A. Poppe,[107] dans l'*Izbornik* de 1076, recueil manuscrit qui

---

[103] Cf. D. Skalalski, *La Principauté de Galicie-Volhynie au XIIIᵉ s.*, exemplaires dactylographiés (Paris, 1969), ii, 32; *PSRL*, ii, col. 826–7 sqq., G. A. Perfecky, op. cit. (n. 68), 67–8 sqq., et D. Skalalski, op. cit., i, 143–4 sqq. (traduction française du texte).
[104] Cf. n. 22. Bien entendu, chaque fois où, dans la Bible, il s'agit de distinguer les *basilès* (latin: *reges*) et les *archontes* (latin: *principes*), on trouve régulièrement *cari* et *knjazi*.
[105] On peut remarquer que, chez les Slaves méridionaux, même dans la langue politique, le grec *basileus* pouvait avoir pour équivalent un terme autre que *car'*, ainsi avant le couronnement impérial de Stefan Dušan (1346), la formule byzantine *en Christô tô theô pistos basileus* était rendue par *v Christa Boga blagověrni kral'*, cf. K. Jireček, op. cit. (n. 1), 10, et G. Ostrogorsky, op. cit. (n. 1), 152–4.   [106] *Russkie dostopamjatnosti*, i (M., 1815), 10.
[107] A. Poppe, 'Le prince et l'Église' (n. 12), 109, n. 37.

reflète assez fidèlement les conceptions intellectuelles et morales de l'élite cultivée de Kiev au XIe siècle.[108] Ainsi, par exemple, dans un extrait inspiré par le même passage de saint Pierre, on trouve βασιλεύς encore une fois rendu par *knjaz'*: Боиться ученикъ учителева слова, паче же самого учителя, такоже боꙗся Б(ог)а, боиться и *князя*, имьже казняться съгрѣшяюштии. *Князь* бо есть Б(о)жии слуга къ чл(о)в(ѣ)комъ милостью и казнью зълыпимъ.[109] On peut également citer cette traduction d'une homélie de saint Jean Chrysostome: ...то, чл(о)в(ѣ)че, видѣвъ, понѣ акы земльному *князю* такоже и къ н(е)-б(е)сьному ц(а)рю приступи сь боꙗзнью,[110] où le russe *knjaz'* rend probablement le grec βασιλεύς.[111]

Des exemples similaires peuvent être relevés dans un texte dont la rédaction définitive date du début du XIIe siècle, le Récit sur le meurtre de Boris et Gleb conservé dans la *Povest' vremennych let*. En particulier, le passage de l'*Ecclésiaste*, x, 16 ...οὐαί σοι πόλις ἧς ὁ βασιλεύς σου νεώτερος... est rendu ainsi: ...Лютѣ бо граду тому, в немь же *князь* унъ. Mais, un peu plus haut, on trouve une citation assez libre du *Livre de Daniel* (v, 21) où, à deux reprises, la fonction de prince est explicitement rapprochée de celle de l'empereur: Святополкъ... помысливъ высокоумьемь своимь, не вѣдыи яко 'Богъ даеть власть, ему же хощеть; поставляеть бо *цесаря* и *князя* вышнии, ему же хощеть, дасть'. Аще бо кая земля управится пред Богомь, поставляеть еи *цесаря* или *князя* праведна, любяща судъ и правду...[112]

Cette identification a été exprimée de façon encore plus explicite par le métropolite Nicéphore dans l'une de ses épîtres à Vladimir Monomaque où, après avoir recommandé à celui-ci la lecture du *Psaume* ci ('Le Miroir des princes'), il écrit: ...тыи есть истиныи икунникъ *царское* и *княжьское* икуны.[113]

La conception identique qu'avaient les lettrés russes du Moyen Âge des fonctions princières et impériales est encore attestée par le *Merilo pravednoe*, une compilation juridique refondue sous sa forme définitive à Tver' au XIVe siècle.[114] On y trouve, entre autres, dans une nouvelle

---

[108] Cf. N. P. Popov, 'L'Izbornik de 1076, dit de Sviatoslav, comme monument littéraire', *Revue des études slaves*, xiv (1934), 5–25.

[109] *Izbornik 1076 goda* (M., 1965), 242.   [110] Ibid. 675.

[111] Ibid. 816; et J. P. Migne, *Patrologiae cursus completus, series graeca*, lxiii (Paris, 1860), col. 898–9.

[112] *PVL*, 94–5; le rapprochement avec le texte de Daniel a été proposé par A. S. L'vov, op. cit. (n. 5), 198. Sur la genèse de ce texte, cf. A. A. Šachmatov, *Razyskanija o drevnejših russkich letopisnych svodach* (Spb., 1908), 29–97.

[113] *Russkie dostopamjatnosti* (n. 106), 74–5. Les termes *car'* et *knjaz'* se trouvent également rapprochés dans 'les Réponses canoniques' (*Kanoničeskie otvety*) du métropolite Jean II (XIe siècle), *RIB*, vi, col. 5, mais dans ce texte, dont l'original était écrit en grec, il peut s'agir d'une transposition du groupe οἱ βασιλεῖς καὶ οἱ ἄρχοντες attesté dans la Bible (cf., par exemple, *Jérémie*, ii, 26, xvii, 25, xlix, 38).

[114] Cf. G. I. Vzdornov, 'Iz istorii iskusstva russkoj rukopisnoj knigi X–XIV vv.', *Drevnerusskoe iskusstvo* (M., 1972), 166–70.

citation de la 1ᵉʳᵉ *Épître de saint Pierre* (ii, 13), le grec βασιλεύς traduit, cette fois, par *cesar'*, mais sous le titre: Отъ бчелы избрано о княженьи. Un peu plus loin, le terme *knjaz'* rend βασιλεύς dans le célèbre passage d'Agapet.[115]

A la même époque, Akindin, dans son épître à Michail Jaroslavič, sur les termes de laquelle nous reviendrons encore, rapprochait explicitement le rôle des empereurs de celui des princes dans le gouvernement de l'Église.[116] A la fin du XIVᵉ siècle, l'identité du pouvoir impérial et princier en matière législative était soulignée par le métropolite Cyprien, dans une épître adressée à Pskov en 1395, où, à propos de la charte accordée à la cité, au XIIIᵉ siècle, par Aleksandr Nevskij, il écrivait: ...въ томъ воленъ всякіи *царь* въ своемъ *царствѣ*, или *князь* въ своемъ *княженьи*, всякая дѣла управляеть и грамоты записываеть.[117]

Ces exemples nous montrent qu'il n'y avait, pour les Russes du Moyen Âge, aucune différence de nature entre l'institution impériale et l'institution princière. Toutefois, il faut remarquer que, si dans une première période, correspondant au XIᵉ siècle, le terme *knjaz'* est le plus employé pour désigner *in abstracto* le détenteur du pouvoir monarchique, celui de *car'* semble l'emporter à partir du XIIᵉ siècle. C'est ainsi que, à cette époque, l'évêque Cyrille de Turov, par exemple, pour parler, dans la Parabole sur l'âme (*Povest'... o belorizce čelovece i o duši i o pokajanii*), d'un 'roi' imaginaire, utilise exclusivement le terme *car'*.[118] Il en va de même dans une œuvre traduite, attestée en Russie à partir du XIIᵉ siècle, le Roman de Barlaam et de Joasaph (*Žitie Varlaama i Ioasafa*).[119]

On peut remarquer que la substitution du terme *car'* à celui de *knjaz'* pour désigner un souverain quelconque coïncide avec le moment où le premier des deux termes commence à être utilisé avec une relative fréquence pour désigner des princes russes.

Ainsi, l'étude du rapport qui pouvait exister entre les termes *car'* et *knjaz'* confirme nos premières constatations: l'attribution, dans les sources narratives, du titre de *car'* à des princes russes ne reflète aucune réalité institutionnelle nouvelle; elle est liée à une évolution du lexique politique russe qui élargit la valeur du terme *car'*.

[115] *Merilo pravednoe* (Moscou, Bibl. Lénine, fonds 304, n° 15), f. 27–27ᵛ, édition en facsimilé de M. N. Tichomirov (M., 1961), 53–4. Une étude globale du vocabulaire politique du *Merilo pravednoe* serait certainement très instructive. Notons, d'ores et déjà, certaines données statistiques publiées: le terme *cĕsar'* s'y trouve 51 fois, celui de *knjaz'* 65 fois, cf. L. V. Vjalkina et G. N. Lukina, 'Materialy k častotnomu slovarju drevnerusskich tekstov', *Leksikologija i slovoobrazovanie drevnerusskogo jazyka* (M., 1966), 268.

[116] Cf. *infra*, p. 35 et n. 166.

[117] *RIB*, vi, col. 233.

[118] Texte publié par I. P. Eremin, 'Literaturnoe nasledie Kirilla Turovskogo', *TODRL*, xii (1957), 348–54.

[119] *Žitie Varlaama i Ioasafa*, éd. en fac-similé dans *Izdanija Obščestva ljubitelej drevnej pis'mennosti*, lxxxviii (Spb., 1887), cf. en particulier p. 448. Sur la date d'apparition de ce texte en Russie, cf. I. Ševčenko, op. cit. (n. 56), 148.

Il faut également noter que, lorsqu'apparaît, au début du xvᵉ siècle, à la cour lituanienne, un nouveau vocable pour désigner le souverain, en plus du terme traditionnel de *knjaz'*, celui-ci n'est pas *car'*, mais *hospodar'* (ou *hosudar'*). Ce nouveau titre, dont l'origine reste à déterminer, est attesté dans les sources lituano-russes tant narratives que diplomatiques, d'où, d'ailleurs, il est passé à Moscou au milieu du xvᵉ siècle.[120] Dans le Panégyrique de Vitovt, le mot *hosudar'* est employé régulièrement pour désigner le grand-prince de Lituanie et même, au début du texte, il se trouve opposé au terme *car'* utilisé pour désigner un empereur indéterminé.[121] Quant à l'emploi du mot *car'* dans le passage cité plus haut (n° 44), il s'explique aisément par le désir de l'auteur du Panégyrique de souligner, en mettant en parallèle le '*car'* de toute la terre' (c.-à-d. l'empereur germanique) et le '*car'* Alexandre' (Vitovt), la puissance de ce dernier.[122]

Cette interprétation nous amène à poser une question plus générale : si le terme *car'* appliqué aux princes russes du Moyen Âge n'exprime aucune réalité institutionnelle, peut-on estimer qu'il reflète une situation politique concrète, un rapport de forces favorable au prince auquel les sources attribuent le titre de *car'* ?

Certes, on peut supposer cette valeur au terme *car'* dans certains des extraits cités plus haut, par exemple dans les chartes galiciennes où Vladimir est non seulement appelé *car'*, mais qualifié aussi de *velikyi* (n° 39–41), ou bien dans la *Zadonščina* où le rappel des liens généalogiques unissant Dmitrij Donskoj et 'Vladimir de Kiev, le *car'* russe' peut être interprété comme un titre de gloire destiné à rehausser le prestige du vainqueur de Kulikovo (n° 42). Il est indéniable que la proposition его о(те)ць бѣ ц(е)с(а)рь в Рускои земли devait, sous la plume du chroniqueur de Daniil Romanovič de Galicie, rappeler la puissance politique qu'avait eue dans la *Rus'* méridionale le père de celui-ci (n° 25). On peut également remarquer que le titre de *car'* est attribué à des princes qui bénéficièrent d'un prestige politique certain, même si celui-ci n'est guère évoqué dans le contexte; tel est, par exemple, le cas de Jaroslav le Sage (n° 1, 2), d'Andrej Bogoljubskij (n° 13–15), de

[120] Cf. G. Alef, 'The Political Significance of the Inscriptions on Muscovite Coinage in the Reign of Vasili II', *Speculum*, xxxiv (1959), 6, n. 26.
[121] Cf. *PSRL*, xvii, col. 102, et M. Hruševs'kyj, op. cit. (n. 88), 6.
[122] Nous avons relevé un autre exemple d'attribution du titre de *car'* à un membre de la dynastie de Gedimin: Semen Aleksandrovič, prince de Kiev, arrière petit-fils d'Ol'gerd, est, en effet, qualifié de *car'* dans les chroniques moldaves sous l'année 6871 (1463) où on lit le passage suivant: *prijat Stefan' voevoda sebě gospodža kjaginja Eudokija ot Kieva, sestra Semena carja* (*Slavjano-Moldavskie letopisi XV–XVI vv.* (M., 1976), 26; cf. également, p. 63, 69, 106). Cette attribution du titre de *car'* au prince lituanien de Kiev s'explique probablement par des considérations politiques moldaves: les voïévodes de ce pays ont, en effet, tenté à cette époque de se présenter, par différents moyens, y compris les alliances matrimoniales, comme les héritiers de Byzance, c'est pourquoi le titre de *car'* aurait été attribué au beau-frère d'Étienne le Grand, cf. P. Ş. Nasturel, 'Considérations sur l'idée impériale chez les Roumains', *Byzantina*, v (1973), 403.

Michail Jaroslavič (n° 33, 34) et de Michail Aleksandrovič (n° 43, 45) de Tver', d'Ivan Kalita (n° 35–8) ou de Vitovt (n° 44). Mais, à côté de ces exemples, on peut en citer d'autres où le même titre est utilisé pour des princes dont la puissance était moindre, même parfois pour ceux qui apparaissent comme les vaincus des querelles dynastiques, comme Boris et Gleb (n° 3–5) ou Roman Rostislavič de Smolensk chassé deux fois (1173, 1176) de Kiev (n° 20)[123] ou, enfin, Igor' Ol'govič de Černigov qui avait renoncé à la gloire princière pour prendre l'habit monacal (n° 11). Le prestige politique ne saurait, par conséquent, être considéré comme une condition essentielle pour qu'un prince russe soit qualifié de *car'*.

Bien plus, la puissance politique d'un prince est, le plus souvent, au moins jusqu'au XIIIe siècle, exprimée par un autre terme, celui de *samoderž'c'* (ou *samovlastec'*). Ainsi, dans le passage de la Chronique de Galicie qui vient d'être rappelé (n° 25), le terme *car'*, emprunté, nous l'avons vu, à l'*Aleksandrija*, sert à exprimer la puissance politique de Roman Mstislavič,[124] mais dans un autre passage de la même œuvre, tout au début, la même réalité est traduite par l'expression 'autocrate de toute la Russie': ...по см(е)рти же великаго князя Романа, приснопамятнаго *самодержьца* всея Руси...[125]

Le même terme sert à rappeler, au début du Dit sur la passion de Boris et Gleb, que, avant la période troublée où périrent les deux frères, Vladimir régnait en maître absolu sur 'tout le pays russe': ...сущю *самодрьжьцю* вьсеи Русьскѣи земли Володимиру, с(ы)ну Святославлю...[126]

Un peu plus tard, le mot *samovlastec'* est utilisé par le chroniqueur pour souligner le fait que, à la mort de son frère, Mstislav de Tmutorokan' (1036), Jaroslav devint le souverain unique de la Russie: Мьстиславъ... умре..., посемь же перея власть его всю Ярославъ и бысть *самавластець* Русьстѣи земли.[127] La version hypatienne emploie d'ailleurs le terme plus explicite de *edinovlastec'* (littéralement 'monocrate').[128] En fait, dans ce cas, les termes *samovlastec'* et *edinovlastec'* expriment la même réalité qu'une expression telle que ...бѣ володѣя единъ в Руси..., utilisée par la *Povest' vremennych let* pour caractériser le pouvoir qu'exerçait, en 977, Jaropolk.[129]

Dans un autre exemple, le terme *samovlastec'* sert à exprimer l'exercice d'un pouvoir monarchique absolu face aux autres forces sociopolitiques; il s'agit du passage de la Chronique de Kiev où est

[123] Cf. B. A. Rybakov, *Russkie letopiscy* (n. 48), 26.
[124] Aussi nous paraît-il difficile d'accepter la traduction anglaise de G. A. Perfecky, op. cit. (n. 68), 58, 'His father was the Emperor of Rus'', dans la mesure où cette expression confère au terme *car'* une valeur institutionnelle que rien ne vient corroborer dans le contexte.
[125] *PSRL*, ii, col. 715.
[126] *Die altrussischen hagiographischen Erzählungen* (n. 43), 27; *Uspenskij sbornik* (n. 45), 43, f. 8b.
[127] *PVL*, 101.   [128] *PSRL*, ii, col. 138.   [129] *PVL*, 54.

relatée l'expulsion par Andrej Bogoljubskij de l'évêque local, des membres de la famille princière et de certains conseillers de Jurij Dolgorukij, et qui se termine par cette remarque: ...хотя *самовластець* быти всѣи Суждальскои земли.[130]

On voit, à l'aide de ces quelques exemples, que c'est le terme *samoderž'c'*, ou *samovlastec'*, et non pas *car'* qui sert à souligner le caractère monarchique et absolu du pouvoir exercé par un prince, sans d'ailleurs avoir, pour autant, une valeur institutionnelle.[131]

Une dernière question doit être soulevée à propos de la valeur politique qu'aurait eue le terme *car'*. Dans le commentaire qu'il a donné du passage extrait du Récit sur la mort de Michail Jaroslavič (n° 34), V. A. Kučkin a présenté l'emploi du verbe *carstvovati* comme une affirmation des droits souverains des princes de Tver' sur la Russie face au pouvoir du khan tatar.[132] Cette interprétation d'un exemple isolé ne paraît pas convaincante. Ne faudrait-il pas voir plutôt dans cet emploi du verbe *carstvovati* un effet littéraire destiné à opposer la gloire passée du prince aux humiliations qu'il eut à subir au moment de son exécution, comme débiteur insolvable, à la Horde d'Or? Ce passage doit, à notre avis, être rapproché de celui de la Chronique galicienne où la gloire 'impériale' de Roman Mstislavič est opposée à l'humiliation de son fils Daniil (n° 25). D'autre part, comme nous le verrons plus bas, il est possible que l'emploi d'un dérivé de *car'* s'explique par le martyre de Michail Jaroslavič.

Ainsi, l'examen des sources auquel nous venons de procéder nous permet, pour l'instant, de proposer deux conclusions négatives: le titre de *car'* appliqué aux princes russes ne comporte aucune valeur institutionnelle précise permettant de l'opposer au terme *knjaz'*; il n'exprime, d'autre part, aucune réalité politique concrète et ne sert pas davantage à affirmer une quelconque revendication d'ordre politique.[133]

Néanmoins, les emplois du titre de *car'* sont suffisamment nombreux pour que nous tentions d'en déceler les raisons.

La première remarque que permettent de formuler les exemples donnés plus haut s'appuie sur la chronologie des textes cités, autant que celle-ci peut être établie avec certitude. L'emploi du terme *car'*

---

[130] *PSRL*, ii, col. 520.

[131] Notons là encore une nette différence avec la terminologie politique des Slaves méridionaux où le terme 'autocrate' a une valeur officielle, qu'il soit associé à celui d' 'empereur' (cf. n. 96) ou qu'il soit employé seul, chez les Serbes notamment, cf. G. Ostrogorsky, op. cit. (n. 1), 141–60.

[132] Cf. n. 79.

[133] Cette dernière constatation diffère totalement de celle à laquelle a abouti un examen de l'emploi du terme *car'* dans les sources narratives roumaines de la fin du xve et du xvie siècle où il traduit une revendication de l'héritage byzantin, cf. P. Ş. Nasturel, op. cit. (n. 122), 410–11.

pour désigner un prince russe connaît une relative faveur à partir du début du XIIᵉ siècle, c'est-à-dire à un moment où les théories politico-religieuses de Byzance pénètrent de façon plus intensive en Russie, comme en témoignent tout particulièrement les épîtres du métropolite Nicéphore (1104–21) adressées à Vladimir Monomaque[134] ou la diffusion des écrits d'Agapet dans le recueil de la *Pčela* (*Μέλισσα*).[135] L'identité entre la nature du pouvoir princier et celle du pouvoir impérial, admise déjà au XIᵉ siècle, mais affirmée de façon particulièrement explicite par un homme comme Nicéphore,[136] a pu favoriser l'emploi du terme *car'* pour désigner des princes russes, d'autant plus que, d'une façon générale, ce vocable, à la suite probablement de la diffusion de nombreuses traductions de textes byzantins, a connu une certaine extension au XIIᵉ siècle, comme nous l'avons montré plus haut.

Ainsi l'usage du terme *car'* dans la titulature princière russe apparaît comme un témoignage de la transposition en Russie des théories byzantines sur la nature du pouvoir monarchique, mais il n'est pas, beaucoup s'en faut, la seule expression de cette évolution de la pensée politique russe. Il doit être rapproché de ces autres témoignages que sont, par exemple, l'usage des épithètes *blagověrnyi* (traduction du grec εὐσεβής, εὐσεβήστατος) ou *christoljubivyi* (grec, φιλόχριστος, φιλοχριστότατος),[137] appliquées aux princes russes — dont la diffusion reste à étudier — et surtout la présence de certains attributs impériaux dans l'iconographie princière russe.[138]

Dans ces conditions, on comprend aisément que, parallèlement à *knjaz'* et à ses dérivés, les lettrés russes aient pu utiliser occasionnellement *car'* et ses dérivés pour parler des princes russes. Cet usage était, de surcroît, favorisé, par exemple, pour le verbe *carstvovati* ou le substantif *carstvie*, largement attestés les textes slavons, par le fait que *knjažiti* et *knjaženie* semblent être apparus tardivement et avoir connu une expansion limitée.[139]

---

[134] Cf. F. Dvornik, 'Byzantine Political Ideas in Kievan Russia', *Dumbarton Oaks Papers*, ix/x (1956), 110–14. Le règne de Vladimir Monomaque constitue, par conséquent, une étape dans l'utilisation du titre de *car'* en Russie, comme l'a pensé V. S. Ikonnikov (cf. n. 11), mais les raisons sont différentes de celles qu'avait avancées l'historien russe.

[135] Cf. I. Ševčenko, op. cit. (n. 56), 144.

[136] Cf. *supra*, p. 23 et n. 113. Il faut, toutefois, remarquer ici que si Nicéphore identifie le pouvoir princier au pouvoir impérial, il prend soin, sur le plan généalogique, de distinguer les origines 'princières' de Vladimir Monomaque (par son père) de ses origines 'impériales' (par sa mère), cf. *Russkie dostopamjatnosti* (n. 106), 63.

[137] Sur l'emploi de ces épithètes à Byzance, cf. R. Guilland, *Études byzantines* (Paris, 1959), 218, L.-P. Raybaud, *Le Gouvernement et l'administration centrale de l'Empire byzantin sous les premiers Paléologues, 1258–1354* (Paris, 1968), 93.

[138] Cf. la bibliographie donnée par M. Cherniavsky, '*Khan or Basileus*' (n. 15), 461, n. 5, et par A. Poppe, 'Le prince et l'Église' (n. 12), 113, n. 54 et du même Auteur, *Państwo i Kościół na Rusi w XI wieku* (Warszawa, 1968), 79–82; voir également M. B. Sverdlov, 'Izobraženie knjažeskich regalij na monetach Vladimira Svjatoslaviča', *Vspomogatel'nye istoričeskie discipliny*, iv (1972), 151–9.

[139] Cf. A. S. L'vov, op. cit. (n. 5), 200–2.

Cependant, l'usage du titre de *car'* par les princes russes paraît avoir été freiné à partir du xiiie siècle, très probablement à cause de la soumission de la Russie au *car'* tatar, ce qui donnerait partiellement raison à la thèse d'I. I. Sreznevskij et de T. Wasilewski qui voyaient dans l'attribution aux princes russes du titre de *car'* une affirmation de l'indépendance politique de leurs États,[140] et à celle de M. Cherniavsky selon laquelle le khan de la Horde d'Or était considéré par les Russes des xiiie–xve siècles comme le détenteur du pouvoir 'impérial', un pouvoir beaucoup plus immédiat que celui qui était reconnu au lointain *basileus*.[141]

Néanmoins, cette situation n'élimina pas totalement l'usage du terme *car'* pour désigner un prince russe. C'est pourquoi nous pensons que, si l'adoption par les milieux dirigeants russes des doctrines politiques byzantines justifie la *possibilité* pour des princes russes d'être qualifiés de *cari*, les raisons essentielles de l'usage de ce titre dans des circonstances ou dans un contexte précis doivent être cherchées hors du domaine politique.

Un examen rapide des textes cités fait apparaître une constatation importante: la majorité de ces témoignages (32 sur 46) concerne des princes morts plus ou moins longtemps avant la rédaction du texte (no 1–5, 10–12, 15, 16, 19–21, 25, 28–32, 34–46).

Parmi ceux-ci, cinq exemples se rapportent à des princes martyrs ou, plus exactement, 'qui ont souffert la passion' (*strastoterpcy*), sans que ce soit pour la cause du Christ: Boris et Gleb (no 3–5, 10, 16) et, au xiie siècle, Igor' de Černigov (no 11). A ces exemples on peut également rattacher le passage sur Roman Rostislavič, dont le prénom de baptême a permis un rapprochement explicite avec Boris–Roman (no 20), réutilisé par le chroniqueur volhynien pour Vladimir Vasil'kovič (no 29): l'attribution du titre de *car'* à ces deux princes au moment de leur mort semble liée aux 'vexations' (*dosady*) qu'ils auraient subies, de leur vivant, l'un de la part des 'gens de Smolensk', l'autre de la part de 'sa famille'.

Parmi les textes que nous avons utilisés, deux autres œuvres consacrées à des princes assassinés, Andrej Bogoljubskij et Michail Jaroslavič de Tver', ont été, du point de vue littéraire, influencées par le thème de Boris et Gleb;[142] et on peut se demander si l'attribution indirecte du titre de *car'* — à l'aide de la citation d'Agapet — au premier (no 15) et surtout l'usage du verbe *carstvovati* pour le second (no 34) ne doivent pas être mis en liaison avec leur mort violente.

Enfin, sur les trois exemples concernant Izjaslav Mstislavič de Kiev,

[140] Cf. nn. 2 et 4.
[141] Cf. *supra*, p. 6 et n. 29.
[142] Cf. N. N. Voronin, op. cit. (n. 55), 88, V. A. Kučkin, op. cit. (n. 79), 238–41, et M. Cherniavsky, *Tsar and People: Studies in Russian Myths* (New Haven–London, 1961), 11–16.

l'un d'entre eux nous offre l'image d'un prince, sinon assassiné, au moins blessé (n° 18).

Nous retrouvons là le thème du 'roi martyr' (rappelons que le latin *rex*, tout comme le slave *car'*, traduit le grec βασιλεύς) connu dans la pensée politico-religieuse du Bas-Empire et du Haut Moyen Âge. Il est, par exemple, explicitement évoqué dans les Dialogues de saint Grégoire le Grand: en parlant de l'assassinat du prince wisigoth Herménégilde (orthodoxe) par son père Léovigilde (aryen), l'auteur décrit un phénomène miraculeux apparu sur la tombe de la victime et le commente en ces termes: 'Nam coepit in nocturno silentio psalmodiae cantus ad corpus ejusdem *regis* et *martyris* audiri, atque ideo veraciter *regis* quia *martyris*.'[143] Il ne nous est pas possible, dans le cadre de cet article, d'entreprendre une étude comparée du thème du 'roi martyr' dans la chrétienté médiévale, mais il ressort du rapprochement qui vient d'être esquissé qu'une analyse de ce thème dans un cadre exclusivement russe, comme cela a été fait jusqu'à maintenant,[144] ne peut être que partielle; celle-ci ne saurait être menée à bien que dans une étude globale de l'image du *rex-basileus* chez les peuples héritiers, à un titre ou à un autre, de la tradition impériale romaine marquée par l'influence biblique.[145]

En ce qui concerne notre propos, le thème du 'roi martyr' permet de justifier, peut-être, l'attribution du titre de *car'* dans 11 ou 12 citations au maximum (si l'on admet que l'emploi du terme *car'* dans l'exemple n° 28 est une conséquence de son usage dans le texte des lamentations de la veuve de Vladimir Vasil'kovič, n° 29). Il ne saurait expliquer l'emploi du terme *car'* dans les 22 passages où des princes décédés sont qualifiés de *car'*. Cependant, pour la plupart, ces passages présentent comme caractéristique commune — si l'on excepte ceux qui évoquent sous une forme très lapidaire saint Vladimir ou ses prédécesseurs — de mettre en valeur les vertus religieuses ou morales du prince défunt.

Déjà dans l'inscription de Sainte-Sophie, l'emploi du mot *uspen'e* pour parler de la mort de Jaroslav le Sage (n° 1) donne à cet événement, comme l'a fait remarquer S. A. Vysoc'kyj, une coloration religieuse très nette; en effet, ce terme, utilisé dans la liturgie orthodoxe pour désigner la 'Dormition' (l'Assomption dans la terminologie latine) de la Vierge (15 août), n'est attesté, dans les textes russes de l'époque kiévienne, qu'à l'occasion de la mort de saint Théodose, abbé du Monastère des Grottes.[146]

---

[143] *Gregorii Magni Dialogi libri IV* (Rome, 1924), 206.

[144] Cf. G. P. Fedotov, *Svjatye Drevnej Rusi* (New York, 1960), 18–31, et du même Auteur, *The Russian Religious Mind*, i: *Kievan Christianity* (Harvard, 1946), 94–106.

[145] Pour l'Occident latin à la fin de l'Antiquité, cette étude vient d'être faite par M. Reydellet, *La Royauté dans la littérature latine de Sidoine Apollinaire à Isidore de Séville*, 3 vol., exemplaires dactylographiés (Paris, 1977).

[146] S. A. Vysockij, op. cit. (n. 42), 39, et *PVL*, 122.

Le caractère religieux du Panégyrique de Rostislav Mstislavič (n°
12), un texte destiné, d'après Ja. N. Ščapov, à préparer la canonisation
du prince,[147] ne fait pas de doute: le défunt a mérité le Ciel et... le
trône de Kiev (ц(а)рствовати в всеи Рускои земли) par le zèle qu'il
a manifesté pour l'Église de Smolensk.

Dans le passage sur la mort d'Izjaslav Mstislavič de Kiev, celui-ci
n'est pas seulement qualifié de *car'*, mais aussi de 'vénérable, orthodoxe
et ami du Christ' (n° 19).

Le Panégyrique d'Ivan Kalita (n° 35–8) ne mentionne pas seulement
l'action du prince en faveur de l'Église, sur laquelle nous reviendrons,
mais aussi son entrée dans les Ordres, peu avant sa mort, sous le nom
d'Ananij.[148]

De même, l'emploi du substantif *carstvo*, pour parler du règne de
Michail Aleksandrovič de Tver' (n° 43), apparaît dans un texte élaboré
dans l'entourage immédiat de l'évêque Arsène, où la prise d'habit du
prince, célébrée par ce même prélat, occupe une place essentielle.[149]

Dans d'autres cas, c'est la valeur morale du prince défunt qui est
soulignée parallèlement à l'attribution du titre de *car'*: c'est parce
qu'il 'aimait sa *družina* et châtiait les méchants' que David Rostislavič
de Smolensk est jugé digne d'être comparé aux *cesari* (n° 21). Plus tard,
pour dire que les divertissements de l'adolescent Michail Aleksandrovič
de Tver' étaient chastes et pieux, l'auteur de son Panégyrique les qualifie
de *carskye* (n° 45).

Ces liens que l'on constate, dans les exemples qui viennent d'être
cités, entre l'attribution du terme *car'* à un prince russe et son martyre
ou ses vertus religieuses et morales nous incitent à rapprocher l'usage
du terme *car'* du problème général du culte religieux des princes russes
défunts.

Parmi les princes mentionnés dans cette étude, certains ont fait
l'objet d'une canonisation générale, tels Vladimir reconnu comme
saint, au moins *de facto*, à partir du xiiie siècle,[150] c'est-à-dire à une
date antérieure à celle où furent rédigés les textes où il est qualifié de
car' (n° 39–42, 46), Boris et Gleb canonisés officiellement dès 1072
semble-t-il,[151] Igor' Ol'govič dont la canonisation paraît antérieure à
l'invasion mongole et dont le culte local existait à Černigov dès 1150
environ,[152] Andrej Bogoljubskij canonisé seulement en 1702, mais
vénéré dans le cadre d'un culte local peu après sa mort,[153] de même

[147] Ja. N. Ščapov, op. cit. (n. 6), 54.
[148] Cf. N. A. Meščerskij, op. cit. (n. 80), 96.
[149] Cf. *PSRL*, xv (1), col. 168–76. Sur la coutume de la prise d'habit par les princes russes
avant leur mort, cf. M. Cherniavsky, *Tsar and People* (n. 142), 34–5.
[150] Cf. E. E. Golubinskij, *Istorija kanonizacii svjatych v russkoj cerkvi* (M., 1903), 63–4.
[151] Cf. A. Poppe, 'O vremeni zaroždenija kul'ta Borisa i Gleba', *Russia mediaevalis*, i (1973),
6–29 (résumé en allemand).
[152] Cf. E. E. Golubinskij, op. cit. (n. 150), 58.   [153] Cf. ibid. 59, 134.

Michail Jaroslavič de Tver' dont le culte local fut sanctionné officiel-lement par le Concile de 1549.[154] D'autres, s'ils n'ont jamais été reconnus comme saints par l'ensemble de l'Église russe, paraissent néanmoins avoir fait l'objet d'un culte local: tel semble être le cas de Jaroslav le Sage, de Rostislav Mstislavič, d'Ivan Kalita et de Michail Aleksandrovič.[155] Seuls parmi les princes qualifiés de *car'* à leur mort, Roman Rostislavič de Smolensk et Vladimir Vasil'kovič de Vladimir en Volhynie ne semblent avoir fait l'objet d'aucun culte, mais nous avons vu que le premier d'entre eux était comparé à Boris–Roman (n° 20) et que l'attribution du titre de *car'* à Vladimir Vasil'kovič était calquée sur le modèle de Roman Rostislavič (n° 29).

D'une façon générale, comme l'a montré M. Cherniavsky, nos in-formations sur le culte dont pouvait être entourée la mémoire des princes russes sont fragmentaires et très probablement incomplètes, si bien qu'il est difficile de tracer des frontières précises entre les princes qui ont fait l'objet d'un culte et les autres, tout prince étant susceptible d'être considéré, tant dans la tradition populaire que dans la doctrine politico-religieuse de la Russie médiévale, comme un saint.[156] Aussi, l'attribution du titre de *car'* le plus souvent à des princes morts et dans des écrits destinés à célébrer leur mémoire (n° 1, 3–5, 10–12, 15, 16, 19–21, 28, 29, 34–8, 43–5) peut-elle être interprétée comme l'un des moyens de proclamer la sainteté d'un prince, soit pour reconnaître ainsi une canonisation officielle de l'Église, soit pour exprimer une dévotion locale et frayer la voie à cette canonisation. L'emploi du titre de *car'* avec une valeur religieuse et morale a subsisté jusqu'au milieu du XVe siècle, où elle est attestée dans le Panégyrique de Dmitrij Donskoj.[157]

Il va sans dire que l'attribution du titre de *car'* n'était que l'un des moyens d'affirmer la sainteté d'un prince et que le recours à ce pro-cédé lexical n'était nullement obligatoire; il serait aisé de citer de nombreux exemples de princes dont la mémoire fut entourée d'une dévotion certaine, tel Aleksandr Nevskij, et qui semblent n'avoir jamais été, pour autant, qualifiés de *car'* dans les sources.

D'un autre côté, l'attribution du titre de *car'* à Vladimir Svjato-slavič, aussi bien dans les fausses chartes de Lev Danilovič (n° 39–41) que dans la *Zadonščina* (n° 42), est justifiée peut-être par sa sainteté (reconnue depuis le XIIIe siècle), mais surtout par sa puissance politique, ainsi que l'atteste, nous l'avons vu, l'emploi de déterminants précis; cette puissance politique était utilisée, soit pour renforcer les droits temporels de l'Église orthodoxe en Galicie à la fin du XIVe siècle, soit pour rehausser le prestige du prince de Moscou. Bien plus, dans la

---

[154] Cf. E. E. Golubinskij, op. cit. (n. 150), 67, 104.   [155] Cf. ibid. 350–1, 365, 355, 362.
[156] Cf. M. Cherniavsky, *Tsar and People* (n. 142), 32.
[157] Cf. ibid. 25–8.

version galicienne de la *Povest' vremennych let*, tous les princes de Kiev, y compris les princes païens, sont appelés *cari* (n° 30), et le verbe *carstvovati* est utilisé pour Rjurik et Oleg (n° 31, 32). Ainsi, à côté de la sainteté des princes, le titre de *car'* peut exprimer la puissance politique, mais uniquement pour des souverains appartenant à un passé lointain, tout comme, par exemple, il pouvait désigner, nous l'avons dit, des souverains païens dans la Bible ou dans le Roman d'Alexandre.

Enfin, les liens que nous avons identifiés entre la sainteté des princes, ou leur prestige politique dans certains cas, et l'usage du terme *car'* ne sauraient, cependant, rendre compte de l'attribution de ce titre à des princes vivants et régnants (n° 6–9, 13, 14, 17, 18, 22–4, 26, 27, 33).

Le premier prince à être explicitement qualifié de *car'* de son vivant est Mstislav Vladimirovič de Kiev dans le colophon de son Évangéliaire rédigé par Naslav (n° 7–9). Au XIIIᵉ siècle, le prince de Vladimir en Volhynie est également appelé *car'* dans un colophon de manuscrit, patristique cette fois (n° 26, 27).

Ces deux témoignages doivent, à notre avis, être rapprochés des nombreux manuscrits grecs où le nom de l'empereur régnant est mentionné dans le colophon, souvent pour dater ainsi le volume.[158] L'influence d'un modèle byzantin est très probable pour l'Évangéliaire de Mstislav, puisque nous savons que l'auteur du colophon s'était rendu à Constantinople pour faire relier le volume, et on peut supposer qu'en rédigeant un colophon de type byzantin, il a emprunté à son modèle le titre de *car'* qui, au XIIᵉ siècle, traduisait systématiquement le grec βασιλεύς. On peut également supposer que, dans le carrefour d'influences culturelles qu'étaient les pays de Galicie et de Volhynie au XIIIᵉ siècle, le scribe du manuscrit de saint Éphrem le Syrien destiné à un familier du prince Vladimir Vasil'kovič a pu avoir sous les yeux un manuscrit grec daté d'après le règne d'un empereur et qu'il a servilement adapté ce modèle à la réalité politique de son pays.

C'est également par l'influence d'un modèle byzantin que l'on peut tenter d'expliquer l'emploi, par trois fois, de la titulature 'impériale' dans le texte rédigé par Moïse, abbé de Vydubič, à la gloire du grand-prince de Kiev, Rjurik Rostislavič (n° 22–4). Ce texte est, en effet, un morceau de rhétorique sans aucun rapport avec la réalité institutionnelle ou politique contemporaine que Ju. K. Begunov rattache avec vraisemblance à la tradition littéraire byzantine.[159] Notons que, en ce qui concerne la titulature, l'influence grecque ne se limite pas à l'emploi des dérivés de *car'*, elle apparaît encore plus nettement dans l'usage du terme *kjur''* (n° 22), transcription livresque et maladroite du grec κύρ(ιος).

[158] Cf. K. Treu, 'Byzantinische Kaiser in den Schreibernotizen griechischer Handschriften', *Byzantinische Zeitschrift*, lxv (1972), 9–34, en particulier, 16–21.
[159] Cf. *supra*, p. 13 et n. 66.

Nous avons examiné plus haut la citation nᵒ 18 où le terme *car'* s'applique à un prince blessé.

Parmi les autres exemples concernant un prince vivant, seul le nᵒ 17 a une valeur exclusivement politique, difficile à définir au demeurant : le verbe *carstvovati* aurait pu, semble-t-il, être remplacé dans ce passage de la Chronique par *knjažiti*. En revanche, tous les autres exemples qui nous restent à analyser sont extraits, tout comme les citations nᵒ 22–4, d'un contexte religieux ou ecclésiastique.

Dès le début du XIIᵉ siècle, le métropolite Nicéphore utilisait le verbe *carstvovati* pour parler du règne des princes russes (nᵒ 6). Or, ce prélat grec, dans une autre épître, a précisé les devoirs religieux d'un prince chrétien : celui-ci devait non seulement obéir aux règles morales que l'Église impose à tout chrétien, mais était considéré comme responsable du salut de ses sujets : ...молю Бога до конца ти съблюдену быти цѣлу : съблюдено же ти се будеть, аще въ стадо Христово не даси влъку внити, и аще въ виноградъ, иже насади Богъ, не даси насадити трънїа, но съхраниши преданїа старое (*sic*) отецъ твоихъ.[160]

Le prince est, par conséquent, convié à exercer un pouvoir dans l'Église. Ce pouvoir ne pouvait, dans la mentalité des clercs grecs ou russes, qu'être de même nature que celui de l'empereur dans la 'Grande Église'. Tout comme ce dernier avait, depuis le Vᵉ siècle au moins, la haute main sur les dyptiques où étaient, entre autres, consignés les noms des défunts proposés à la vénération des fidèles,[161] le prince russe était amené à intervenir dans la canonisation des saints ; c'est dans ces circonstances que Jaroslav est qualifié, sous la plume du moine Nestor, de *car'* (nᵒ 2). Beaucoup plus important était le pouvoir disciplinaire que le prince pouvait être amené à exercer dans l'Église ; ainsi, pour l'auteur, très probablement ecclésiastique, du Récit sur la déposition de l'évêque Théodore, Andrej Bogoljubskij a destitué celui-ci 'de son bras impérial' (nᵒ 13).[162] Plus tard, pour inciter le grand-prince Michail Jaroslavič à agir de même avec le métropolite Pierre, le moine Akindin lui rappela qu'il était '*car'* dans son pays' en ajoutant qu'il devrait rendre compte devant Dieu de sa passivité s'il ne sévissait pas contre le chef de l'Église russe accusé de simonie (nᵒ 33). Les princes russes se trouvaient ainsi investis du droit de destituer le métropolite ou un évêque tout comme, à Constantinople, l'empereur pouvait destituer le patriarche.[163] Ajoutons que Michail Jaroslavič semble s'être rendu

---

[160] *Russkie dostopamjatnosti* (n. 106), 70.

[161] Cf. A. Michel, *Die Kaisermacht in der Ostkirche, 843–1204* (Darmstadt, 1959), 88–98.

[162] Certes, l'usage de l'adjectif *carskyi* peut s'expliquer par le caractère 'impérial' de la Chronique d'Andrej Bogoljubskij, cf. B. A. Rybakov, *Russkie letopiscy* (n. 48), 74, mais il n'en reste pas moins que dans ce texte, où les épithètes solennelles ne manquent pas, l'adjectif *carskyi* n'est employé que pour décrire le prince dans l'exercice de ses fonctions 'ecclésiales' et dans un récit d'origine ecclésiastique, cf. *supra*, p. 11 et n. 52.

[163] Cf. A. Michel, op. cit. (n. 161), 70–2, et L.-P. Raybaud, op. cit. (n. 137), 105–8.

aux arguments d'Akindin et, exerçant sur le plan local un pouvoir de
type impérial,[164] convoqua en 1310 à Perejaslavl'-Zaleskij un synode —
où le grand-prince était représenté par ses fils — afin de juger Pierre.[165]

Le fait qu'Akindin, en qualifiant son souverain de *car'*, n'ait envisagé
que l'aspect ecclésiastique de la fonction impériale est confirmé par
un autre passage de son épître où, après avoir explicitement rapproché l'action dans l'Église des empereurs de celle de 'nos princes',
il souligne le parallèle entre les fonctions 'impériale' (au sens large?) et
épiscopale : А церкви Христовою благодатію отъ нужи приречен-
н(ы)е свобожьшися отъ благочестивыхъ *царь* и *князь* нашихъ, (и)
изрядныхъ іерѣи, яко кринъ въ благоуханіе Христови процвѣтши.
Святительство бо и *ц(е)с(а)рьство* съединеніемъ и бес порока закон-
ныя уставы твердо и неподвижимо должни суть держати и творити:
ово же божественымъ служа, ово же человѣчьскыми обладая;
единѣмъ же началомъ вѣры и закономъ обое происходя, человѣчь-
ское украшаетъ житіе.[166]

Ce même aspect de la fonction impériale exercée par des princes
russes qualifiés de *car'* est attesté dans certains des textes consacrés
à la mémoire de princes morts. Ainsi le Panégyrique d'Ivan Kalita fait
clairement allusion au rôle joué par ce prince dans la vie interne de
l'Église russe de son temps; l'auteur de ce texte évoque non seulement
l'activité de bâtisseur que déploya le prince (c'est à elle que l'on
doit la première cathédrale de l'Assomption à Moscou), mais aussi
l'action qu'il aurait menée contre 'les hérésies': ...безбожнымъ
ересамъ преставшимъ при его державѣ.[167] Peu importe la nature
exacte de ces 'hérésies', qui n'ont guère laissé de traces dans d'autres
sources (il s'agissait probablement, comme à l'époque de Michail
Jaroslavič, tout simplement de simonie),[168] retenons, pour notre étude,
qu'un prince qualifié dans son Panégyrique, plus ou moins directement, de *car'* se voit attribuer les fonctions impériales de gardien de
l'orthodoxie.[169]

D'autre part, l'emploi du verbe *carstvovati* pour Rostislav Mstislavič
s'explique certainement, nous l'avons dit, par le désir de l'auteur
de son Panégyrique de préparer la canonisation du prince, mais les
mérites de celui-ci sont constitués non pas tant par la pratique des
vertus chrétiennes que par l'initiative qu'il a prise dans l'administration de l'Église, en fondant la chaire épiscopale de Smolensk et en lui
attribuant un temporel.[170]

---

[164] Cf. A. Michel, op. cit. (n. 161), 62–9.
[165] Cf. V. S. Borzakovskij, *Istorija Tverskogo knjažestva* (Spb., 1876), 96–7.
[166] *RIB*, vi, col. 155.
[167] N. A. Meščerskij, op. cit. (n. 80), 96.
[168] Cf. A. I. Klibanov, *Reformacionnye dviženija v Rossii v XIV — pervoj polovine XVI v.* (M.,
1960), 120–1.   [169] Cf. A. Michel, op. cit. (n. 161), 78–87.
[170] Cf. Ja. N. Ščapov, op. cit. (n. 6), 59.

Enfin, Andrej Bogoljubskij, en plus de l'exemple commenté plus haut, est qualifié de *car'* dans un texte lié à un culte local, celui de saint Léonce, premier évêque de Rostov (n° 14), mais, nous l'avons vu, la tradition manuscrite de ce passage ne paraît pas certaine.

Il ressort de ce qui vient d'être dit, surtout d'après les témoignages très précieux que sont les épîtres du métropolite Nicéphore et du moine Akindin, que la hiérarchie ecclésiastique accordait aux princes russes en général, mais surtout au prince de Kiev et, plus tard, à celui de Vladimir, une place privilégiée face à l'épiscopat et en particulier au métropolite. Celui-ci étant, au moins *de facto*, investi, dans le cadre de l'Église russe, de pouvoirs comparables à ceux qu'exerçait le patriarche dans l'Église 'universelle', le souverain russe se voyait attribuer, conformément aux structures ecclésiastiques grecques, toujours sur le plan local, des pouvoirs analogues à ceux qui revenaient, dans le cadre de l'*oikouménè*, à l'empereur.

Cette position du prince, ou, à partir de la fin du XIIᵉ siècle, du grand-prince, dans l'édifice ecclésial russe est confirmée par un autre fait, relevé depuis longtemps par les historiens: il est très probable que les noms des princes russes étaient mentionnés dans les offices là où l'Église grecque plaçait ceux des empereurs.[171] L'évocation du nom des princes dans les colophons de manuscrits, surtout liturgiques, comme un Évangéliaire (n° 7–9), peut être également considérée comme une confirmation de cet usage.

Enfin, la coïncidence chronologique entre le moment où le titre de *car'* commence à être attribué plus fréquemment à des princes russes et celui où est diffusée, par un homme comme Nicéphore, la doctrine selon laquelle le prince exerce des responsabilités de chef religieux n'est peut-être pas fortuite. On peut y voir une nouvelle preuve de ce que le pouvoir de nature impériale qu'exerçaient occasionnellement les princes russes n'appartenait pas au domaine politique, mais aux domaines religieux et ecclésiastique. C'est pourquoi les princes russes purent continuer à porter épisodiquement le titre de *car'*, même lorsqu'ils reconnurent le pouvoir politique du *car'* tatar: pour des raisons évidentes, ils ne pouvaient pas abdiquer entre les mains d'un khan païen ou musulman les responsabilités que la tradition byzantine leur avait attribuées en matière ecclésiastique.

[171] Cf. M. A. D'jakonov, op. cit. (n. 7), 24, n. 2, M. Cherniavsky, '*Khan or Basileus*' (n. 15), 461, n. 7, et A. Poppe, 'Le prince et l'Église' (n. 12), 112–13. Il faut remarquer ici que, au moment où le grand-prince de Moscou Vasilij I eut la velléité d'interdire la commémoration du nom de l'empereur (cf. n. 25), il ne s'agissait que de la commémoration par le métropolite dans sa cathédrale et non pas par l'ensemble du clergé (cf. *RIB*, vi, col. 271–2). De plus, cette commémoration n'excluait pas celle des princes russes, puisque, à la même époque, le métropolite Cyprien, cherchant à étendre les pratiques liturgiques de sa cathédrale à l'ensemble de la province ecclésiastique russe, écrivait au clergé de Pskov, dans les dernières années du XIVᵉ siècle: *da priložili esmy k″ tomu, kak″ pravoslavnych carii pominati takože i knjazei velikich″ i mertvych″ i živych″, jakože my zdě v″ mitropol'i pominaem″*, *RIB*, vi, col. 239.

Cette fonction impériale qu'exerçaient les princes russes dans le cadre de leur Église locale fut apparemment reconnue par Byzance, à condition que l'autorité de l'empereur à la tête de l'*oikoumènè* fût respectée, jusqu'à la fin de l'Empire grec: en 1439–41, le grand-prince de Tver' Boris Aleksandrovič l'exerça, au nom de tous les princes russes, y compris celui de Moscou, en se faisant représenter par l'un des ses *bojare* au Concile de Ferrare–Florence.[172] C'est ce qui explique, peut-être, la fréquence de l'emploi du terme *car'* dans le *Slovo pochval'noe* du pseudo-Thomas, en particulier dans la première partie de cette œuvre consacrée précisément à la participation du grand-prince au Concile, mais nous dépassons là les limites de notre étude.

Il reste cependant une prérogative impériale, dans le domaine ecclésiastique toujours, que les princes russes ont par moments revendiquée, mais que Byzance ne semble guère leur avoir accordée, tout au moins de façon durable, celle d'intervenir dans la nomination du chef de l'Église.[173] Parmi les textes cités, nous n'avons trouvé qu'une seule allusion à cette prérogative, dans l'épître du grand-prince Vasilij II au patriarche Mitrophane (nº 46). Nous pensons, en effet, que l'attribution du titre de *car'* à saint Vladimir n'est pas seulement destinée à souligner son baptême,[174] mais, comme le suggère tout le contexte, à rappeler que 'le nouveau Constantin' était intervenu dans la nomination du premier métropolite russe, ce qui ne pouvait pas ne pas constituer, aux yeux de Vasilij II et de son entourage, un argument supplémentaire pour autoriser, au milieu du XVe siècle, l'élection d'un métropolite, sans l'intervention de Constantinople, par un synode d'évêques locaux convoqué par le souverain russe.

Il est, d'autre part, intéressant de constater que, parmi les princes des XIe et XIIe siècles le plus souvent qualifiés de *car'*, on trouve trois souverains qui ont précisément tenté d'exercer la prérogative impériale de nommer le chef de l'Église russe ou d'une partie de celle-ci: en effet, Jaroslav le Sage, en faisant élire le moine Hilarion à la chaire métropolitaine de Kiev (1051), a usé, comme l'écrit A. Poppe, 'des mêmes droits que ceux qui, selon l'opinion du clergé byzantin, revenaient à l'empereur';[175] de même, bien que les circonstances fussent différentes, Izjaslav Mstislavič usa, lui aussi, de prérogatives impériales en faisant nommer, en 1147, comme métropolite, contre la volonté

---

[172] Cf. *Inoka Fomy Slovo pochval'noe*, éd. par N. P. Lichačev (n. 17), 3–5, et introduction, p. xviii–xxi.

[173] Sur le rôle de l'empereur dans ce domaine à Byzance, cf. A. Michel, op. cit. (n. 161), 27–35, et L.-P. Raybaud, op. cit. (n. 137), 104–5.

[174] Cf. D. Obolensky, op. cit. (n. 39), 29.

[175] A. Poppe, 'Le prince et l'Église' (n. 12), 99, cf. également du même Auteur, 'La tentative de réforme ecclésiastique en Russie au milieu du XIe siècle', *Acta Poloniae historica*, xxv (1972), 23; D. Obolensky, 'Byzantium, Kiev and Moscow: a Study in Ecclesiastical Relations', *Dumbarton Oaks Papers*, xi (1957), 60–4 (reproduit dans *Byzantium and the Slavs* (n. 39)); et L. Müller, *Des Metropoliten Ilarion Lobrede* (n. 23), 1–11.

de Byzance et d'une fraction de l'épiscopat russe, Clément de Smolensk (Klim Smoljatič);[176] enfin, Andrej Bogoljubskij tenta, vers 1164, de faire créer dans sa nouvelle capitale, Vladimir, une chaire métropolitaine indépendante de celle de Kiev et d'y faire nommer un clerc de son choix.[177] L'attribution à Jaroslav du titre de *car'* à une époque où son usage n'est guère attesté par ailleurs, la relative fréquence avec laquelle ce titre est décerné à Andrej Bogoljubskij et surtout à Izjaslav Mstislavič seraient-elles dues — en plus des autres raisons déjà analysées — aux initiatives prises par ces trois princes pour s'arroger le droit de nommer le chef de l'Église russe? Il est difficile de répondre à cette question. Toutefois, quelques témoignages tardifs permettent de suggérer une réponse affirmative: en plus des épîtres d'Akindin à Michail Jaroslavič (n° 33) et de Vasilij II au patriarche Mitrophane (n° 46), on peut encore citer le *Slovo na latynju* rédigé vers 1460.[178] En effet, dans cette œuvre, le grand-prince de Moscou est fréquemment appelé *car'*, alors que dans un autre texte consacré à l'apologie de Vasilij II défenseur de l'orthodoxie face à l'hérésie latine et à l'apostasie grecque, le Récit du huitième Concile œcuménique de Siméon de Suzdal' (*Povest' Simeona Suzdal'skogo ob Osmom sobore*), écrit vers 1444, le même souverain n'est qualifié que de православныи ou благовѣрныи великыи князь.[179] Cette différence dans la terminologie utilisée par les deux textes ne s'explique-t-elle pas par le fait qu'entre 1444 et 1460 eut lieu l'élection du premier métropolite russe autocéphale, Jonas, par un synode d'évêques convoqué à l'initiative du grand-prince Vasilij II (1448)? Il est permis, dans ces conditions, de supposer — sans l'affirmer — que l'intervention d'un prince dans la nomination du chef de l'Église aux XIᵉ et XIIᵉ siècles pouvait contribuer à lui faire donner par ses contemporains le titre de *car'*.

Mais l'absence, constatée une fois de plus, de tout emploi systématique du terme *car'* rend cette explication historique de l'usage du titre de *car'* hypothétique. L'historien ne peut qu'avancer une ou plusieurs raisons pour lesquelles l'attribution du titre de *car'* à un prince russe est possible, tout en traçant les limites de la valeur que pouvait revêtir ce terme. Pour rendre compte des raisons précises de l'usage de ce vocable dans un texte donné, il convient peut-être d'étudier de plus près la tradition littéraire dont il est le produit.

Parmi les exemples que nous avons cités, il est possible d'identifier, au moins approximativement, quelques unes de ces traditions. Ainsi,

---

[176] Sur cet événement, cf. D. Obolensky, op. cit. (n. 175), 64–72.
[177] Cf. W. Vodoff, op. cit. (n. 52), 202–11.   [178] Cf. n. 18.
[179] Les deux versions de ce texte ont été reproduites par V. Malinin dans *Starec Eleazarova monastyrja Filofej i ego poslanija* (Kiev, 1901), addendum, 89–114. La première des deux versions a été traduite en français par J.-P. Arrignon, 'Les Russes au Concile de Ferrare-Florence', *Irénikon*, xlvii (1974), 193–208; sur la date de l'œuvre, cf. p. 190.

dans la Chronique de Kiev, telle qu'elle est conservée dans le manuscrit de l'Hypatienne, le titre de *car'* est attribué aux princes martyrs (n° 10, 11, 16) dans la partie de la Chronique qui serait due à Polycarpe, abbé du Monastère des Grottes (milieu du XIIe siècle). Un sens plus large semble avoir été donné au terme *car'*, un demi-siècle plus tard, par Moïse, abbé du Monastère Saint-Michel de Vydubič, qui a montré son goût pour un lexique 'impérial' dans le discours adressé à Rjurik Rostislavič (n° 22-4); il n'est pas impossible que cet ecclésiastique, qui refondit la Compilation de 1198, soit responsable d'un certain nombre d'emplois du terme *car'*, par exemple dans la notice nécrologique de David Rostislavič (n° 21); les notices consacrées aux Rostislaviči (les descendants de Rostislav Mstislavič, petit-fils de Vladimir Monomaque) semblent être, en effet, de la main de Moïse,[180] mais il faut remarquer ici que les textes dédiés à la mémoire de Mstislav et de Roman Rostislavič ne contiennent pas le mot *car'*;[181] on ne sait pas, d'autre part, s'il faut attribuer à l'abbé de Vydubič les lamentations de la veuve du second de ces deux princes (n° 20). Il n'en reste pas moins que l'usage du terme *car'* ou de ses dérivés paraît avoir été relativement répandu dans l'entourage des Rostislaviči, qu'ils aient régné à Kiev ou seulement à Smolensk (n° 12, 16, 20-4). Ces princes semblent avoir récupéré à leur profit la tradition qui se créait à Kiev au début du XIIe siècle de désigner, officieusement, le prince par le terme *car'* (n° 7-9, 17-19).

Plus tard, aux XIVe-XVe siècles, dans la Russie du nord-est, il semblerait que l'usage du titre de *car'* ait été plus répandu dans la tradition littéraire tvérienne que dans celle de Moscou: on relève, en effet, le terme *car'* ou ses dérivés à Tver' dans trois ou quatre œuvres différentes (n° 33, 34, 43, 45), alors qu'à Moscou tous les exemples cités appartiennent au même texte, le Panégyrique d'Ivan Kalita (n° 35-8).

Au terme de cette étude — dont les conclusions devront être, répétons-le, complétées, voire corrigées, par un dépouillement systématique de toutes les sources et une étude globale du vocabulaire politique de la Russie ancienne —, nous pouvons nous hasarder à formuler quelques constatations.

Le terme *car'* et ses dérivés, attestés essentiellement dans les sources narratives, ne sont jamais appliqués à des princes russes de façon systématique et ne se substituent jamais au terme *knjaz'* et à ses dérivés. Employé, de plus, indifféremment pour le prince de Kiev ou pour un prince de moindre importance (aux XIe-XIIe siècles), pour des souverains puissants ou pour des princes faibles, le titre de *car'* ne semble recouvrir aucune réalité institutionnelle et n'exprime, à la différence du terme

[180] Cf. B. A. Rybakov, *Russkie letopiscy* (n. 48), 335, 65.
[181] Cf. *PSRL*, ii, col. 610-12, 617.

samoderž'c', aucun rapport de forces politiques, à l'exception peut-être des princes de Kiev du Xᵉ siècle, de saint Vladimir notamment, dans les sources tardives. Néanmoins, il est difficile de voir dans l'attribution à un prince russe du titre de *car'* le simple désir d'utiliser une formule laudative, comme ce fut le cas, à l'origine, pour l'usage de l'épithète *velikyi* devant le terme *knjaz'*.[182]

Attesté surtout au XIIᵉ siècle, l'emploi du terme *car'* pour désigner un prince russe peut être rapproché de la pénétration plus intensive à cette date des idées politiques byzantines: la nature du pouvoir princier, pour les théoriciens byzantins ou russes (tels que le métropolite Nicéphore, contemporain de Vladimir Monomaque), était identique à celle du pouvoir impérial; les princes russes, tout en reconnaissant la légitimité du pouvoir du *basileus* sur l'*oikoumênê* chrétienne, participaient, dans une certaine mesure, à la dignité et à la fonction impériales.[183] Cependant, il faut souligner que l'usage du titre de *car'* n'est que l'un des moyens, utilisé au demeurant assez rarement, dont disposaient les lettrés russes pour exprimer la vision qu'ils avaient du pouvoir princier.

Cette possibilité que la doctrine politique professée par le clergé byzantin laissait aux écrivains russes du XIᵉ au XVᵉ siècle de décerner à leurs princes le titre de *car'* ne semble avoir été utilisée que de façon très inégale selon la tradition littéraire à laquelle appartenait chacun d'entre eux, ce qui rend aléatoire toute tentative de dégager un sens précis du terme *car'* pour l'ensemble des exemples relevés. En fait, ceux-ci nous ont permis de définir, au moins approximativement, deux valeurs du vocable *car'* qui nous paraissent être le plus fréquemment attestées dans les sources: l'une est d'ordre religieux et moral, l'autre a trait aux fonctions que les princes russes se voyaient attribuer à l'intérieur de l'Église locale.

Les liens que nous avons relevés entre l'usage du terme *car'* et la mise en valeur des vertus chrétiennes d'un prince généralement défunt et, en particulier, l'attribution du titre de *car'* aux princes martyrs ou à ceux qui leur étaient, plus ou moins artificiellement, assimilés, permettent de supposer que, pour les lettrés russes du Moyen Âge, ce titre avait une valeur essentiellement religieuse et morale. L'emploi du terme *car'* pour désigner des princes russes au moment

---

[182] Cf. L. K. Goetz, 'Der Titel "Grossfürst" in den ältesten russischen Chroniken', *Zeitschrift für osteuropäische Geschichte*, i (1911), 23–35.

[183] Il est intéressant de noter qu'une conclusion assez proche a été tirée d'une étude de la fonction royale dans l'Occident barbare par rapport à l'institution impériale : 'La royauté est conçue non comme une délégation du pouvoir impérial, une lieutenance, mais comme la participation à l'idéal de gouvernement élaboré par l'Empire au cours des siècles' (M. Reydellet, op. cit. (n. 145), 213). Malheureusement l'absence, en Russie, d'une culture politique et juridique aussi élaborée que celle qu'a héritée l'Occident barbare ne nous permet pas de trouver des témoignages qui permettraient de définir d'une façon aussi limpide le pouvoir princier russe par rapport au pouvoir impérial.

de leur décès ou plus tard doit être, par conséquent, rapproché du culte — sanctionné parfois officiellement — dont ceux-ci, en très grand nombre, voire en majorité, faisaient l'objet après leur mort.

Mais l'attribution du titre de *car'* à quelques princes de leur vivant nous interdit de nous limiter à l'explication qui vient d'être proposée. Si on laisse de côté les cas où l'usage du titre de *car'* pour désigner un prince russe peut être dû à l'influence directe d'un modèle grec (dans les colophons de manuscrits notamment), il apparaît que ce titre est décerné à un prince vivant — comme d'ailleurs à certains princes morts — lorsque celui-ci a été amené à exercer (ou est convié à le faire), dans les limites de l'Église russe, des pouvoirs analogues à ceux que la tradition ecclésiastique byzantine attribuait à l'empereur dans le cadre de l'Église universelle. Aussi est-il permis de voir, dans l'emploi du terme *car'* pour désigner un prince, une preuve, parmi d'autres, de ce que les clercs voyaient dans les princes russes les détenteurs, en matière ecclésiastique, d'un pouvoir de type impérial.

Le fait que l'usage du terme *car'* ait été limité, pour les princes russes, aux domaines religieux ou ecclésiastique, explique que cet usage ait persisté à l'époque mongole, lorsque la Russie reconnaissait le pouvoir politique direct du *car'* de la Horde d'Or. Mais il est probable que c'est le joug mongol qui empêcha, pendant plus de deux siècles, le terme *car'* d'acquérir, lorsqu'il s'agissait de princes russes, une valeur politique; cela explique peut-être aussi la lenteur avec laquelle, même après la constitution de l'État moscovite, le titre de *car'* fut adopté dans le vocabulaire politique russe,[184] puisqu'il s'écoula près d'un siècle entre le moment où les princes de Moscou commencèrent à être désignés, avec une relative fréquence, par le terme *car'* dans la littérature, parfois dans les documents diplomatiques, et celui où Ivan le Terrible en fit le titre officiel des souverains russes (1547).[185]

[184] Cette lenteur tranche particulièrement avec la rapide fortune politique que connut, dans la seconde moitié du XVe siecle, à la cour de Moscou, le terme *gosudar'*, cf. n. 120, G. Stökl, op. cit. (n. 1), 114–15, et J. Raba, 'The Authority of the Muscovite Ruler at the Dawn of the Modern Era', *Jahrbücher für Geschichte Osteuropas*, xxxiv (1976), 322.

[185] Nous tenons à remercier ici ceux qui nous ont apporté leur aide, soit pour interpréter certains textes, soit pour compléter la documentation bibliographique, en particulier Mme H. Ahrweiler, Professeur à l'Université de Paris i, MM. A. Guillou, Directeur d'études à l'É.H.É.S.S., P. Ş. Nasturel, J.-M. Olivier, ainsi que ceux des participants à notre séminaire qui ont fait profiter cette étude de leurs remarques, enfin M. J. Fontaine, Professeur à l'Université de Paris iv, qui a eu l'obligeance de nous communiquer la thèse de M. M. Reydellet peu après sa soutenance.

Osip Nepea and the Opening of Anglo-Russian Commercial Relations

By SAMUEL H. BARON

ON 28 February 1557 a Russian, who had been shipwrecked three months earlier on the coast of Scotland, was treated to a remarkable reception in England. One hundred and forty merchants, mounted, and attended by servants in livery, escorted him to London. At the city's outskirts Viscount Montague, representing the Queen, accompanied by three hundred mounted knights, esquires, gentlemen, and yeomen, met and embraced him. As the assembly proceeded into the city, it stopped to be greeted first by four finely dressed merchants, who presented the Russian with a richly caparisoned gelding, and then by the Lord Mayor of London and the aldermen. Flanked by Viscount Montague and the Lord Mayor, and followed by a numerous and distinguished company, the Russian rode through the city of London, whose streets were thronged with curious and excited onlookers, to the luxuriously appointed quarters in which he was installed. By the time he set sail for his native land eight weeks later he had been solicitously attended, lavishly entertained, showered with gifts, and twice received by the King and Queen. The recipient of all these attentions and honours was Osip Nepea, Russia's first ambassador to England.[1]

The merchants who welcomed him were members of the Muscovy Company, chartered in 1555 to exploit the opportunities created by Richard Chancellor's voyage of exploration two years before, which had taken him to a Russian harbour in the White Sea. The notables who presented Nepea with the gelding were undoubtedly Sebastian Cabot, the governor of the Company, and George Barne, Anthony Hussey, and John Southcote, three of the four consuls, who, with the governor, constituted the Company's directorate. The Lord Mayor was William Garrard, the fourth consul; and Barne, a former mayor,

---

[1] Richard Hakluyt, *The Principal Navigations, Voyages, Traffiques and Discoveries of the English Nation*, ii (Glasgow, 1903), 350–62. Hakluyt's materials on Anglo-Russian affairs, which appear in the second and third volumes of his collection, constitute the single most important source for the problems we are concerned with here. Joseph Robertson's 'The First Russian Embassy to England', *Archaeological Journal*, xiii (1856), is misleadingly titled, for it offers only a few short documents on Nepea between the time of his shipwreck and his arrival in London.

was one of several Company members who were also aldermen.[2] Closely connected with the leadership of the City of London, the Company also had intimate ties with the Crown. The Crown had supported the expedition in 1553 and had granted the Company its charter. Some of its high officials were charter members, and it was to prove unstinting in support of the Company's welfare. The lavish reception accorded to Nepea indicated the great advantages anticipated in England from the newly opened commercial relations with Russia.[3]

'We know little of this person whose name does not have a Russian ring', I. Lyubimenko wrote of the ambassador, whom England welcomed—according to William Camden—as it had no other before.[4] Nepea (English sources usually refer to him as Osep, sometimes Osiph or Joseph, Napea; Anthony Jenkinson, the merchant-diplomat, gives his patronymic as Gregoriwich)[5] seems to have had a meteoric career. He appears from nowhere, bursts upon London for a moment of brilliant display, and then disappears into the obscurity whence he came. Such at least is the impression one gets from writings on early Anglo-Russian relations. It may, though, be possible to draw a fuller and more realistic, if less sensational, sketch. Writers who have sought to identify Nepea associate him with the town of Vologda. J. Hamel speaks of him as 'the boyar of Vologda', Yu. Tolstoy as 'namestnik [viceroy or governor] of Vologda', and N. E. Nosov as a Vologda merchant.[6] Tolstoy evidently based his identification on the contemporary English account of Nepea's reception, in which he is described as the

[2] For the charter, see Hakluyt (n. 1), ii, 304–16. The first governor and the consuls are named in the charter. For biographical material on these men, see T. S. Willan, *The Muscovy Merchants of 1555* (Manchester, 1953), 78, 84, 97–8, 104–5, 122.

[3] On the government's concern that the ambassador be handsomely treated, see *Acts of the Privy Council*, vi (1893), 27, 52–3, 54, 56. Among the more notable works on early Anglo-Russian relations are the following: E. A. Bond (ed.), *Russia at the Close of the Sixteenth Century* (1856); I. Kh. Gamel', *Anglichane v Rossii v XVI i XVII stoletiyakh*, 2 parts (Spb., 1865–9); Yu. Tolstoy (ed.), *Pervye sorok let snoshenii mezhdu Rossieyu i Anglieyu, 1553–1593* (Spb., 1875); E. D. Morgan and C. H. Coote (eds.), *Early Voyages and Travels to Russia and Persia*, 2 vols. (1886); A. J. Gerson, 'The Organization and Early History of the Muscovy Company', in: *Studies in the History of English Commerce in the Tudor Period* (Philadelphia, 1912); I. Lyubimenko, *Istoriya torgovykh snoshenii Rossii s Angliei* (Yur'ev, 1912); id., *Les Relations commerciales et politiques de l'Angleterre avec la Russie avant Pierre le Grand* (Paris, 1933); M. Wretts-Smith, 'The English in Russia during the Second Half of the Sixteenth Century', *Transactions of the Royal Historical Society*, 4th series, iii (1920); K. H. Ruffman, *Das Rußlandbild im England Shakespeares* (Göttingen, 1952); N. T. Nakashidze, *Russko-angliiskie otnosheniya vo vtoroi polovine XVI v.* (Tbilisi, 1955); T. S. Willan, *The Early History of the Russia Company, 1553–1603* (Manchester, 1956).

[4] Lyubimenko, *Les Relations* (n. 3), 29; Camden, as cited by Lyubimenko, ibid. 29, note.

[5] Hakluyt (n. 1), ii, 350, 411, 425; *Sobranie gosudarstvennykh gramot i dogovorov* (hereafter *SGGiD*), v (M., 1894), no. 113.

[6] J. Hamel, *England and Russia* (1854), 146; Tolstoy, op. cit. (n. 3), 9; N. E. Nosov, *Stanovlenie soslovno-predstavitel'nykh uchrezhdenii v Rossii* (L., 1969), 563. In his later work, *Anglichane v Rossii* (n. 3), Gamel' (Hamel) labels Nepea a 'Vologda dvoryanin' (p. 56). Though in error here, this book is fuller and more reliable than the better known *England and Russia*.

Russian Emperor's 'high officer in the town and country of Vologda'. Elsewhere, however, he observes that the title was honorary rather than actual—the tsar regularly bestowed honorary titles on representatives he sent abroad—and that Nepea had no real connection with Vologda.[7] There is reason to believe that Nepea was probably a native of Kholmogory rather than Vologda, for when he returned from England, as Jenkinson (in whose company he travelled) relates, he was there 'of all his acquaintances *welcomed home* and had presents innumerable sent to him'.[8]

Tolstoy renders the Russian ambassador's name Osip Grigor'evich Nepea, probably following Jenkinson in this. Whether or not he agreed with Hamel's description of Nepea as a boyar, he obviously considered him a member of the noble-servitor class, for only the names of such persons included the patronymic. Both Hamel and Tolstoy were wrong, however. References in the early Russian sources render the name Osip Nepeya or Nepeya Grigor'ev, and a number of authorities have agreed in combining these elements into what is most likely the complete, correct name—Osip Nepeya Grigor'ev.[9] Such a form was customary for those who, while not members of the servitor class, ranked well above ordinary men—notably, important merchants. High-ranking, non-noble officials in the government administration (*d'yaki* and *pod'yachie*) also had surnames but no patronymics.[10] Nosov seems to be correct in identifying Nepea as a merchant,[11] but we should not therefore dismiss the possibility that he also played some part in the government administration.

The conjecture that Nepea was a merchant is based partly on the evidence of certain business undertakings he hoped to carry out in

---

[7] Hakluyt (n. 1), ii, 350; Tolstoy, op. cit. (n. 3), 189, note. Nosov evidently shares Tolstoy's scepticism about Nepea's provenance, referring to him as a Vologdan, but putting the word in quotation marks (op. cit. (n. 6), 258). On the other hand the Patriarchal or Nikon Chronicle refers to 'Osip Nepea vologzhanin'—see *Polnoe sobranie russkikh letopisei* (hereafter *PSRL*), xiii (M., 1965), 270. The chronicle may be mistaken on this point, as it is in stating that Philip and Mary granted Russian merchants the right to trade in England without payment of customs (p. 286).

[8] Hakluyt (n. 1), ii, 426. The italics are mine. All quotations from the sixteenth-century English sources are given in modern orthography.

[9] Tolstoy, op. cit. (n. 3), 9 and 189, note. For contemporary source references see *Sbornik Imperatorskogo russkogo istoricheskogo obshchestva* (hereafter *SIRIO*), xxxviii (Spb., 1883), 36; *SGGiD* (n. 5), i, 553; A. A. Zimin (ed.), *Tysyachnaya kniga 1550 g. i Dvorovaya tetrad' 50-kh godov XVI v.* (M.–L., 1950), 117; S. O. Shmidt (ed.), *Opisi Tsarskogo arkhiva XVI veka i arkhiva Posol'skogo prikaza 1604 goda* (M., 1960), 48; V. I. Buganov (ed.), *Razryadnaya kniga 1475–1598* (M., 1966), 182. The authorities referred to are N. N. Bantysh-Kamensky, *Obzor vneshnikh snoshenii Rossii (po 1800 god)*, i (M., 1894), 91; Shmidt, op. cit., 167; S. B. Veselovsky, *D'yaki i pod'yachie XV–XVII vv.* (M., 1975), 135. Though, strictly speaking, Nepeya is the correct transliteration, we follow the established usage and render the name Nepea.

[10] For the rendering of the names of the Stroganovs, other leading merchants, and the *d'yaki*, see *Dopolnenie k aktam istoricheskim* (hereafter *DAI*), iii (Spb., 1848), nos. 117–19; *SGGiD* (n. 5), i, 553–4.

[11] Bantysh-Kamensky had earlier done so (loc. cit. (n. 9)).

conjunction with his embassy to England. His voyage was made on an English ship, one of three under the command of Richard Chancellor, which sailed from the Bay of St. Nicholas (near the future town of Arkhangel'sk) on 20 July 1556. The ships were loaded partly with cargo collected by the Company's agents, but partly also with wax, train-oil, tallow, furs, yarn, and other wares shipped by Russian merchants on their own account. The goods of the Russians were valued at the very considerable sum of £26,000 and, according to Tolstoy, £6,000 worth belonged to Nepea. A contemporary source is unclear on the value of his portion, but plainly conveys that a substantial share 'was laden at the adventure of the foresaid ambassador [Nepea]'.[12] It was not uncommon for Russian envoys to engage in trade while on diplomatic missions, for the tsar generally paid them in furs or other goods rather than cash. However, Nepea's venture appears to have been of quite a different order of magnitude and, accordingly, we may conclude that he was a wealthy Kholmogory merchant.

But why should the Tsar have sent a merchant, who is not known to have had any diplomatic experience, to represent him on a mission to which he clearly attached much importance? Here we must first recall the Muscovite government's preoccupation with protocol, and especially with reciprocity. The Englishman who first came to the Russian court and persuaded the Tsar to allow the English to trade in his country and to conclude with them a treaty on favourable terms was the sea-captain Richard Chancellor.[13] He returned to Russia the following year with George Killingsworth and Richard Gray, who secured for the English many privileges. Though they carried a letter to the Tsar from the King and Queen, Killingsworth and Gray were not officials of the Crown, nor directors or even members of the Muscovy Company, but the Company's agents. The Tsar was no doubt informed that they were merchants, and it would have seemed to him proper to send a merchant rather than someone of higher standing to negotiate terms for the Russians in London.[14] A merchant was also an appropriate envoy in view of the fact that the mission was largely concerned with commercial relations.

None the less, the choice of Nepea remains puzzling. If a merchant were to be sent as the Tsar's emissary, then why not a leading Moscow

[12] Hakluyt (n. 1), ii, 351; Tolstoy, op. cit. (n. 3), 9. Morgan and Coote (op. cit. (n. 3), i, p. iv) assert that the pound in the mid sixteenth century was worth five times its value when they wrote (1886).
[13] See letter of Ivan IV of 1554, printed in Hakluyt (n. 1), ii, 271-2.
[14] Nepea was accompanied on his mission by two other substantial merchants, Feofan Makarov and Mikhail Grigor'ev (Kositsyn?). Makarov had been town magistrate of Kholmogory when Chancellor first appeared in Russia and had assisted him on his way to Moscow. See Drevnyaya rossiiskaya vivliofika, 20 vols. (M., 1788-91), xviii, 10-14; and, on Makarov and the Kositsyns, Nosov, op. cit. (n. 6), 355-7. It is noteworthy that all three Russian merchants were from Kholmogory.

merchant rather than a seemingly obscure provincial? Although the privileged merchant corporations of Moscow—the *gosti*, *gostinnaya sotnya*, and *sukonnaya sotnya*—had not as yet taken shape, individual merchants (*gosti*) who enjoyed high status and were close to the throne had long occupied an established position in Moscow life.[15] The question here posed turns out to be especially germane when one considers the circumstances surrounding the negotiation of the English privilege in 1555. After an audience with the Tsar, Killingsworth and Gray presented to officials of the *Posol'skii prikaz* a memorandum setting forth the privileges the Company desired. When the Tsar was informed of this, he directed that 'his best merchants of Moscow [i.e. the *gosti*] be spoken to, to meet and talk with' the English.[16] Leading Moscow merchants were, then, involved in the negotiations and were consequently well informed on what had taken place. One of them would seem to have been ideally qualified to continue and conclude in London the negotiations begun in Moscow.

It is scarcely conceivable that the Tsar would have appointed to serve as his envoy in England someone who had taken no part in the Moscow talks, and we may therefore conjecture that—for reasons still to be determined—Nepea in some way participated in the negotiations of 1555. Apart from the Moscow merchants, three Russian officials are reported to have been involved in the discussions. One, according to Hamel, was Aleksey Fedorovich Adashev. Hamel gives no details, but Adashev must have been concerned in the matter, since he had control of the activities of many officials and was deeply involved in diplomatic affairs.[17] Killingsworth, who wrote the only surviving account of these events, makes it plain that he and his colleagues conducted their business with the 'secretary' and the 'under-chancellor' of the *Posol'skii prikaz*. Killingsworth's laconic narrative gives the name of the 'secretary' (*d'yak*) of the Chancellery of Foreign Affairs, who was then Ivan Mikhailovich Viskovaty (Weskawate, in Killingsworth's rendering), but it does not record the identity of the 'under-chancellor' (*pod'yachii*). Providing a tantalizing clue, he asserts that the 'under-

---

[15] On the *gosti* before the sixteenth century, see V. E. Syroechkovsky, *Gosti-Surozhane* (M.–L., 1935); L. V. Cherepnin, *Obrazovanie russkogo tsentralizovannogo gosudarstva v XIV–XV vekakh* (M., 1960), 415–22 and *passim*.

[16] Hakluyt (n. 1), ii, 293.

[17] Hamel, *England and Russia* (n. 6), 139; I. I. Smirnov, *Ocherki politicheskoi istorii russkogo gosudarstva 30–50-kh godov XVI veka* (M.–L., 1958), 218–19, 226. Smirnov's long account of Adashev's activities (pp. 212–31) stresses his deep involvement in diplomatic affairs, but makes no suggestion that he, together with I. M. Viskovaty, headed the *Posol'skii prikaz*, as does I. P. Shaskol'sky (probably erroneously) in his article 'Russko-livonskie peregovory 1554 g. i vopros o livonskoi voine', *Mezhdunarodnye svyazi Rossii do XVII v.* (M., 1961), 383. Smirnov's list of the negotiations in which Adashev participated (p. 219) does not include those with the English in 1555. Thus, it seems that Hamel had access to a source unknown to Smirnov, which, unfortunately, he failed to cite.

chancellor' 'was not two years past the Emperor's merchant, and not his Chancellor'.[18] May we not conclude that this unnamed person was Osip Nepea?

If we are right, then Nepea was a prosperous Kholmogory merchant, who at some point served as a commercial agent of the Tsar and was later appointed to a high-ranking post in a government department. If not commonplace, such careers were known in those times. As the Englishman John Hasse reported in 1554, the Tsar was 'a great merchant himself of wax and sables'[19]—and, we would add, of other commodities as well. He did not, of course, personally engage in commercial operations, but from time to time called upon leading merchants to serve as his factors. The merchants who usually performed such duties were *gosti*, such as Ivan Afanas'ev, who traded at Antwerp on the Tsar's behalf in 1567, and Dmitry Ivashev, who in the same year travelled to Ormuz, on the Persian Gulf, on the Tsar's business.[20] The *gosti* were often, but by no means always, natives of Moscow. Some of them were prominent merchants from other regions of the country whom the Tsar summoned to the capital.[21] Kholmogory was one of the chief towns of the Dvina district, a region which enjoyed a striking upsurge of economic prosperity and produced many energetic and affluent merchants in the sixteenth century.[22] Nepea was evidently one of them and, even though positive evidence is lacking, there is nothing implausible in the proposition that he attracted the government's attention and was engaged as the Tsar's agent.

There is ample evidence that at some point Nepea settled in Moscow and, then or later, became a government official. From at least the late fifteenth century close links had developed between the *gosti* and the nascent bureaucracy, and in the next two centuries a member of a *gost'* family was occasionally recruited to serve permanently as a *d'yak* or *pod'yachii* in the government administration.[23] In Nepea's time there was Stepan Tverdikov, who traded on the Tsar's behalf in England in 1567 and at Antwerp in 1568, and was a *d'yak* at the *Kazennyi dvor* in 1584.[24] The Ivashev and Tarakanov families, both of which included at least one *gost'*, also had each a member who served as a *d'yak* in the financial administration in the second half of the

[18] Hakluyt (n. 1), ii, 293–5.
[19] Ibid. 277.
[20] V. A. Kordt, 'Ocherk snoshenii Moskovskogo gosudarstva s Respublikoyu Soedinennykh Niderlandov do 1631 g.', *SIRIO*, cxvi (Spb., 1902), p. xviii; M. V. Fekhner, *Torgovlya russkogo gosudarstva so stranami vostoka v XVI v.*, 2 ed. (M., 1956), 28. Both were among the *gost'* representatives at the 1556 zemskii sobor. See *SGGiD* (n. 5), i, no. 192.
[21] S. V. Bakhrushin, *Nauchnye trudy*, i (M., 1952), 162–5.
[22] See Nosov, op. cit. (n. 6), 240–84.
[23] Syroechkovsky, *Gosti-Surozhane* (n. 15), 87–92. On gosti who became d'yaki in the seventeenth century, see my article 'Who were the gosti?', *California Slavic Studies*, vii (1973), 34.
[24] Kordt, op. cit. (n. 20), p. xvii; *DAI* (n. 10), i, 199–200.

sixteenth century.[25] Nepea's career followed an analogous pattern, for we find him listed as a *d'yak* in several contemporary records, of which the earliest is dated 1559. He well exemplifies S. B. Veselovsky's statement that 'it is possible to point to a whole series of *pod'yachie* who were given the rank of *d'yak* and various [other] rewards for participation in embassies'.[26]

If we assume that Nepea was the 'under-chancellor' of the *Posol'skii prikaz* in 1555, we may accept Killingsworth's testimony that he had been appointed to that post two years earlier. His appointment may have been consequent on Chancellor's arrival in Moscow, for an expansion of Russia's foreign trade could then certainly be anticipated, as might also the value to the Chancellery of Foreign Affairs of an experienced merchant who had undertaken, presumably with success, commercial assignments for the Tsar. Nepea's Kholmogory origins and his intimate knowledge of the Dvina district might have counted specially in his favour. The Northern Dvina was the obvious artery of communication between the White Sea and the Russian interior; and Kholmogory, situated on the Dvina only seventy versts from its mouth at St. Nicholas Bay, was sure to figure prominently in the development of Anglo-Russian trade relations. As Chancellor and Hasse had observed, Kholmogory was a bustling centre of trade in fish, salt, train-oil, furs, and walrus ivory; and, in addition, it was in lively communication with Vologda and Novgorod, towns which marketed large quantities of hemp, flax, wax, honey, and tallow.[27]

Between 1553 and 1555 Nepea may have been the official primarily concerned with Anglo-Russian relations. He must anyway have been a key figure in the negotiations with the English in Moscow in 1555, for Viskovaty lacked his commercial experience and the Moscow merchants his official standing. A careful reading of Killingsworth's account confirms our supposition. Of the beginning of the negotiations he writes: 'a day was appointed, and we met in the secretary his office, and there was the under-chancellor, who was not past two years since the Emperor's merchant, and not [i.e. rather than] his chancellor.'[28] Here, and throughout the account, Killingsworth invariably speaks of the person

[25] SGGiD (n. 5), i, no. 192 (p. 533); DAI (n. 10), i, 196, 271, 273–4; ibid. iii, 158–60.

[26] Razryadnaya kniga 1475–1598 (n. 9), 182; SGGiD (n. 5), i, 553; Veselovsky, D'yaki i pod'yachie (n. 9), 135; Veselovsky, as cited in Smirnov, op. cit. (n. 17), 216.

[27] Hakluyt (n. 1), ii, 224–5, 262–3, 276–7.

[28] Ibid. 293. Much of the case made above on circumstantial grounds is confirmed by a piece of evidence I encountered only after the completion of this article. In 1584, in reviewing the chief moments in the history of Anglo-Russian relations, Ivan IV told the English ambassador, Sir Jerome Bowes, that after Chancellor's second visit to Russia he, the Tsar, had sent 'our merchant Osip Nepea Grigor'ev' to negotiate with the English crown (see SIRIO, xxxviii, 109). This source confirms the full and correct name of the ambassador and the suggestion that he had been a merchant. As it accords with Killingsworth's statement that the 'under-chancellor' had until recently been the Tsar's merchant, it also lends weight to the claim that Nepea was a *pod'yachii* in the *Posol'skii prikaz*.

he took to be the head of the *Posol'skii prikaz* as the 'secretary', as distinct from his chief assistant, whom he calls, interchangeably, the 'underchancellor' or the 'chancellor'. The following paragraphs make plain that the 'chancellor'—the term Killingsworth favours—was actively involved in the negotiations on the Russian side. It is safe to assume that Nepea, whom we take this 'chancellor' to be, acquitted himself well, for otherwise he would hardly have been named the Tsar's envoy to continue the negotiations in England. But let us first see what we can learn of the negotiations in Moscow.

The Chancellor expedition of 1553 carried a letter from King Edward VI, asking any sovereign whose country the Englishmen might reach to treat them well. For his part, he promised: 'We shall with like humanity accept your subjects.'[29] In 1555 Queen Mary and King Philip devoted most of the communication they sent with Killingsworth to Ivan IV to thanks for favours already bestowed and a request that further grants and privileges be extended to the English merchants. In what seems like a *pro forma* afterthought, they wrote: 'Which your benevolences so to be extended, we be minded to requite towards any your subjects merchants that shall frequent this our realm.'[30] The Company did not bother with such frills. An instruction it handed at the same time to the agents leaving for Russia admonished them to keep their eyes and ears open, to learn all they could about the country and its resources, to be alert to promising opportunities for trade, and to continue the search for trade routes to China and elsewhere. They were to learn 'the natures, dispositions, laws, customs, manners and behaviours . . . of the nobility as of the . . . merchants, mariners, and common people; and to note diligently the subtleties of [the merchants'] bargaining, buying and selling.' But, as might be expected, the Company did not envisage, and it certainly did not propose to encourage, competition to itself through the grant of reciprocal rights for Russians in England. Indeed, the directors considered it possible that they should have no dealings at all with private merchants. Having learned of the Tsar's interest in trade, they thought they might arrange to sell their stocks of goods to him, and he in turn would dispose of them to his subjects.[31]

Killingsworth's account indicates that the negotiations in Moscow touched on such matters as prices, weights and measures, and procedures to ensure delivery and payment. More sustained attention was evidently devoted to the question of where the English should establish their trading post or factory. Hasse had recommended Vologda, but

[29] Hakluyt (n. 1), ii, 211.
[30] Ibid. 278–81.
[31] The instruction is printed in ibid. 281–9. The ensuing negotiations demonstrated that the Tsar was not minded to serve as wholesale buyer for all Russia.

the Company apparently had no strong preference. In the instruction to its agents it advised that 'provision be made in Moscow or elsewhere, in one or more good towns', for residences for the agents, warehouses and offices.[32] In the light of our earlier discussion, the so-called 'chancellor's' recommendation is specially noteworthy. 'Methinks', Killingsworth reports him as saying, 'you shall do best to have your house at Kholmogory'. Both the English and the Russian merchants involved in the discussions had misgivings, but the chancellery officials succeeded in dispelling them.[33] The English were assured at the same time that they might establish stations at other towns as well, but in fact Kholmogory served very satisfactorily as their chief centre for a number of years. When, in 1567, the English ambassador Thomas Randolph passed through, he found Kholmogory to be 'a great town', in which 'the Englishmen have lands of their own, given them by the emperor, and fair houses with offices for their commodity, very many'. The townspeople, he added, were 'much at the commandment of the English', because they profited from the latter's commercial activity there.[34]

In 1555 the Company had drawn up a considerable list of desiderata to be sought in Moscow by its agents. It did not secure everything it wanted, but it did not fall far short, and it gained some advantages not included in the original list.[35] Consistent with this outcome is the conspicuous absence of discord in Killingsworth's account of the negotiations. He was perhaps surprised to learn of the inclusion of Russian merchants in the discussions, but this proved to be no cause for dismay. He says nothing reproachful of the merchants; he represents the 'chancellor' as helpful and reasonable; and, as for Viskovaty, he describes him as 'our very friend'.[36] In all this there is not the slightest hint that the Russians advanced any demands in return for the generous privileges the English were granted. Their needs might in fact have been passed over in silence in Moscow, but they were no less real on that account. Indeed, the fulfilment of these needs, two in number, was precisely the object of Nepea's embassy to London, which followed the negotiations in Moscow.

---

[32] Hakluyt (n. 1), ii, 277, 282–3.

[33] Ibid. 310–11.

[34] Morgan and Coote, op. cit. (n. 3), i, pp. lxi–lxii; Hakluyt (n. 1), ii, 103–4.

[35] The document which Hakluyt printed (ii, 297–303) as the text of the privilege Ivan granted to the English in 1555 is now generally considered to be only a memorandum stipulating the Company's desiderata. For the substance of the privilege actually granted, see Gamel', *Anglichane v Rossii* (n. 3), 253–5. Gamel' is misleading in asserting that the English obtained more than they asked. A major privilege which they sought but were evidently denied in 1555—it does not appear in Gamel''s account—was the right to travel freely through Russia to other countries on business. This right was first granted to Anthony Jenkinson in 1558.

[36] Hakluyt (n. 1), ii, 293–6.

One of them, the Tsar's desire to recruit artisans who might help to overcome Russia's technological inferiority *vis-à-vis* its unfriendly neighbours, is cited by most writers as the prime reason for Russia's generosity to the English.[37] The frustration by the Holy Roman Emperor and Livonia of Hans Schlitte's effort, a few years earlier, to enlist scores of skilled Germans for service in Russia supports this view. And the strenuous objections raised by a number of states from the mid 1550s against English technical assistance and military supplies being sent to Russia underlines the significance of this factor. Killingsworth says nothing directly on the point, though he observes in passing that the Tsar is 'troubled with preparations to wars'.[38] If the matter did not come up in Moscow—it was of course a political rather than a commercial question, and therefore beyond the competence of the Company's agents—it certainly did in London. Mary and Philip in their letter to Ivan (April 1557), written after the talks with Nepea, gave this commitment: 'And we be also pleased that such artificers and craftsmen our subjects, as will repair from hence unto you, shall and may pass at their liberty with our good favour and licence.'[39]

As is apparent from this same royal letter, the other Russian demand —it must have come as a very unpleasant surprise to the Company— was for reciprocity of commercial rights. Killingsworth makes no mention of this and, indeed, the subject may not have arisen during the Moscow talks. The Russians may rightly have considered that the English agents had no authority to treat such questions. In any event, the Russian negotiators probably took it for granted that reciprocal rights would be forthcoming, on the basis of the pledge Mary and Philip had given in their letter of April 1555. Even before the negotiations in London and the formal grant of trading rights there to Russian merchants, Nepea behaved as if reciprocity had already been established. He travelled to England not only as the Tsar's envoy, it should be recalled, but also as a merchant with valuable goods which he intended to sell. He may well have encouraged the ten other Russian merchants who, at the same time and on their own account, sent large quantities of produce for sale in England. At least two other Kholmogory merchants, Feofan Makarov and Mikhail Grigor'ev (Kositsyn?), accompanied Nepea, and possibly all ten whose goods were loaded travelled with him. On the basis of this evidence, Hamel understandably asserted that the Russians meant to establish 'direct trade relations' with

---

[37] Karamzin supposed that the English gained so much because they paid the Tsar a large sum. Lyubimenko considered it more probable that the English bribed the officials and the Russian merchants involved in the negotiations. See Lyubimenko, *Les Relations* (n. 3), 31, note. Neither author adduced substantiating evidence.

[38] S. F. Platonov, *Moskva i zapad v XVI–XVII vv.* (L., 1925), 9–13; H. Zyns, *England and the Baltic in the Elizabethan Era*, tr. H. C. Stevens (Manchester, 1972), 44–5; Hakluyt (n. 1), ii, 293. [39] *SGGiD* (n. 5), v, no. 113.

England. This attempt was not made immediately, however, for two of the three ships in the English flotilla were wrecked on the Norwegian coast, and the Russian merchants and their cargoes were lost. The surviving vessel, under Chancellor's command, was later wrecked on the coast of Scotland. Chancellor helped save Nepea's life but was himself drowned, as were nine of Nepea's Russian attendants, and only a small fraction of the merchandise in which Nepea had invested was salvaged.[40]

Nepea must have been badly shaken by the disaster that had befallen him and his compatriots, but in a little while he dutifully proceeded to London to carry out his mission. We have no records of the negotiations, but after they had ended Mary and Philip wrote to Ivan that they had received his 'dear and well-beloved messenger and ambassador . . . and caused such matters as were by him on your behalf proponed to be at good length considered in sundry conferences by certain of our council, to whom we gave special charge to commune and conclude with your said ambassador touching [his] charge.'[41] Clearly, one of the matters the Tsar had 'proponed' was the question of trade rights for Russian merchants in England, for most of the substantive part of the royal letter consisted of a considerable list of favours granted them. They could enter, trade throughout, and depart from England freely and without interference. They should be as free from customs payments as other foreign merchants trading in England. They were to be given residences and warehouses in London, and in other towns as they desired. They were free to sell wholesale or retail; their property would enjoy royal protection; and any disputes in which they became involved were to be resolved swiftly and fairly by the High Chancellor.[42] These rights established as solid a legal basis for Russian trade in England as

[40] Hakluyt (n. 1), ii, 351–2; Hamel, *England and Russia* (n. 6), 147; Nosov, op. cit. (n. 6), 355–7; Tolstoy, op. cit. (n. 3), p. x.

[41] *SGGiD* (n. 5) v, no. 113. Virtually no documentation on the London negotiations has survived. The great fire of London in 1666 destroyed the records of the Muscovy Company; and there is no trace of the written report (*stateinyi spisok*) Nepea must have submitted, for the records of the *Posol'skii prikaz* for that year have not survived. See Willan, op. cit. (n. 3), 19; Ya. S. Lur'e, 'Russko-angliiskie otnosheniya i mezhdunarodnaya politika vtoroi poloviny XVI v.', in *Mezhdunarodnye svyazi Rossii do XVII v.* (n. 17), 427.

[42] *SGGiD* (n. 5), v, no. 113. The rights granted are of interest not only in themselves but because they help us to ascertain the rights granted the English in Russia, the details of which are not entirely certain. As pointed out above, Hakluyt erroneously identified a document detailing the Company's desiderata as the privilege Ivan IV granted to the English. Gamel', who first raised questions about the Hakluyt document, presented the substance but not the text of the actual privilege, which he said he had found in the English archives. However, he gave no reference, and no one else has ever located the document he claimed to have seen. These matters are treated in Willan, op. cit. (n. 3), 10–13. Lyubimenko (*Istoriya torgovykh snoshenii* (n. 3), 37) rightly suggests the need for caution in using Gamel''s account. We infer that the rights granted to the Russians were much like those the English had secured, because the former are said in the letter of Mary and Philip to be given in return for ('in the like consideration of') those given to their own subjects.

the English had secured in Russia. In at least two important respects, however, the Russian and English privileges differed. First, reciprocity was not established in relation to customs liability—a point which may have escaped Nepea's notice because of the circuitous way it was expressed in the royal letter of 1557. While the English had earlier gained the right to trade in Russia without payment of duty, Russians trading in England were to pay no more than other foreign merchants, but they were to pay. Secondly, the Muscovy Company was in effect given a monopoly of the English trade with Russia, but, as the Russians had no analogous organization, they neither sought nor were granted a comparable status.

Judging from the results as set down in the letter of Mary and Philip, Nepea carried out the negotiations with skill and success. The same is attested by the admiration he won from persons at the highest levels of government. The royal counsellors with whom he dealt, Sir William Petre and the Bishop of Ely, were impressed with his 'gravity, wisdom, and stately behaviour', and the royal couple wrote to Ivan that Nepea had 'very well and wisely demeaned himself in his charge with us here'.[43] In striking contrast, the Company's directors took a distinctly negative view of him by the time the negotiations had ended. A letter from them to their agents in Russia did not mince words:

We do not find the ambassador as conformable to reason as we had thought we should. He is very mistrustful, and thinks every man will beguile him. Therefore you had need to take heed how you have to do with him or with any such, and to make your bargains plain, and to set them down in writing. For they be subtle people, and do not always speak the truth, and think other men to be like themselves.[44]

It may seem rash to attempt an interpretation of this arraignment, couched as it is in such general terms. Nevertheless, some interpretation is necessary, since this passage forms the essential link between the preceding and following parts of our analysis. Although it has some larger implications, the passage clearly suggests the reasons for the Company's disenchantment with Nepea. He had not been 'conformable to reason', that is, to the Company's view of how relations between the two sides should be arranged. Instead, he proved to have an independent position, defended it stubbornly, and thus made hard and disagreeable bargaining inevitable. All this came as a distasteful revelation, because Killingsworth's report of the negotiations in Moscow had predisposed the Company's directors to find the Russian ambassador complaisant. Besides, they had gone to great pains and expense to win his favour—the Company had paid for Nepea's magnificent reception

[43] Hakluyt (n. 1), ii, 357; SGGiD (n. 5), v, no. 113. Nepea later recalled that he had steadfastly refused to make engagements respecting matters for which he had no commission (Morgan and Coote, op. cit. (n. 3), ii, 262).   [44] Hakluyt (n. 1), ii, 391.

and entertainment in England—only to discover that, while he accepted the handsome treatment graciously, it had no effect on his conduct as a negotiator.

In describing Nepea as mistrustful and inclined to think that others were out to beguile him, the Company's directors inadvertently paid tribute to his skill as a negotiator. They certainly strove in every way to maintain the privileges they had won in Moscow while denying the Russians equivalent rights. To agree to the latter would be to invite competition from Russian merchants in England and seriously diminish the value of their privilege. Nepea's refusal to be taken in by their arguments accounts for the accusation of 'mistrustfulness'. His instructions undoubtedly precluded making concessions, and he had besides, in the sovereigns' promise of reciprocity of April 1555, a trump card. The Crown, of course, wished to give all possible support to the Company, but it could not repudiate the commitment it had made. If, as suggested above, the promise had been a *pro forma* afterthought, in the negotiations Nepea could transform it into a device with which to frustrate the Company's design. He probably got the better of the Company by using its would-be protector against itself. No wonder that vexation at having been outwitted is the feeling we sense underlying this passage of the Company's letter to its agents.

The defeat would have been especially humiliating because the Company's directors were men of the world—educated, affluent, and experienced in commercial and political affairs; yet they had been bested by the representative of a 'rude and barbarous kingdom'. They expected Nepea to be naïve, perhaps overawed by all he was exposed to in London, and compliant; but he turned out to be a shrewd, tough, and formidable adversary. Hence the cautionary words to their agents that they 'take heed how you have to do with him or with any such'.

The charge that Nepea suspected others of mendaciousness is of a piece with his purported wariness. Whether he knowingly agreed to an arrangement on customs which put the Russians at a disadvantage, or in this instance was caught out, it is impossible to say. But a matter of far greater significance emphasizes that Nepea's wariness was by no means misplaced. For, having been outwitted in the formal negotiations, the Company's directors immediately set out to reduce the privileges the Crown had granted and, in effect, to deprive the Russians of their gains. Immediately following the passage we have been analysing, they wrote: 'Therefore we would have none of them to send any goods in our ships at any time, nor none to come as passengers, unless the Emperor do make a bargain with you, as is aforesaid, for his own person.'[45]

---

[45] Hakluyt (n. 1), ii, 391. Whether the government at the highest level was aware of, or connived in, the Company's intrigue is a matter beyond the scope of the present inquiry,

The privileges the Crown had extended could be enjoyed only when the Russian merchants and their merchandise reached England. Russia had plenty of craft suitable for traffic on the Dvina, the Volga, and other rivers, and also vessels which made considerable voyages along the coasts of the Barents Sea. But it lacked ships sufficiently large and sea-worthy to undertake the five or six weeks' journey from the White Sea to England. Therefore, if the Russians and their goods were denied passage on English ships, their privilege would become a dead letter. Instead of having the direct trade relations with England they apparently wished, the Russians would be entirely dependent on the Company. If they were to trade with England, they would be obliged to buy from and sell to the Company's agents in Russia; and the Company would thus have a monopoly not only of English trade in Russia but of the distribution of Russian products in England as well. As the English had gained the right of wholesale and retail trade in Russia, they were in a position to reduce still further the role of native merchants in the trade with England.

The Company dispatched the letter to its agents on one of four ships which left England for Russia on 12 May 1557. Unaware of this duplicity, Nepea sailed on board another of the ships, carrying to the Tsar the letter of Mary and Philip listing the privileges granted to the Russian merchants. The flotilla also carried goods purchased for the Tsar's treasury, a number of men who had contracted to enter the Tsar's service, and ropemakers, a furrier, and other artisans engaged by the Company to process Russian products for export. The ships were commanded by Anthony Jenkinson, who was also responsible for escorting Nepea back to Russia in his flagship, the *Primrose*. When they arrived in Russia, Nepea escorted Jenkinson to Moscow, where the Tsar received the Englishman cordially and granted his request for permission to travel through Russia to Persia and other lands.[46] In the four and a half months the two travelled together from Gravesend to Moscow Nepea and Jenkinson became well acquainted. The Russian must have become favourably disposed towards his companion, for he later went out of his way to render him an important service.

After reporting to the Tsar on his embassy to London, Nepea evidently returned to his position in the Chancellery of Foreign Affairs. Our sparse but illuminating information on his continuing interest in Anglo-Russian trade relations comes mainly from a letter of Henry Lane, who in 1557 was appointed, in addition to Killingsworth and Gray, the Company's agent in Russia and assigned to Kholmogory.

but a fact which has hitherto escaped attention is worth noting: Sir William Petre, one of the royal counsellors who negotiated with Nepea, was a charter member of the Muscovy Company. On Petre's membership, see Willan, *The Muscovy Merchants* (n. 2), 10, 117.

[46] Hakluyt (n. 1), ii, 375, 381, 382, 387, 413, 425–30, 436.

Lane's letter, which was mostly concerned with other matters, mentioned to the Company's management that Nepea, after his return from England, had persuaded 'sundry Russian merchants . . . to freight goods and pass in our ships to England'. Nepea obviously wanted the Russians to take advantage of the privileges the crown had granted, and encouraged some merchants to do so. Moreover, through his mediation the merchants had 'obtained letters from the emperor' supporting their action. For his part, Lane reported: 'upon good consideration I answered and refused'.[47] By so doing, he drew attention to the conflicting signals from the Crown and the Company, and courted a showdown with the Russians.

Lane's letter is dated 1560, although the events he describes must have occurred before or during the spring of 1558. He must have earlier communicated more fully with London on a matter of such obvious importance. But the few lines of the 1560 letter give no hint of the immediate Russian response. Whatever then occurred, later, as Lane wrote, 'they were driven to credit us . . . until the next return'. In other words, the Russian merchants either chose not to fight back or fought and lost, for they ended by selling their commodities to the agent for shipment to England, with payment to be made the following year. The Company had embarked on a hazardous course, but it achieved its end.

The argument here presented, it may be objected, rests on a number of questionable assumptions: (i) that the Russian government wanted not only formal, but actual reciprocity; (ii) that the Russians could in fact have effectively exploited the rights they were granted; (iii) that the Company had real cause to be alarmed by the demand for and grant of reciprocity to the Russians. If we cannot be absolutely certain on the first count, we can hardly ignore the fact that in the first half of the reign of Ivan IV the government quite aggressively sought to conclude commercial treaties which would gain for Russian merchants the right to trade not only in England but in Sweden and Denmark, as well as provide for the nationals of these countries to trade in Russia.[48] The second and third points are of course opposite sides of the same coin. If the Russians were capable of exploiting the rights they had been granted, then the Company had reason to be alarmed; on the other hand, if they were incapable, then it made no sense for the Company to oppose the grant of rights to the Russians.

At first glance the latter proposition seems true and our argument refuted, but closer inspection supports the opposite conclusion. At the

---

[47] Hakluyt (n. 1), ii, 411.

[48] Kordt, op. cit. (n. 20), pp. xiii–xviii; W. Kirchner, *Commercial Relations between Russia and Europe 1400 to 1800* (Bloomington, 1966), 37–9. Russian merchants also traded in Holland a number of times in the 1560s and 1570s.

time of the negotiations in London, the Company's directors certainly knew that Nepea and a number of other Russian merchants had embarked for England with cargoes of goods for sale. They were bound to view Nepea's insistence on the legitimization by the Crown of Russian trading activity as evidence of intent to pursue it also in the future. That they would have been correct in so reasoning is evident from Lane's letter of 1560, relating that after Nepea's return the Russians had tried to ship goods to England for sale on their own account. The Company had reason, then, to be alarmed, and in order to protect its interests it thrust at the Achilles' heel of the Russians— their lack of shipping. In so doing, the Company made it clear that genuine, as opposed to formal, reciprocity was unattainable between partners of unequal strength. Though the Russians still had the privilege to trade, they could not use it, because they were without the means to transport their products to England.

This deficiency was bound to make them dependent upon those who were better equipped, unless they could build a seagoing commercial fleet or exact concessions from the English. There is no evidence that they entertained the idea of establishing a merchant marine. Far more strangely, after having striven to achieve reciprocity the Russians apparently surrendered what they had gained without a struggle. In attempting to explain this perplexing chain of events, we once again enter the realm of speculation, for the documentation which might clearly resolve our problem is lacking. At issue is the role of the merchants, of Nepea, and of the Tsar.

As we know, some Russian merchants had undertaken to trade in England, personally or through agents, in 1556, and others attempted, unsuccessfully, to follow suit in 1557–8. To what extent the merchants themselves had taken the initiative and to what extent they were responding to government pressure it is impossible to say. It may be asserted with some confidence, however, that the merchantry as a whole was inclined to conservatism and caution, and the bolder spirits who took an interest in developing trade relations with England were undoubtedly an unrepresentative minority. Because traffic with England was new and untried, even they were likely to have viewed the undertaking as risky and to have joined on a tentative, experimental basis. Accordingly, when they met with resistance from the English side, they may have had little inclination to fight back—especially in the light of the history of the trade to that point.

Thus far, the English effort to develop trade relations with Russia was far from being a brilliant success. The entire crews of two of the three ships in the original expedition of 1553 had frozen to death, after losing their way and attempting to winter in Lapland. Perhaps the Russian merchants were unaware of it, but on the return voyage the third ship, under Chancellor's command, was intercepted by Dutch vessels and stripped of its cargo. The English ships sent on the second voyage, in 1555, reached St. Nicholas safely, but on the way back three of the four ships foundered, with great loss of life and cargo. Virtually all the merchandise loaded on behalf of Russian merchants went to the bottom in these disasters, together with seventeen Russians.[49] In the light of this the risks must have seemed daunting, and the Russian merchants may have been relieved to have them taken by the English, so long as they themselves could sell their goods at a profit.[50]

Nepea is unlikely to have given in so readily. He personally had suffered heavy losses and had come near to losing his life in the shipwreck on the Scottish coast. Yet he had pressed on, in England and after his return to Russia, with the project to establish Anglo-Russian trade relations on a reciprocal basis. He could not have viewed with equanimity the frustration of a programme in which he deeply believed, to which he had devoted so much effort, and the advancement of which had evidently won him promotion to the rank of *d'yak*. However, neither could he dragoon the merchants into a course of action to which they were unaccustomed, and which also seemed fraught with hazards. Even if the merchants could be rallied for a fight, they could not expect to prevail without the Tsar's backing. Therefore, Nepea could bring counter-pressure to bear on the English only if the Tsar would intervene.

The Tsar had ample means to make the Company reconsider, for its future depended on his good will. As the Company's stance in effect nullified the privilege the English Crown had granted the Russian merchants, he could threaten in turn to cancel what he had granted. Alternatively, he might have taken action less drastic, but still sufficiently damaging to compel a change of attitude. The Company placed great store on further exploration to find a new route to the East, and he could deny its agent, Jenkinson, permission to travel through Russia to Persia and other lands. However, the Tsar declined to challenge the Company on either the broader or the narrower issue. In April 1558—about the time when Lane rebuffed the Russian merchants, or later—Ivan graciously granted Jenkinson's request and sent him on his way.[51] Without the Tsar's support Nepea's design could not be implemented, and whatever representations he or his superiors in the *Posol'skii prikaz* may have made evidently went unheeded.

---

[49] Henry Lane's review of the Company's experience notes that 1560 was the first year in which the vessels sent from England to Russia arrived safely and returned without mishap (Hakluyt (n. 1), iii, 335).

[50] As A. A. Nikitina has recently noted ('Anglo-russkie otnosheniya v svete khroniki V. Kemdena', in: *Feodal'naya Rossiya vo vsemirno-istoricheskom protsesse* (M., 1972), 320): 'there are many data in the literature on the struggle of the Russian merchants against the English monopoly in the seventeenth century, [but] for the sixteenth century such evidence is very slight.'   [51] Hakluyt (n. 1), ii, 436.

We noted above that Ivan had aggressively sought to secure commercial rights for Russian merchants in a number of foreign countries. He certainly appreciated the advantages, fiscal and perhaps others, that trade might bring. In rebuffing the Russian merchants, to whom the Tsar had given supporting letters, Lane had flouted the ruler's will and diminished prospective state revenues from trade, and Ivan in deciding not to retaliate against the English must have had compelling reasons. Other considerations may have influenced his decision, but Russia's involvement in the Livonian War is likely to have been crucial. The conflict had been brewing since 1554, and in January 1558 the Russian forces invaded Livonia. The time was well chosen, for in the preceding years Russia had secured her eastern flank by conquering Kazan' and Astrakhan', and in 1556 and 1557 had signed a six-year armistice with Poland and ended the war with Sweden.[52] Though Russia was in a strong position, both diplomatically and militarily, it would have been imprudent to risk alienating England at this time. Russia hoped for English aid, and the Tsar may have resolved to be forbearing, because some assistance had already been delivered and there could be little doubt that more would be forthcoming.

On behalf of his master, Nepea had asked the English Crown to permit artificers and craftsmen to work in Russia, and his request had been granted. As Russia was then preparing for war, it is hardly farfetched to suppose that Nepea particularly requested men whose skills would enhance Russia's military capacity. The Russian government appreciated the advantages such men might confer. When in 1547 Schlitte was sent to Germany to recruit men for the Tsar's service, he engaged among others engineers and architects, ironworkers, and bellfounders (who might also cast artillery). In 1552 Razmysl Petrov, a Lithuanian, had helped the Russians take Kazan', thanks to his skill at mining the town walls.[53] There was apprehension among Russia's neighbours that—as a Venetian source in London had reported— Nepea had come to London to acquire artillery and ammunition. Before and after his arrival Poland and Sweden made representations in London against such a transaction.[54] Their protests were unavailing, for England did aid Russia, though stoutly denying it.

The letter of Mary and Philip of April 1557 spoke both of rights granted to Russian merchants and of permission for skilled artisans to go to Russia. While fairly detailed and specific on the first score, they were, however, terse and general on the second. They refrained from

[52] W. Kirchner, *The Rise of the Baltic Question* (Newark, Del., 1954), 99.

[53] Platonov, *Moskva i zapad* (n. 38), 10; Kirchner, *Commercial Relations* (n. 48), 79; A. A. Zimin, 'Uchastnik vzyatiya Kazani v 1552 g. Litvin Razmysl Petrov', *Voprosy voennoi istorii Rossii*, vi (1969), 273–8.

[54] *Calendar of State Papers and Manuscripts relating to English Affairs in the Archives and Collections of Venice*, vi, pt. 1, p. 143; pt. 2, p. 1005.

writing longer letters, they told the Tsar, trusting Nepea 'at good length [to] declare [their] offers and good will'. The 'secret instructions ... transmitted to Nepea orally' (the formulation is D. S. Likhachev's)[55] must have related to the technical and material assistance England was prepared to give. The pledge was not declared precisely in writing because of the matter's sensitivity. When Nepea returned home, he was accompanied by English specialists whom he had engaged. The Tsar obviously valued them highly, for he invited them to dine with him and presented each with a fur-trimmed robe of velvet or damask and thirty roubles. Except for one, a doctor, who was treated still more generously, we do not know their number or specializations. Jenkinson mentions these people several times, but never in precise terms, e.g. 'men as came to serve the emperor', or 'the rest of our men of our occupations'.[56] His reticence mirrors that of the King and Queen, and lends support to our suspicion that they were specialists in war-related arts. Their number and value, and the expectation of further aid, may have helped to persuade the Tsar not to press the trade question.

The Tsar may also have calculated that Russia would actually lose little or nothing if he ignored the Muscovy Company's provocation. Among his objectives in the war against Livonia was the acquisition of one or more ports on the Baltic, which would give Russia unimpeded access to trade with any number of European states. In 1557 Ivan had vainly attempted to negotiate with Narva an agreement that would have breached Riga's and Reval's control of the Baltic trade routes with Russia.[57] In the early stages of the Livonian War Russia's armies promised to achieve by force of arms what the Tsar had failed to gain by negotiation. When Jenkinson's petition lay before the Tsar, the capture of an outlet into the Baltic may have seemed imminent, and with it the undercutting of the English advantage in the Russian trade. In any event, in May 1558 the Russians laid siege to Narva, and the next month the town capitulated. In the following years the port of Narva was crowded with ships from Lübeck, Hamburg, Antwerp, and ports in Holland, Denmark, and Sweden. As early as 1560 the competition thus created led officers of the Muscovy Company to lament (prematurely) the possibility that they 'might be out of hope of doing any good' in the trade with Russia.[58] After some hesitation as to how

[55] SGGiD (n. 5), v, no. 113; D. S. Likhachev (ed.), Puteshestviya russkikh poslov XVI–XVII vv. (M.–L., 1954), 394.

[56] Hakluyt (n. 1), ii, 426, 429, 430. A Russian chronicle entry indicates that 'many skilled craftsmen, doctors, and prospectors for gold and silver, and smiths, and many other artisans' came from England with Nepea (PSRL, xiii, 286).

[57] W. Kirchner, 'The Role of Narva in the Sixteenth Century: a Contribution to the Study of Russo-European Relations', in: Kirchner, Commercial Relations (n. 48), 59–77. A full-scale treatment is given in the same author's Rise of the Baltic Question (n. 52).

[58] Hakluyt (n. 1), ii, 404.

to deal with the situation, the Company in 1566 persuaded Parliament to extend its monopoly right to Narva. Thereafter, it traded regularly there as well as at St. Nicholas, but it had to contend with the competition of other European nations, and the many English merchants who ignored the ordinance of Parliament.[59]

Russia's seemingly abject, if partly understandable, surrender of its reciprocal trading rights had remarkable consequences. One of the most striking was the considerable English penetration of Russia and the contrasting lack of any such penetration of England by the Russians. Through its pursuit of profit in Russia the Company created a body of Englishmen who knew Russia's language and people, its geography and resources, its customs and institutions, while to the Russians England remained a closed book. The Company established stations at Rose Island (near St. Nicholas), Kholmogory, Vologda, Moscow, and Yaroslavl', and also carried on occasional trade at Narva, Novgorod, Pskov, Kazan', and Astrakhan'. The Company's agents undertook the processing of Russian raw materials and created a rope and cordage industry which employed a hundred Russians and supplied a large part of the needs of the English navy. The Russians, on the other hand, did not set up a station in London or anywhere else in England, much less establish industrial enterprises there. The Company used Russia as a base for the exploration of the Barents Sea and contiguous waters and for travel to Persia and beyond, while of course the Russians made no similar use of England.

It would be simplistic, however, to attribute Russia's inactivity and lack of response solely to the Company's manœuvres in 1557–8 which we have discussed above.[60] Its lack of response raises a whole series of questions, for example: why did the Russian merchants not resist the granting of extraordinary rights to foreigners at a time when the conquest of Kazan' and Astrakhan', the opening of the northern route from Western Europe, and the capture of Narva offered unprecedented opportunities for unimpeded trade with both East and West? Why did Russia not recognize how much a fleet would improve her economic situation and therefore build one? Why did the Russian merchants not form associations akin to the Muscovy Company, and advance their interests through collective action? Why did their government not give the Russian merchants the kind of support which so materially assisted the English merchants to prosper? Why was England able to free

[59] Willan, op. cit. (n. 3), 68–77, 79, 85, 98. For a more recent examination of the role of Narva, see Zyns, *England and the Baltic* (n. 38), ch. II, especially pp. 46 seqq.

[60] Queen Elizabeth renewed the offer of rights for Russian merchants in 1569, 1572, 1584, and 1597. However, these offers brought no response from the merchants, and, in 1585, Tsar Fedor wrote to Elizabeth: 'As our merchants have not gone to your land in the past, neither will they have need to hereafter.' See Morgan and Coote, op. cit. (n. 3), ii, 303; Tolstoy, op. cit. (n. 3), 79, 248, 259; *SIRIO*, xxxviii, 246–7; Willan, op. cit. (n. 3), 112–14.

herself from subordination to the Hanseatic League and become a dominating commercial power, while Russia ended the Hanse domination only to fall into dependence upon the English (and then the Dutch)?[61]

These large questions obviously cannot be answered here, but in the last of our data on Nepea there may be a few clues. In 1561 Jenkinson again appeared in Moscow to ask the Tsar's permission to travel to Persia to trade on the Company's behalf. He met strong resistance and saw so little hope of overcoming it that he was ready to abandon his quest and return to England. Then an unexpected sequence of events brought a reversal of his fortunes:

Having received my passport, ready to depart [Jenkinson relates], there came to our house there Osep Napea, who persuaded me that I should not depart that day, saying that the Emperor was not truly informed, imputing great fault to the frowardness of the Secretary, who was not my friend: before whom coming the next day, and finding the Secretary and Osep Napea together, after many allegations and objections of things, and perceiving that I would depart, I was willed to remain until the Emperor's Majesty was spoken with again touching my passage. . . . And within three days after sending for me, he declared that the Emperor's pleasure was that I should . . . pass through his dominions into Persia.[62]

It is impossible to determine whether the secretary's antipathy was directed against Jenkinson personally or instead reflected a fear of English competition which Russian merchants trading in Persia may have already begun to entertain. The conduct of Nepea and the Tsar is more susceptible to analysis. The Tsar ultimately decided in Jenkinson's favour, we may assume, in the expectation of services in return. Jenkinson wrote cryptically of having been dismissed by the ruler 'with certain [of] his affairs committed to my charge, too long here to rehearse'. It is known that he took with him to Persia valuables from the Tsar's treasury, which he sold at a handsome profit; and it has been suggested that he carried out a political assignment as well.[63] Nepea, who was well acquainted with Jenkinson, evidently recommended him to the Tsar as a man of talent and flair who would be worth employing. In this he proved his perspicacity again, but now in a manner adverse to the Russian merchants whose interests he had earlier championed. Before long, rumblings of discontent with English competition—which

[61] Kirchner has written: 'In the sixteenth century Russia found herself on a level of economic development in relation to the Western powers which made impossible the successful initiation of an active foreign trade' (*Commercial Relations* (n. 48), 39). Lyubimenko earlier made a similar assessment (see *Istoriya torgovykh snoshenii* (n. 3), 38). This judgement provides a good point of departure, but leaves a great deal open for further investigation.

[62] Hakluyt (n. 1), iii, 17–18.

[63] Ibid. 18, 43; Morgan and Coote, op. cit. (n. 3), i, p. xxvii; Willan, op. cit. (n. 3), 58.

Jenkinson's voyage had made possible—were issuing from Russian merchants trading in Persia.[64]

The reason for Nepea's volte-face may be surmised. In 1561 he had been in government service for eight years and had been a *d'yak* since 1558–9.[65] In his first years as a state servant he displayed an unusual awareness of and commitment to the interests of the group from which he came, no doubt believing that the advancement of Russian commerce would work also to the advantage of the state. Over the years, however, he could hardly avoid adopting the government's viewpoint. From his bitter experience in 1558 he knew that the Tsar placed political considerations above commercial interests and, when they appeared to conflict, was prepared to sacrifice the latter to the former. Besides, the Tsar's concept of what was 'political' was unusually broad: it embraced anything in which the ruler had an interest, not only international relations, military affairs, and the exchequer, but also the commercial affairs in which he himself was involved. So well had Nepea learned the lesson that even this unusually keen and adroit erstwhile merchant and defender of merchant interests later lent himself to a policy clearly disadvantageous to the Russian merchants. He might have said in 1561 what Ivan IV said to Jenkinson a decade later: 'We know that merchant matters are to be heard, for that they are the stay of our princely treasures. But first princes' affairs are to be established and then merchants'.'[66] This attitude became a constant in official Russian political economy, and guided decision-making for a long time. It placed insurmountable obstacles in the way of the kind of economic development that propelled England to the forefront of the commercial nations of Europe.[67]

[64] Hakluyt (n. 1), iii, 52. Had the Russian merchants known of English plans calculated to damage them still further (ibid. 51–2), their rumblings might have been audible in Moscow.

[65] Veselovsky, *D'yaki i pod'yachie* (n. 9), 135.

[66] Tolstoy, op. cit. (n. 3), 129. We have one further reference to Nepea's involvement in Anglo-Russian relations, again as a friend of the English. In 1568 he advised William Rowley, the Company's agent in Russia, that Jenkinson had unwisely led the Tsar to expect certain concessions from Queen Elizabeth that probably would not be forthcoming. See Morgan and Coote, op. cit. (n. 3), ii, 262. The reference was undoubtedly to Ivan's bid for a political alliance with England, a bid repeatedly frustrated, with the Company suffering the consequences more than once.

[67] See my articles 'The Weber Thesis and the Failure of Capitalist Development in "Early Modern" Russia', *Jahrbücher für Geschichte Osteuropas*, xviii (1970), and 'Who were the *gosti*?', *California Slavic Studies*, vii (1973).

I wish to express my gratitude to the National Endowment for the Humanities and the American Philosophical Society for support which made this study possible; and to Professors Robert O. Crummey of the University of California, Davis, and David M. Griffiths of the University of North Carolina, Chapel Hill, for helpful comments and suggestions.

Music in Sixteenth-century Moldavia: New Evidence

By A. E. PENNINGTON

THE existence of an important centre of church music in the monastery of Putna during the sixteenth century has been known for some time: seven notated bilingual akolouthiai are generally acknowledged to have been written in Putna.[1] These survive in eight sixteenth-century manuscripts: Shchukin 350 in the State Historical Museum (GIM) in Moscow (henceforth referred to as Shchukin 350); MS. 13.3.16 in the Library of the Academy of Sciences (BAN) in Leningrad (henceforth BAN 13.3.16: this manuscript and Shchukin 350 constitute one book, written in or about 1511 by the monk Evstatie—they will henceforth be referred to jointly as Evstatie's book); ff. 1–84ᵛ of MS. 56/576 in the library of the monastery of Putna (henceforth Putna 56); MS. 1.26 in the Central University Library, Iaşi, written in 1545 by the hieromonk Antonie (henceforth Iaşi 1.26); MS. 52/1886 in the library of the monastery of Dragomirna (henceforth Dragomirna 52); MSS. 283 and 284 in the library of the Rumanian Academy of Sciences, Bucharest (henceforth B283 and B284 respectively); and MS. 816 in the library of the Ecclesiastical Museum, Sofia (henceforth Sofia 816). The undated manuscripts may be dated approximately by watermarks and internal evidence: Putna 56 to the first decade of the century, Dragomirna 52, B283 and Sofia 816 to the middle of the century, and B284 to the third quarter. To these seven akolouthiai must be added ff. 85–160ᵛ of MS. Putna 56/576 (henceforth Putna B), a fifteenth-century akolouthia, apparently written by a Greek, but with a repertory very similar to that of the seven listed. Recently Dr. J. Raasted identified one more manuscript—MS. Sl. 12 in the University Library at Leipzig—as belonging to the Putna school, and Dr. D. Conomos, on the basis of the catalogue description by Dr. M. K. Hadjiyakoumis[2] recognized that MS. 258 in the monastery of Leimonos on the island of Lesbos must also belong to this tradition. This article attempts to describe these two manuscripts, placing them in the context of the

[1] See especially Diac. G. Panţiru, 'Şcoala muzicală de la Putna', *Studii de muzicologie*, vi (Bucharest, 1970), 31–67; G. Ciobanu, 'Şcoala muzicală de la Putna', *Muzica*, xvi (9) (Bucharest, 1966), 14–20; id., 'Les manuscrits de Putna et certains aspects de la civilisation médiévale roumaine', *Revue roumaine d'histoire de l'art. Série Théâtre, Musique, Cinéma*, xiii (Bucharest, 1976), 65–77; A. E. Pennington, 'Seven Akolouthiai from Putna', *Studies in Eastern Chant*, iv (Oxford, 1978, forthcoming); see the last for further bibliography.

[2] M. K. Chatzēgiakoumis, Μουσικά χειρόγραφα τουρκοκρατίας (*1453–1832*), i (Athens, 1975), 31–5. References to this author will be by the preferred form Hadjiyakoumis.

nine listed above, and pointing out particular features of interest, as far as these are evident to one who is not a musicologist.

MS. Sl. 12 in the University Library of Leipzig (henceforth referred to as Leipzig Sl. 12) is a small book: the binding is 16·4 × 10·3 cm., the paper 15·8 × 9·9 cm. The binding is new, cloth on boards (which may be older). At both front and back there is one new paste-down and one new flyleaf, without any visible watermark. The older part of the book consists of iii+134 folios—that is, three old flyleaves and 134 leaves of text. Ff. i–iiiᵛ and 1–3ᵛ are quite badly damp-stained and damaged, and ff. 1–8ᵛ have been repaired at the spine, but the constitution of the book has not been much changed, as can be seen by the scribe's gathering signatures (in Cyrillic), most of which survive. The collation is as follows: ff. i–iiiᵛ and ff. 1–2ᵛ are unsigned and outside the gatherings. I⁶ (ff. 3–8ᵛ, one or two leaves missing between ff. 5ᵛ and 6), II⁶ (ff. 9–14ᵛ), III–XVII⁸ (ff. 15–134ᵛ; there is, however, no signature on f. 134ᵛ). There are at least two watermarks: one an anchor in a circle with countermark M and a trefoil, not unlike Briquet 559 (1573)[3], and the other some type of armorial bearing too fragmentary for identification. The anchor watermark indicates an Italian paper, such as was certainly in use in Putna. Inside the front cover is a bookplate, showing that it belonged to Andreas Acoluthus, Professor of Oriental Languages in Breslau, and the stamp of the city library of Leipzig.

On ff. i–iiiᵛ, the old flyleaves, are a number of scribbles and inscriptions, the most important of which are:

f. i. The date (in Cyrillic) 7166 (= 1658).[4]

f. iᵛ. (a) Въ лѣ⟨то⟩ 7131 (= 1623) м⟨е⟩с⟨е⟩ца ап⟨риля⟩ 27 прѣставис⟨а⟩ пан Семiωн Строич . и при егѹменѣ ⟨i⟩е⟨р⟩ом⟨о⟩нах Мардарie.[5]

(b) въ дны Iω⟨на⟩ Стефан⟨а⟩ воевода Томшович на второе г⟨о⟩с⟨ѹ⟩д⟨арст⟩ва его . когда пришед въ земля Молдавскоу. (Stefan II Tomşa was voevoda of Moldavia 1611–15, so this was presumably written in 1612.)

f. ii. A different hand, using ink which has faded badly, has written in Cyrillic a Greek theotokion: Тѵпермахѹ стратига (sic) and, similarly, the Easter troparion: Х⟨ри⟩с⟨то⟩с анести ек некрон.

[3] C.-M. Briquet, Les Filigranes, 3 vols. (Geneva, 1907). Other repertories referred to are: G. Piccard, Die Ochsenkopfwasserzeichen (Veröffentlichungen der Staatlichen Archivverwaltung Baden-Württemberg), ii (Stuttgart, 1966); V. Mošin, Anchor Watermarks (Monumenta Chartae Papyraceae historiam illustrantia, 13) (Amsterdam, 1973).

[4] In quotations from manuscripts Cyrillic letters used as numerals are rendered by Arabic numerals. Superscript letters are brought into the line and abbreviations are expanded, letters supplied being in angle brackets. Final jer, if not written in the text, is not supplied.

[5] No Mardarie is known as abbot of Putna at this time. In 1613 the abbot was Agafton and in 1629 Anastasie (see D. Dan, Mănăstirea şi comuna Putna (Bucharest, 1905), 118). It is possible that there was an abbot Mardarie between these two, but if not, then this inscription is evidence that the manuscript was not in Putna by 1623.

f. iii. In a different hand again, with darker ink:

(*a*) в лѣтѡ 7079 (= 1570) м⟨е⟩с⟨е⟩ца декеврие 9

(*b*) вь тъжде теченіе лѣтѡм . м⟨е⟩с⟨е⟩ць мартіе

(*c*) в лѣтѡ 88 (= 7088 = 1580) м⟨е⟩с⟨е⟩ца февръарі . 6 по сълоучаю

(*d*) въ нед⟨е⟩лѣ мѣс⟨о⟩поустна . в лѣтѡ 7091 (= 1583) м⟨е⟩с⟨е⟩ца генварі 15. (These four inscriptions appear to have been written at the same time in one hand, so do not permit the dating of the manuscript to before 1570; it seems reasonable to suppose they were written in or soon after 1583, so that the manuscript could have been written during the third quarter of the century, a date suggested also by the watermark.)

(*e*) в л⟨ѣ⟩тѡ 7137 (= 1629) м⟨е⟩с⟨е⟩ца генвар⟨іе⟩ 19 прѣстависа архіеп⟨ис⟩к⟨о⟩пъ Анастасіе митрополит въ дворѣ Іаском напрасно и скоро прѣд лицем г⟨о⟩сп⟨о⟩д⟨е⟩во Б⟨ог⟩а си(?) а тогда Мирон Барновски Могила воевода . и п⟨ог⟩ребоша его въ своем новосъзданѣ его монастирю Драгомирна. (This must refer to Anastasie Crimca, the founder of Dragomirna monastery, and is a useful indication that the manuscript was probably still in Moldavia in 1629. Miron Barnovschi-Movilă was voevoda of Moldavia from January 1626 to August 1629 and again in 1633.)

In the main part of the manuscript—ff. 1–134ᵛ—there are two hands. The principal scribe evidently left certain leaves blank, some of which (ff. 1–3ᵛ) he later filled himself, others (ff. 92–3, 129–34) were written in a somewhat smaller hand, in ink which has faded more than that used by the first scribe. The main hand is very similar in style to that of the scribe of Sofia 816, but slight differences, especially in the formation of certain neumes, make it clear it is not the same scribe. Both hands of Leipzig Sl. 12 write nine lines of text and music to the page, and both are neat bookhands, with cursive elements. Text and neumes are in black ink, with headings, initials, rubrics, martyriai, and cheironomiai in red. On ff. 4, 10 and 95 are headpieces in red ink, using interwoven fillets in patterns similar to those found in the known Putna manuscripts.

Like the other manuscripts, Leipzig Sl. 12 shows a mixture of Greek and Slavonic. Most of the neumed texts are Greek, but there are two (on ff. 93ᵛ–94ᵛ) in Slavonic. Attributions to composers and headings are usually in Greek, except for the attribution of a Slavonic composition on f. 93ᵛ (see below, p. 70). In the seven known akolouthiai names of feasts are in Slavonic: Leipzig Sl. 12 does not generally name feasts, but the one mention of a feast date (on f. 95) is indeed in Slavonic: м⟨е⟩с⟨е⟩ца септевріа 8. The spelling of both Greek and Slavonic is similar to that of the other manuscripts.

The manuscript contains an akolouthia very similar to those of the seven familiar works. The contents are listed below by items, indicating

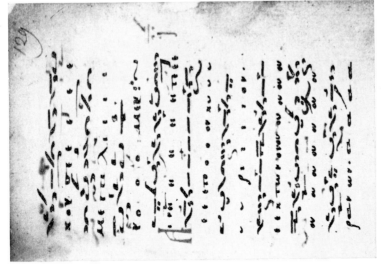

(ii) MS. Leipzig Sl. 12 f. 129. The beginning of the Koinonikon *Αἰνεῖτε τὸν Κύριον*, mode 1 in the second hand

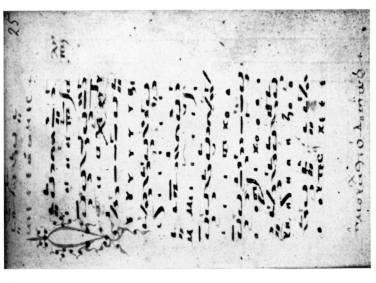

(i) MS. Leipzig Sl. 12 f. 25. The beginning of the Cherubic hymn *Οἱ τὰ χερουβίμ*, mode 2 pl. by the Monk Theodosios

I

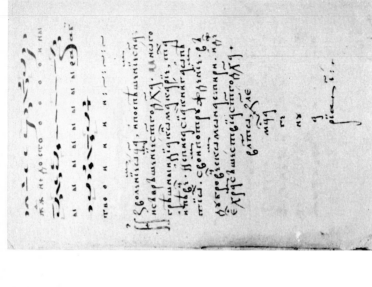

(iii) MS. Leimonos 258 f. 255^v. The beginning of the koinonikon Σῶμα Χριστοῦ, mode I pl. by Stefan (the Serb)

(iv) MS. Leimonos 258 f. 413. The colophon of the scribe, deacon Makarie

II

the mode and composer, if specified, and with a reference to other manuscripts of the group if an item appears in them. If, however, the item occurs in Sofia 816 or Leimonos 258 no reference will be made to the other manuscripts, since the concordance for these two manuscripts is available elsewhere.[6] Supplementary or contradictory information about modes or composers that appears in the other manuscripts cited is put in the appropriate columns in brackets, opposite the relevant reference. The other manuscripts of the group are abbreviated here as Sofia, Shchukin, BAN, Putna, Putna B, Iaşi, B283, B284, Dragomirna, and Leimonos respectively, and the reference given is to the folio on which the particular composition begins, whether it is in place in the manuscript or not.

Item	Folios	Mode	Composer	Other manuscripts
1. Cherubic hymn: Οἱ τὰ χερουβίμ	1–3	1	Chrysaphes	Sofia 49^v
2. Psaltike techne	4–7			Shchukin 1 Iaşi 1 B283 4
3. Δι' εὐχῶν τῶν ἁγίων πατέρων ἡμῶν	7	1		
4. Koinonikon for Sunday: Αἰνεῖτε τὸν Κύριον	7^v–9^v	1	Theodosios	
GREAT VESPERS				
5. Part of the prooemiac psalm which begins: Ἀνοίξαντός μου τήν χεῖρα	10–24^v	4 pl.		Shchukin 2 B283 7 B284 1
6. Cherubic hymn: Οἱ τὰ χερουβίμ	25–8	2 pl.	Monk Theodosios	B283 69
7. Koinonikon for Sunday: Αἰνεῖτε	28–30	3 pl.	Stefan the Serb	Sofia 97^v
LITURGY				
8. Trisagion: Ἅγιος ὁ Θεός	31–33^v	4 pl.		Sofia 232
9. Festal trisagion: ὅσοι εἰς Χριστόν	33^v–35	2 pl.	Monk Evstatie	Sofia 34
10. Cherubic hymn: Οἱ τὰ χερουβίμ	35^v–39	1 pl. (2 pl.)	Monk Agathonos	Sofia 39^v
11. Cherubic hymn	39–43	2	Agallianos	Sofia 42

[6] Pennington, op. cit. (n. 1), and below, pp. 74–80.

Item	Folios	Mode	Composer	Other manuscripts
12. Cherubic hymn	43–6	4	Monk Anthimos	Sofia 47^v
13. Cherubic hymn	46–49^v	3	Monk Evstatie	Sofia 45
14. Cherubic hymn	49^v–52^v	1 pl.	Monk Evstatie	Sofia 56
15. Πατέρα υἱόν	52^v–53^v	4 pl.	Moschianos	Sofia 67^v
16. Sanctus: Ἅγιος, ἅγιος, ἅγιος	53^v–55	2		
17. Theotokion: 'Επὶ σοὶ χαίρει κεχαριτωμένη	55–58^v	4 pl.	(Koronis)	Sofia 70

Koinonika for the Days of the Week

18. Sunday: Αἰνεῖτε τὸν Κύριον	58^v–60^v	1	(Raidestinos)	Sofia 72
19. Sunday	60^v–62^v	1		Sofia 73^v
20. Wednesday: Ποτήριον σωτηρίου	62^v–64^v	1	('tou autou', i.e. Raidestinos)	Sofia 74^v
21. Sunday	64^v–66	2	(Moschianos)	Sofia 77
22. Wednesday	66–8	2	(Gerasimos)	Sofia 79^v
23. Tuesday: Εἰς μνημόσυνον	68–9	3	('tou autou', i.e. Gerasimos)	Sofia 81
24. Tuesday	69–71	3		Sofia 82^v
25. Sunday	71–72^v	nenano	The lampadarios	Sofia 93^v
26. Sunday	72^v–74^v	3 pl.	(Vlatyros)	Sofia 96
27. Sunday	74^v–76^v	4 pl.	(Manouil)	Sofia 98^v
28. Wednesday	76^v–78^v	4 pl.		Sofia 105

Liturgy of the Presanctified

29. Cherubic hymn: Νῦν αἱ δυνάμεις	78^v–81	2 pl.	(Longinos)	Sofia 108^v
30. Koinonikon: Γεύσασθε καὶ ἴδετε	81–82^v	nenano		Sofia 110^v
31. Koinonikon: Εὐλογίσω τὸν Κύριον	82^v–83	2 pl. (1 pl.) (1 pl.) (1 pl.) (1 pl.)		Putna 41^v Iaşi 118^v B283 130 B284 87^v
32. Cherubic hymn for Holy Thursday: Τοῦ δείπνου σου	83–5	2 pl.	Monk Longinos	Sofia 111

Item	Folios	Mode	Composer	Other manuscripts
33. Cherubic hymn for Holy Saturday: Σιγησάτω πᾶσα σάρξ	85ᵛ–88	4 pl.		Sofia 112
34. Koinonikon: Σῶμα Χριστοῦ	88–90	(nenano)		Sofia 114
35. Koinonikon: Σῶμα Χριστοῦ	90–91ᵛ	4 pl.		Sofia 115ᵛ
36. Theotokion in Slavonic: Възбраннои воеводѣ (kontakion for the Annunciation)	93ᵛ–94ᵛ	4 pl.	Theodosios	
37. Easter Troparion in Slavonic: Христос въскресе	94ᵛ	2 pl.		Sofia 195 (in Greek)

STICHERA AND OTHER TEXTS FOR VARIOUS FEASTS

38. Nativity of the Mother of God: Ἐξ ἀκάρπου γὰρ ῥίζης	95–8	2 pl.	Koukouzeles	Leimonos 262
39. Nativity of Christ: Δόξα ἐν ὑψίστοις Θεῷ	98–100ᵛ	1 (3 pl.)		Sofia 127ᵛ
40. Nativity of Christ: Μεγάλυνον ψυχὴ μου τὸν ἐν τῷ σπηλαίῳ	101–4	1		Sofia 133
41. Easter: Χριστὸς ἀνέστη	104–109ᵛ	2 pl.		Sofia 195

THEOTOKIA

42. Ἄνωθεν οἱ προφῆται	109ᵛ–116	1		Sofia 227ᵛ
43. (For the Dormition): Χαῖρε κεχαριτωμένη Παρθένε	116–20	nenano		Sofia 174ᵛ
44. (For the Dormition): Ἀλλ' ὦ παρθένε ἄχραντε	120–125ᵛ	2 pl.		Sofia 234ᵛ
45. Σὲ μεγαλύνομεν τὴν ὄντως Θεοτόκον	125ᵛ–129	2 pl.		Sofia 212

ADDITIONS IN THE SECOND HAND

46. Cherubic hymn: Οἱ τὰ χερουβίμ	92–3	4		

Item	Folios	Mode	Composer	Other manuscripts
47. Koinonikon for Sunday: Αἰνεῖτε	129–129ᵛ	I		Sofia 73ᵛ
48. Cherubic hymn: Οἱ τὰ χερουβίμ	131–4	I	Chrysaphes	Sofia 49ᵛ⁷

On f. 130 the second hand has written in Cyrillic the Greek theotokion Аѯїωн естин and the polychronion Тон деспотин and on f. 130ᵛ in Slavonic the theotokion О тебѣ радуетсѧ. These texts are not neumed.

It can be seen from this list that the book is very similar in content to parts of Sofia 816. The most important divergence is that it contains three compositions attributed to Theodosios: the Sunday koinonikon in mode 1 on f. 7ᵛ, with the attribution τοῦ Θεοδοσίὸς, the cherubic hymn in mode 2 plagal on f. 25, with the attribution τοῦ μοναχ⟨ου⟩ Θεοδοσίως, and the Slavonic theotokion in mode 4 plagal (with a supplementary modal signature in Slavonic: глас 8) with the attribution твореніе Θεωδ⟨ο⟩σιός.⁸ The first and last of these have not yet been found in other manuscripts, but the cherubic hymn occurs in B283 with the attribution (in mixed Greek and Cyrillic letters) tou Theod⟨o⟩-sie Zotika. Theodosios of Leipzig Sl. 12 must therefore be the same person.

It has been argued elsewhere that Theodosie Zotik(a) may be a local composer,⁹ and the appearance of these two compositions, so far only in one Moldavian manuscript, strengthens the argument against his being Greek, particularly since one of the compositions is in Slavonic —the Rumanian Evstatie certainly composed to Slavonic texts, and it is less probable that a Greek would have done so. The attribute 'Zotika' found in B283 becomes, however, more puzzling. Panţiru suggested that it might be a surname, and Theodosie therefore a lay figure, but Leipzig Sl. 12 specifically attributes the same composition to Theodosios as a monk. It seems probable that Leipzig Sl. 12 is later than B283, and Theodosie might have become a monk in the interval. Otherwise it must be presumed to be an attribution by locality. The different forms of the name are also surprising, since there is considerable consistency in the treatment of composers' names in the Putna akolouthiai. All, including Leipzig Sl. 12, put the Serb Stefan into the Slavonic genitive form: τοῦ Cτέφαν⟨α⟩ cрпína and leave the Rumanian Evstatie undeclined, e.g. Leipzig Sl. 12, f. 32: τοῦ μόναχ⟨ου⟩ Εὐστατίε. B283 appears to treat

⁷ This is the same setting as that on ff. 1–3.

⁸ Sic. Greek and Cyrillic alphabets are not always clearly distinguishable in the scribes' practice, but here the name is unmistakably in Greek.

⁹ Panţiru, op. cit. (n. 1), 34–5; A. E. Pennington, 'Stefan the Serb in Moldavian Manuscripts', Slavonic and East European Review, li (1973), 111.

Theodosie as mixed Rumanian (*Theodosie*, the Greek vocative, is the expected Rumanian form) and Slavonic (*Zotika*, though so far unexplained, could well be a genitive singular form). Leipzig Sl. 12, on the other hand, though the accents are erratic, retains the Greek nominative Θεοδόσιος, never using the correct Greek genitive Θεοδοσίου. It is, of course, possible that the scribe thought of -ος as the genitive flexion, but this is not a common type of mistake in the Putna manuscripts.[10]

MS. Leimonos 258 has been very fully described by M. K. Hadjiyakoumis,[11] but in order to characterize the manuscript in the context of the other Moldavian books it will be necessary to repeat some of the information he gives.

The book, catalogued as MS. 258 in the monastery library, is in two parts, bound together, possibly in the nineteenth century in Leimonos, with a binding of dark-brown leather on boards 15·5 × 10·6 cm. There are no clasps. On the upper cover is a stamp with the Virgin and Child, crowned, and on the lower a stamp with King David. On the first flyleaf is a note that the book was given to Leimonos by Σωφρόνιος ψάλτης, and on the third flyleaf is the stamp of the monastery and the date (presumably of acquisition) 1898.

The first part of the book—ff. 1–144^v—is a seventeenth-century notated Greek anthology, which, although it includes a polychronion to the voevoda of Moldavia on ff. 123–4, appears (as Hadjiyakoumis says) to have no connection with the Putna school of music. Slavonic inscriptions on two coloured illustrations in the book do not, unfortunately, prove a bilingual scribe of the Moldavian school—they are merely the formal name of the depicted saint, and the leaves are in any case later additions, not part of the original structure of the book. A third similar illustration has been lost between ff. 93^v and 94— a smudge from a halo is visible on f. 94.

The following observations relate only to the second part of the book —ff. 145–418^v. This part of the book is in good condition, and consists of twenty-five gatherings, signed by the scribe and almost complete: the collation is: I–XIV^8 (ff. 145–256^v), XV^7 (ff. 257–261b^v, with one leaf torn out between ff. 260 and 261; the curious numbering is caused by the first foliation, which numbered only leaves with text: leaves which had been left blank were numbered later as 261a, 261b, etc.), XVI–XXXIV^8 (ff. 262–413^v), XXXV^5 (ff. 414–418^v). Ff. 145–146^v are mended at the spine. The paper is 15·2 × 10·1 cm., probably Italian. It has at least six watermarks: one an ox-head very like Piccard XIII 154 (1522, 1523); one a hill somewhat like Briquet 7922 (1515); two are cardinals' hats with countermark A, one not unlike Briquet 3405 (1518),

[10] Pennington, op. cit. (n. 9), 110.
[11] Loc. cit. (n. 2). No further references will be made to this book for individual points of description.

the other somewhat like Briquet 3402 (1499); two are single-shank anchors in circles with countermark VI and a trefoil; in one the circle is surmounted by a trefoil, in the other by a ring; neither is very like any in the repertories, although they belong to Mošin's groups 595–7 (1494–1523, but with double shanks) and 2025–112 (1580–1650—evidently a later type).

This manuscript is of particular importance because the scribe's colophon survives. It reads:

Изволеніем ѡца, и поспѣшеніем с⟨ы⟩на: и съвръшеніем с⟨вѧ⟩т⟨а⟩го д⟨оу⟩ха . Мнѡгогрѣшныи діакѡн Макаріе, тах и пѣвец . исписа сіа книга ѡ пѣтіѡх . своим потрѫжденіем . въ Дѫбровческѡм мѡнастири . идеж⟨е⟩ ес⟨ть⟩ храм съшествіа с⟨вѧ⟩т⟨а⟩го д⟨оу⟩ха в л⟨ѣ⟩тѡ 7035 (= 1527) м⟨е⟩с⟨е⟩ца генѫаріа 10 (f. 413).

The monastery in question must be Dobrovăţ, where a church dedicated to the Descent of the Holy Spirit (Pentecost) was built by Stefan the Great in 1503–4.[12] The name of the monastery has been found as *Dobrovăţ, Dobroveţ*, and also *Dubroveţs*;[13] it is the last form that would regularly produce the adjective *Dubrovčesk*. There were apparently strong connections between the monasteries of Putna and Dobrovăţ: Putna was active in furnishing Dobrovăţ with books at the time of the latter's foundation—MSS. Sl. 540, 544, and 547 in the library of the Rumanian Academy in Bucharest, menologia for July, November, and March respectively, were all written in Putna, but belonged to Dobrovăţ.[14] In MS. Sl. 547 the scribe Paisie states in his colophon (f. 214ᵛ) that he wrote it in 1504 for the voevoda Stefan to give 'въ монастыр създанныи ѡт него на имѧ идеже ес⟨ть⟩ храм с⟨вѧ⟩тыѧ и нераздѣлимыѫ Троицѫ' when Pachomie was abbot of that monastery.[15] Paisie calls himself *pěv⟨e⟩c*, but MS. Sl. 547 is not neumed, so Leimonos 258 is the first source of evidence for the musical links between the monasteries; its similarities to those books which were certainly written in Putna (Evstatie's books and Iaşi 1.26) as well as to the others which have been ascribed to Putna on the grounds of

[12] See G. Balş, *Bisericile lui Ştefan cel Mare* (Buletinul Comisiunii Monumentelor istorice, Anul xviii) (Bucharest, 1926), 118 and fig. 486 (the dedication tablet).

[13] E. Turdeanu, 'Centres of Literary Activity in Moldavia, 1504–1555', *Slavonic and East European Review*, xxxiv (1955), 109. The stem, referring to the monastery or the eponymous river, appears as Добровц-, Добровец-, and also Дѫбровц- in a document of 6 October 1503 (I. Bogdan, *Documentele lui Ştefan cel Mare*, ii (Bucharest, 1973), 238–40).

[14] E. Turdeanu, 'L'activité littéraire en Moldavie à l'époque d'Étienne le Grand, 1457–1504', *Revue des études roumaines*, v/vi (Paris, 1958), 42–5.

[15] Pachomie was the first abbot of Dobrovăţ, see the document of 6 October 1503: монастир що на връх Добровец, идеже ест храмъ съшѣствіе свѧтаго дѫха и где есть игѫмен молебник наш кир попа Пахоміе (Bogdan, op. cit. (n. 13), 239). The difference in dedication is curious, but perhaps more apparent than real, since the Feast of the Trinity and of Pentecost coincide in Orthodox tradition. This document of 1503, Dr. D. Deletant has pointed out (in a private communication), conflates Stefan's foundation of Dobrovăţ in Vaslui with Alexander's earlier foundation of Dobrovăţ in Iaşi county. However, it seems clear enough that Pachomie was abbot of Stefan's foundation.

common physical appearance, content, and style, suggest that the musical links were strong and the influence of Putna very considerable. The deacon Makarie is so far unidentified. He may have progressed in holy orders and be the same as the hieromonk Makarie, who in 1529 copied a Gospel book in Putna,[16] but the name is not uncommon and a comparison of the hands has not yet been possible.

There are ten lines of text and music to a page. The text and neumes are in black ink, well preserved; headings, initials, rubrics, martyriai, and cheironomiai are usually in red, but, unlike the Putna akolouthiai, gold is also used: on ff. 156, 172, 194, 262 and 381 the main initials are in gold, and in the colophon on f. 413 the first initial and (surprisingly) the 'M' of Мнѡгогрѣшныи are in gold. On ff. 262 and 381 the modal signatures are also in gold. Many of the bigger red initials have blue flourishes or serifs.[17] On ff. 145, 156, 172, 194, and 262 there are headpieces (those on ff. 172 and 262 are elaborate, the others simple), with red fillets interwoven in decorative patterns very like those of the Putna akolouthiai, but, unlike them, coloured blue, green, orange, and brown. In the margins Makarie draws stylized pots of flowers in red, usually to mark the presence of a doxology. Similar flowers are found in Sofia 816, Iaşi 1.26 and B283.

The language mixture in Leimonos 258 is similar to that of the other books: most of the texts are Greek, but there are two compositions in Slavonic (ff. 328ᵛ and 409ᵛ). Names of composers are in Greek, but names of feasts in Slavonic. Most rubrics and the heading for Vespers (f. 145) are in Greek, but the heading for the beginning of the Liturgy (f. 194) is in Slavonic. Modal signatures are in Greek, but gathering signatures are in Cyrillic. The orthography of both languages reflects a characteristic disregard for classical principles and the two alphabets are intermingled to a considerable extent; a remarkable example is on f. 168ᵛ in the attribution to Koukouzeles: τοῦ μαϊστ⟨όρ⟩ου κυρ Ἰωνου τοῦ Κουκουζελь, with a Cyrillic soft *jer* on the end of the name.

The contents of Makarie's akolouthia are also very similar to those of the other books, and since it is fairly long and in very good condition it offers an excellent basis for comparison. The contents are listed below by items, as was done for Leipzig Sl. 12, except that for any item that does not appear in Sofia 816 appropriate references are given for all the other manuscripts of the group. Leipzig Sl. 12 is abbreviated to Leipzig.

Leimonos 258 does not begin with a *psaltike techne* and since f. 145 is signed as the beginning of the first gathering there is no reason to suppose that anything is missing.

[16] E. Turdeanu, 'L'activité littéraire en Moldavie, 1504–1552', *Revue des études roumaines* ix/x (Paris, 1965), 127.

[17] Such flourishes are not found in the other akolouthiai, but do appear in other Putna manuscripts, e.g. in the Psalter, MS. 76 in the monastery library, which also uses gold.

Item	Folios	Mode	Composer	Other manuscripts
GREAT VESPERS				
1. Part of the procemiac psalm which begins: Ἀνοίξαντος	145–55	4 pl.		Sofia 3
Heading: Ἄλαγμα τοῦ ἀριστεροῦ χοροῦ				
2. Kathisma: Μακάριος ἀνήρ	156–163ᵛ	4 pl.		Sofia 1
PROKEIMENA FOR THE WEEK[18]				
3. Sunday: Ἰδοὺ δὴ εὐλογεῖτε τὸν Κύριον	163ᵛ–164	1		
4. Monday: Κύριος εἰσακούσεται	164–5	1 pl.		
5. Tuesday: Τὸ ἔλεος σου Κύριε	165–165ᵛ	1 pl.		
6. Wednesday: Ὁ Θεὸς ἐν τῷ ὀνοματί σου	166–166ᵛ	1 pl.		
7. Thursday: Ἡ βοή- θεια μου	166ᵛ–167	2 pl.		
8. Friday: Ὁ Θεὸς ἀντιλήπτωρ μου	167ᵛ–168	3 pl.		
9. Saturday: Ἐνεδύσατο Κύριος δύναμιν	168ᵛ–171ᵛ	4 pl.	Koukouzeles	
MATINS				
10. Polyeleos, the so-called 'Koukouma'	172–193ᵛ	1	Monk Kornilios	Sofia 11
LITURGY				
11. Trisagion: Ἅγιος ὁ Θεός	194–6	4 pl.		Sofia 4
12. Festal trisagion: Ὅσοι εἰς Χριστόν	196–7	1 pl.	Monk Evstatie	Sofia 34
13. Trisagion for the Holy Cross: Τὸν σταυρόν σου	197–198ᵛ	2	Monk Evstatie	Sofia 35
14. Cherubic hymn: Οἱ τὰ χερουβίμ	198ᵛ–203	1 pl.	Koronis	Sofia 36ᵛ
15. Cherubic hymn	203–205ᵛ	2 pl.	Agathon	Sofia 39ᵛ
16. Cherubic hymn	205ᵛ–208	2 or nenano	Agallianos	Sofia 42

[18] Evstatie also has a full set of prokeimena for the week, but all his settings are different.

Item	Folios	Mode	Composer	Other manuscripts
17. Cherubic hymn	208ᵛ–212	1 and 1 pl.	Monk Evstatie	Sofia 52
18. Cherubic hymn	212–214ᵛ	3	Monk Evstatie	Sofia 45
19. Cherubic hymn	214ᵛ–216ᵛ	(1 pl.)	Monk Evstatie	Sofia 56
20. Anaphora: Πατέρα Υἱόν	217–217ᵛ	4 pl.		Sofia 67ᵛ
21. Sanctus: Ἅγιος, ἅγιος, ἅγιος	217ᵛ–218ᵛ	2		Sofia 68ᵛ
22. Theotokion: Ἐπὶ σοὶ χαίρει κεχαριτωμένη	219–21	4 pl.	Koronis	Sofia 70

KOINONIKA FOR THE DAYS OF THE WEEK

Item	Folios	Mode	Composer	Other manuscripts
23. Sunday: Αἰνεῖτε τὸν Κύριον	221–222ᵛ	1	Raidestinos 'persikon'	Sofia 72
24. Wednesday: Ποτήριον σωτηρίου	222ᵛ–223ᵛ	1	('tou autou', i.e. Raidestinos)	Sofia 74ᵛ
25. Sunday	223ᵛ–225	2	Moschianos	Sofia 78ᵛ
26. Sunday	225–6	2	(Moschianos)	Sofia 77
27. Wednesday	226–227ᵛ	2	Gerasimos	Sofia 79ᵛ
28. Tuesday: Εἰς μνημόσυνον	227ᵛ–228ᵛ	3	tou autou, i.e. Gerasimos	Sofia 81
29. Tuesday	228ᵛ–230	nenano		Sofia 82ᵛ
30. Sunday	230–1	3	The lampadarios	Sofia 83ᵛ
31. Wednesday	231–2	3	Argyropoulos	Sofia 84ᵛ
32. Sunday	232–3	4	The lampadarios	Sofia 86
33. Wednesday	233–234ᵛ	4	Ampelokipiotis	Sofia 88ᵛ
34. Sunday	234ᵛ–235ᵛ	1 pl.	Koronis	Sofia 91
35. Sunday	235ᵛ–236ᵛ	nenano	The lampadarios	Sofia 93ᵛ
36. Wednesday	236ᵛ–237ᵛ	nenano	(The lampadarios)	Sofia 95
37. Sunday	237ᵛ–239	3 pl.	Vlatyros	Sofia 96
38. Sunday	239–40	3 pl.	Argyropoulos	
39. Sunday	240–241ᵛ	3 pl.	Stefan the Serb	Sofia 97ᵛ
40. Wednesday	241ᵛ–243	3 pl.	The lampadarios	

Item	Folios	Mode	Composer	Other manuscripts
41. Sunday	243–244ᵛ	4 pl.	Manouil Argyropoulos 'organikon'	Sofia 98ᵛ
42. Wednesday	244ᵛ–246	4 pl.	David Raidestinos	Sofia 101ᵛ
43. Wednesday	246–247ᵛ	4 pl.	('organikon')	Sofia 105

LITURGY OF THE PRESANCTIFIED

44. Cherubic hymn: Νῦν αἱ δυνάμεις	247ᵛ–249	2 pl.	Monk Longinos	Sofia 108ᵛ
45. Koinonikon: Γεύσασθε καὶ ἴδετε	249–250ᵛ	2 pl.	Moschianos	Putna 40ᵛ
46. Koinonikon: Γεύσασθε καὶ ἴδετε	250ᵛ–251ᵛ	nenano	The lampadarios	Sofia 110ᵛ
47. Verse: Εὐλογήσω τὸν Κύριον καὶ ὑψώσω σε ὁ Θεός μου	251ᵛ	1 pl.		Putna 41ᵛ Iași 118ᵛ B283 130 B284 87ᵛ
48. Cherubic hymn for Holy Thursday: Τοῦ δείπνου σου	251ᵛ–253ᵛ	2 pl.		Sofia 111
49. Cherubic hymn for Holy Saturday: Σιγησάτω πᾶσα σάρξ	253ᵛ–255ᵛ	1 pl. (4 pl.)		Sofia 112
50. Koinonikon for Holy Saturday: Σῶμα Χριστοῦ	255ᵛ–256	1 pl.	Stefan	Putna B 86
51. Koinonikon: Σῶμα Χριστοῦ	256–257ᵛ	nenano		Sofia 114
52. Koinonikon: Σῶμα Χριστοῦ	257ᵛ–259	4 pl.		Sofia 115ᵛ
53. Sunday koinonikon: Αἰνεῖτε	259–259ᵛ	1	Kyr Ioan	
54. Sunday koinonikon: Αἰνεῖτε	260–1	4 pl.		

STICHERA AND OTHER TEXTS FOR VARIOUS FEASTS

55. Nativity of the Mother of God: Ἐξ ἀκάρπου γὰρ ῥίζης	262–4	2 pl.		Putna B 89 Iași 129 B283 140 B284 63 Dragomirna 37 Leipzig 95

Item	Folios	Mode	Composer	Other manuscripts
56. Exaltation of the Cross: Διὰ πιστῶν βασιλέων ἡ πίστις	264–266ᵛ	2 pl.	(Koukouzeles)	Putna B 92ᵛ Iaşi 131ᵛ B284 75ᵛ Dragomirna 38
57. St. John the Theologian: Ἐν ἀρχῇ ἦν ὁ λόγος, καὶ ὁ λόγος ἦν πρὸς τὸν Θεόν	266ᵛ–269	2 pl.	('tou autou', i.e. Koukouzeles)	Putna B 93ᵛ Iaşi 134 Dragomirna 40
58. St. Demetrios: Ἀπόλαυε τῶν θαυμάτων	269–71	1	Koukouzeles	Putna B 95 Iaşi 137
59. St. Demetrios: Φρούρησον πανένδοξε τὴν σὲ μεγαλύνουσαν πόλιν	271ᵛ–273	2 pl. or nenano		Putna B 96 Iaşi 139ᵛ B283 143 Dragomirna 42
60. Archangel Michael: Σκέπασον ἡμᾶς	273–5	nenano		Sofia 117
61. Eisothia of the Mother of God: Ἄσπιλε ἀμόλυντε (part of sticheron)	275ᵛ–278	1 pl.		Sofia 119ᵛ
62. St. Sava: Τῶν δαιμόνων (part of idiomelon)	278–280ᵛ	(2 pl.)		Sofia 122ᵛ
63. St. Nicholas: Τῶν θλιβομένων	280ᵛ–283	2 pl.		Sofia 125
64. Nativity of Christ: Δόξα ἐν ὑψίστοις Θεῷ τῷ ἐκ παρθένου ἀνατείλαντι	283–5	3 pl.		Sofia 127ᵛ
65. Nativity of Christ: Ἀδὰμ ἀνανεοῦται σὺν τῇ Εὔᾳ (part of idiomelon)	285–8	4 pl.	'tou maist⟨or⟩ou', i.e. Koukouzeles	Putna B 102 Iaşi 152 bisᵛ
66. Nativity of Christ: Ὦ βάθος πλούτου (part of sticheron)	288–291ᵛ	4 pl.		Sofia 129ᵛ
67. Nativity of Christ: Μεγάλυνον ψυχή μου τὸν ἐν τῷ σπηλαίῳ	291ᵛ–293ᵛ	1		Sofia 133
68. Epiphany: Διὰ τὰς ἁμαρτίας ἡμῶν (part of idiomelon)	291ᵛ–293ᵛ	1		Sofia 133
69. Epiphany: Ἀλλὰ πᾶσαν ἐπλήρωσας (part of idiomelon)	295ᵛ–299	4 pl.		Sofia 137ᵛ

Item	Folios	Mode	Composer	Other manuscripts
70. Purification (Hypapante): Αὕτη γὰρ θρόνος (part of idiomelon)	299–301ᵛ	4 pl.		Sofia 141
71. Holy three hierarchs: Τοὺς κήρυκας τοὺς ἱερούς (idiomelon)	302–304ᵛ	4 pl.		Sofia 177ᵛ
72. Annunciation: Τῇ ὑπερμάχῳ στρατηγῷ (kontakion)	304ᵛ–308ᵛ	4 pl.		Sofia 144

FROM THE PENTECOSTARION

Item	Folios	Mode	Composer	Other manuscripts
73. Easter: Ἀναστάσεως ἡμέρα (Heirmos of the first Ode of the Canon)	308ᵛ–313	1		
74. Pentecost: Καὶ σοῦ ἀγαθὲ (idiomelon)	313–16	2 pl.		Sofia 205

ADDITIONAL STICHERA FOR FEASTS, THEOTOKIA, AND OTHER TEXTS

Item	Folios	Mode	Composer	Other manuscripts
75. Nativity of St. John: Οὗτος γὰρ ἐκήρυξε	316–19	2		Sofia 156
76. Theotokion: Σὲ μεγαλύνομεν τὴν ὄντως Θεοτόκον	319–321ᵛ	1 pl. (1)	The lampadarios	Sofia 212
77. Theotokion: Χαῖρε τῆς χάριτος πηγὴ	321ᵛ–325ᵛ	1		Sofia 208
78. Heirmos of the ninth Ode of the Canon of the fifth tone: Ἠσαΐα χόρευε ἡ παρθένος	325ᵛ–328ᵛ	1 pl.	The lampadarios	
79. Sticheron from the burial service (Slavonic):[19] Каа житеиска пища прѣбывает печали непричасна	328ᵛ–331	1		
80. Annunciation: Εὐαγγελίζεται ὁ Γαβριὴλ	331ᵛ–334ᵛ	2 pl.		Sofia 148ᵛ

FROM THE PENTECOSTARION

Item	Folios	Mode	Composer	Other manuscripts
81. Palm Sunday: Ὁ διδάσκαλος λέγει (part of idiomelon)	334ᵛ–338ᵛ	2 pl.		Sofia 185

[19] Evstatie also includes 'pokoina' from the burial service, but different texts and settings. The Synodal Church Slavonic text begins: Каѧ житейскаѧ слѧдость ...

Item	Folios	Mode	Composer	Other manuscripts
82. Easter: Αὔτη ἡ κλητὴ καὶ ἀγία ἡμέρα (Heirmos of the eighth Ode of the Canon)	338ᵛ–341ᵛ	1		Sofia 189
83. Easter: Φωτίζου φωτίζου (Heirmos of the ninth Ode of the Canon)	341ᵛ–344	1	Glykes	Sofia 192
84. Easter: Χριστὸς ἀνέστη (troparion)	344–347ᵛ	1 pl. (2 pl.)	Monk Theodoulos	Sofia 195
STICHERON FOR A FEAST				
85. St. George: Τοῦ μεγάλου βασιλέως	348–51	1		Sofia 153
FROM THE PENTECOSTARION				
86. Ascension: Τίς λαλήσει τὰς δυναστείας σου Χριστέ; (idiomelon)	351–353ᵛ	4 pl.	The lampadarios	Sofia 198ᵛ
87. Ascension: Ἀπέστειλας ἡμῶν Χριστέ ὁ Θεός (idiomelon)	353ᵛ–357	4 (1)	Evgenikos	Sofia 201
88. Λόγε Πατρὸς καὶ σύμφυν πνεῦμα[20]	357–360ᵛ	4 pl.	John Laskaris	Putna B 151
ADDITIONAL STICHERA, THEOTOKIA, AND OTHER TEXTS				
89. St. Paul: Παῦλε στόμα Κυρίου (idiomelon)	360ᵛ–363ᵛ	2		Sofia 164
90. St. Peter Ὅθεν πρὸς αὐτὸν ὁ σωτήρ (idiomelon)	363ᵛ–368	4		Sofia 159ᵛ
91. Transfiguration: Οὐρανοὶ ἔφριξαν (idiomelon)	368–71	1		Sofia 168ᵛ
92. Dormition: Ἀλλ' ὦ παρθένε ἄχραντε (idiomelon)	371–5	2 pl.		Sofia 234ᵛ
93. Dormition: Χαῖρε κεχαριτωμένη παρθένε (idiomelon)	375–377ᵛ	nenano		Sofia 174ᵛ
94. Beheading of St. John: Ἀλλ' ἡμεῖς τὸν βαπτιστήν (part of idiomelon)	377ᵛ–381	nenano		Sofia 181

[20] This text probably belongs to Pentecost, but is so far unidentified.

Item	Folios	Mode	Composer	Other manuscripts
THEOTOKIA				
95. Ἄνωθεν οἱ προφῆται	381–5	I	John Kladas the lampadarios	Sofia 227ᵛ
96. Ἄνωθεν οἱ προφῆται	385–8	nenano	Koukouzeles	
97. Ἄνωθεν οἱ προφῆται	388–390ᵛ	3 pl.	'tou maistorou', i.e. Koukouzeles	
98. Τὴν ὄντως Θεοτόκον	390ᵛ–392	2	'tou maistorou'	Putna B 160ᵛ
99. Τὴν ὄντως Θεοτόκον	392ᵛ–395ᵛ	4 pl.	'tou maistorou'	Sofia 220ᵛ
100. Ἐν Σιναίῳ τῳ ὄρει κατεῖδέ σε	395ᵛ–398ᵛ	3	'tou autou', i.e. Koukouzeles (Koronis)	Iaşi 227
101. Ἄπας γηγενὴς σκιρτάτω τῷ πνεύματι (Annunciation: heirmos of the ninth Ode of the Canon)	398ᵛ–401ᵛ	4	Domestikos Konstantinos Magoulas	Iaşi 223ᵛ
102. Δέησιν δέξαι πανάγιε μήτηρ Θεοῦ τοῦ λόγου	402–404ᵛ	2 pl.		
103. Ψαλμοῖς καὶ ὕμνοις σέ ὑμνῶ παρθενομήτωρ κόρη	404ᵛ–409	4 pl.	Manouil Chrysaphes	Sofia 166ᵛ [21]
104. (Slavonic): Тебе бо имам надеждж	409ᵛ–413	4 pl.		Iaşi 230ᵛ B283 225
FROM MATINS				
105. Pasa pnoe: Πᾶσα πνοὴ	413ᵛ–417ᵛ	I		B283 231 Dragomirna 32
FROM THE LITURGY				
106. Trisagion: Ἅγιος ὁ Θεός	417ᵛ–418ᵛ	4 pl.		Iaşi 60ᵛ Dragomirna 7ᵛ

On f. 193ᵛ a later hand has written part of the ninth Ode of the Canon for the Hypapante: Θεοτόκε, ἡ ἐλπὶς πάντων τῶν Χριστιανῶν. This text is not neumed.

Makarie's book is very similar in its repertory and in its arrangement of material to the majority of the Putna manuscripts (Evstatie's book

[21] Only the beginning survives in Sofia 816, and the item was omitted from the concordance of that text. See Pennington, op. cit. (n. 1). Both this and the next item probably also refer to the Annunciation.

is exceptional). He begins with chant for Great Vespers, then for the Liturgy, then the Liturgy of the Presanctified and then gives selected texts for the major feasts of the September year, including one text for Easter and one for Pentecost in the appropriate place between the Annunciation (25 March, therefore almost always before Easter) and the Nativity of St. John (24 June). This pattern is also followed by B283, but Sofia 816, Putna B, Iaşi 1.26 and Dragomirna 52 all finish the texts for fixed feasts before beginning the Pentecostarion. Makarie then proceeds to three theotokia and the Slavonic text of the Canon of St. John Damascene from the burial service—as if he were finishing his anthology. Then, however, he returns to the Annunciation, Palm Sunday, Easter again, and St. George (23 April, therefore almost always after Easter), then the Ascension, and (probably) Pentecost, followed by texts for the rest of the major fixed feasts to the end of the year, where he eventually finishes with another group of theotokia and two standard texts from Matins and the Liturgy, respectively. The material construction of the book offers no evidence to suggest that Makarie added sections as an afterthought: f. 331ᵛ, on which he returns to the Annunciation, is in the middle of gathering 24, and f. 351, on which he returns to the Ascension, is the second leaf of gathering 27. In neither place is there a noticeable difference in ink or style. Nor are the intrusive texts later intercalations, as is the case with some of Evstatie's work.[22] Makarie's idiosyncratic arrangement is a further indication that these small books of chant were personal anthologies or work-books; it may be observed that Makarie says in his colophon (f. 413) that he wrote his book 'своим потр八жденіем . . .', not 'на послышаніе' as hieromonk Stefan of Putna wrote a February menologion in 1530, nor 'повелѣніем . . . воеводы' as deacon Nikodim wrote an April menologion in Putna in 1467.[23] If item 88 is correctly identified as a Pentecost text, it is appropriate that Makarie should include two texts for this day, the feast of dedication of his own monastery; however, he also keeps two for the Dormition (Putna's dedication) as well as a very large group of theotokia.

The selection of settings in the books shows a considerable shared repertory, but some variety—no two books of those found so far are identical in their repertory. Makarie includes many melodies familiar from other sources—Greek as well as Moldavian. He has one setting by Chrysaphes, the mid-fifteenth-century composer,[24] whose work must have been beginning to penetrate Moldavia in the 1520s—none

[22] A. E. Pennington, 'The Composition of Evstatie's Song Book', Oxford Slavonic Papers, N.S. vi (1973), 103–8.

[23] Now MS. Undol'sky 79 F 5/63 and MS. Undol'sky 81 F 5/66 respectively, in the Lenin Library, Moscow.

[24] See D. E. Conomos, Byzantine Trisagia and Cheroubika of the Fourteenth and Fifteenth Centuries (Thessaloniki, 1974), 42.

of his compositions is found in Evstatie's book or Putna 56, but he is more widely represented in the other Putna manuscripts from the mid sixteenth century or later. Makarie includes five compositions by Evstatie, who was protopsaltes of Putna in 1511, and very possibly still alive and active in Makarie's time. He does not include any of Theodosie's work (offering an extra piece of evidence that Theodosie may have lived later in the century), nor does he include the koinonikon of Dometian the Vlach, which appears in four of the later manuscripts (Sofia 816, Iași 1.26, B 283 and Dragomirna 52).

He includes the koinonikon by Stefan the Serb in mode 3 pl., now known from six Moldavian manuscripts, and also a setting of the koino-nikon for Great Saturday in mode 1 pl. attributed simply to 'Stefan'. It is highly probable that this is also Stefan the Serb. No other composer Stefan is mentioned in comparable sources,[25] while the Serb has been cited a few folios earlier. The form of the name also suggests the identity: it is written in the same way as is the Stefan in the full attribution on f. 240, with superscript n showing that the -a- in the line is to be read twice, giving the Slavonic genitive form Stefana. This koinonikon by Stefan also appears, without attribution, in Putna B—the older part of MS. Putna 56, which by its watermarks was tentatively dated to the first half of the fifteenth century. The composer Stefan the Serb has been credibly, though not definitively, identified with the domestik Stefan who copied books at the court of Despot Lazar in Smederevo in the 1450s and 1460s.[26] If Makarie is right in attributing the setting to Stefan, and if Stefan is Stefan the Serb, and if Stefan the Serb is Lazar's domestik Stefan, then Putna B must have been written in the second half, probably the last quarter, of the fifteenth century, and could, consequently, have been written at Putna. There are many uncertainties, but such a conclusion would explain why the repertory of Putna B is so much like that of the later akolouthiai, and also, presumably, why the gathering signatures are in Cyrillic, although the hand seems otherwise to be purely Greek.

If Stefan is Stefan the Serb, this brief koinonikon is important, since it is only the fourth surviving composition attributable to him,[27] and a remarkable testimony to his international reputation.

Nine, or possibly ten notated akolouthiai now appear to be connected with the Putna school of music: the earliest—Putna B—possibly

[25] Cf. M. Velimirović, 'Byzantine Composers in MS. Athens 2406', *Essays presented to Egon Wellesz* (Oxford, 1966), 7–18; N. A. Veēs, Τὰ χειρόγραφα τῶν μετεώρων, κατάλογος περιγραφικός, i (Athens, 1967). Hadjiyakoumis lists both compositions, without comment, under Stefan the Serb and mentions no other Stefan (op. cit. (n. 2), 384).

[26] Dj. Sp. Radojčić, *Književna zbivanja i stvaranja kod Srba u srednjem veku i u tursko doba* (Novi Sad, 1967), 148–9. On the copying activities of Domestik Stefan, see L. Cernić, 'Rukopis Stefana Srbina', *Bibliotekar*, i/ii (Belgrade, 1968), 61–83.

[27] For the most recent information see D. Stefanović, *Stara srpska muzika* (Belgrade, 1975), especially pp. 19–20, 53–66, also his bibliography.

dating from the late fifteenth century (although this manuscript needs further investigation), all the others from the sixteenth century. Two— Evstatie's book and Antonie's (Iași 1.26) were certainly written in Putna; one—Makarie's book (Leimonos 258)—must have been written in Dobrovăț. The similarity of style and repertory shows that the musical links between the two monasteries were very strong, and throws doubt on the provenance of the seven manuscripts which have lost their colophons and which cannot now be safely attributed to Putna itself, although they quite clearly belong to the Putna school. All the manuscripts so far known appear to have been written by different scribes, who were, of course, also singers, and it is much to be hoped that further manuscripts will be identified as stemming from this flourishing centre.[28]

[28] It is a pleasant duty to thank the many people who have helped in tracking down these manuscripts: Dr. J. Raasted and Dr. D. Conomos for drawing my attention to them in the first place; the Board of the Faculty of Medieval and Modern Languages of Oxford University for a grant for travel to Leipzig; Dr. M. Hadjiyakoumis and the Librarian of Leipzig University Library for their courteous reception and for microfilm; Miss A. Tamvaki, Abbot Nikodimos and the monks of Leimonos for their hospitality and patience; Professor D. Obolensky, the Rev. M. Fortounatto, Dr. D. Deletant, N. G. Wilson, and Dr. D. Stefanović for helpful comments, and finally Dr. D. Conomos (again) for contributing and checking musical and Greek information.

N. I. Kostomarov and the Origins of the *Vestnik Evropy* Circle

By ALEXIS E. POGORELSKIN

WRITING in 1955 in a volume dedicated to G. M. Trevelyan, Noel Annan discussed the origins, in the first decade of the nineteenth century, of England's 'new intelligentsia' or 'intellectual aristocracy', which was 'able to move between the worlds of speculation and government' and 'in literary life . . . [formed] the backbone of the Victorian intellectual periodicals'.[1] At first few in number and attracted to each other primarily by a common hatred of the slave trade, in the course of the century these men developed a commitment to a variety of causes and as a group flourished through intermarriage.

By the second half of the nineteenth century Russia, too, could boast a moderate intelligentsia, if not an intellectual aristocracy. A substantial number of its members, having forsaken academic careers, gathered round the journal *Vestnik Evropy*, itself originally based on the model of the English monthly or quarterly reviews. However, these men attached themselves to a journal not because they had suffered a personal or spiritual crisis such as had impelled Leslie Stephen to leave Cambridge and write for the *Cornhill Magazine*, nor because they sought a larger social arena, having tired of academic life altogether. In their case, journalism was one of the few careers open to them after events in the University of St. Petersburg in the early 1860s had made academic positions untenable for them.

It was partly because *Vestnik Evropy* at first attracted those whose careers had been largely associated with academic achievement that uncertainty arose at its inception over which collaborators held primary responsibility for the journal. Turgenev unwittingly expressed the confusion when, noting the journal's inauguration, he singled out the most famous individual connected with it. He wrote to the poet Afanasy Fet: 'This year I have been receiving journals . . . the most agreeable development is . . . the revival of *Vestnik Evropy* by Kostomarov.'[2]

The historian N. I. Kostomarov, in fact, had no responsibility for the revival of *Vestnik Evropy* and remained with it only briefly. Even earlier, in the university, his relations with those who became closely

[1] N. G. Annan, 'The Intellectual Aristocracy', in: *Studies in Social History: a Tribute to G. M. Trevelyan*, ed. J. H. Plumb (1955), 244, 285.
[2] I. S. Turgenev, *Polnoe sobranie sochinenii i pisem. Pis'ma*, vi (1963), 65: letter of 25 Mar. 1866.

connected with the journal were strained. Yet Kostomarov was responsible for the initial success of *Vestnik Evropy*. At the same time the tension between him and the editorial board emphasized the unity within that group which was unusual then—and later—in Russian intellectual life. An account of Kostomarov's association with those who did bear responsibility for the journal is essential for an understanding of its consistency and its regular appearance over more than fifty years.

The Russian intelligentsia suffered from uncertainties and instabilities unknown to the English intellectuals discussed by Annan, who were bound by ties of family and common endeavour within a stable political order. In Russia, however, the experience of dislocation and uncertainty shared and overcome could itself be a source of unity. In this paper I shall attempt to explain the stability of the *Vestnik Evropy* circle in relation to its foundation at a time of academic turmoil and to detail the efforts of its members to bring the talent and the name of Kostomarov under its banner.

In September 1856, when Prince G. A. Shcherbatov became Superintendent of the St. Petersburg Educational District, and *ipso facto* responsible for the university in the capital, he embarked on a series of reforms of that institution which he had long contemplated while an assistant to his patriarchal predecessor, M. N. Musin-Pushkin. Shcherbatov, in fact, nurtured a 'broad plan to transform the university'.[3] Basic to his programme was the encouragement of professors and lecturers who, despite their unquestioned ability, had been forced to abandon all hope of pursuing an academic career because of political repression in the past. The most notable addition to the Historical-Philological Faculty under Shcherbatov was the appointment of Kostomarov to the Chair of Russian History in 1859.

Kostomarov was no ordinary academic. In 1846, while teaching history at the St. Vladimir University in Kiev, he had been arrested for membership of the Cyril and Methodius Society.[4] The group had discussed a Slavonic federation in which the Ukraine would enjoy autonomy. Kostomarov was imprisoned in the Fortress of St. Peter and St. Paul for a year and then exiled to Saratov. While there, he was able to continue his historical work and in the late 1850s published studies on Bogdan Khmel'nitsky and Sten'ka Razin. When, at the instigation of Shcherbatov, E. P. Kovalevsky, the Minister of Education, petitioned Alexander II to allow Kostomarov to be considered

[3] N. V. Shelgunov, *Vospominaniya*, ed. A. A. Shilov (P., 1923), 124; V. D. Spasovich, *Sochineniya*, iv (Spb., 1891), 20.

[4] For these and other biographical facts about Kostomarov see 'N. I. Kostomarov', *Entsiklopedicheskii slovar'*, xv (Spb., 1895), 402–3.

for an impending vacancy as professor of Russian history, the Emperor insisted that he judge Kostomarov's work for himself. During the summer of 1859 he read the study on Razin, was favourably impressed, and approved Kostomarov's candidacy.[5] Within ten years of what had appeared to be total ruin, Kostomarov had managed to resurrect his career both as scholar and as teacher.

He was elected to the St. Petersburg chair and delivered his inaugural lecture on 22 November 1859. The occasion, which marked the resumption of his teaching career after an interval of twelve years, was a triumph. At the end of the lecture the students carried him shoulder-high from the hall—a gesture they often repeated. Not only did Kostomarov's lectures attract students from all faculties of the university, but 'his popularity embraced all of intellectual St. Petersburg of the time'.[6] Kostomarov himself later wrote: 'Hardly any other professor was respected by the students as I was . . . . In the streets strangers raised their hats to me. . . .'[7]

In part, society was honouring Kostomarov for his past martyrdom. Yet his lecture-room would not have been crowded had it not been for the theme of his lectures and the polish of his delivery. Nicholas I and other proponents of 'official nationality' had encouraged the study of Russia's past to justify their conception of autocracy. Academic history and popular history in the form of journalism and belles-lettres 'became a centre of attention and controversy'.[8] Yet a gap existed between the work of professional historians who enjoyed imperial favour (and hence access to government archives) and that of the novelists, journalists, and playwrights who capitalized on historical themes, producing romanticized and often fanciful versions of the past.[9] The general reader found Karamzin obsolete, Solov'ev dry, and Ustryalov, Kostomarov's predecessor, too official. Kostomarov, by contrast, concerned himself with aspects of the Russian national tradition which academic historians had ignored, but which less serious writers had attempted to treat. Lecturing on rebels and separatists and on regions like Novgorod and Pskov, whose democratic heritage contrasted so sharply with that of Muscovy, he satisfied a curiosity which serious historians had aroused, but which, before him, only a handful of secondary writers had exploited in order to sell their works.

Not only the subjects on which he lectured, but also his style made him popular. He employed the skill of an actor to mimic and evoke

[5] N. I. Kostomarov, 'Avtobiografiya', *Russkaya mysl'*, xxxiii (1885), no. 5, p. 33.

[6] V. Ostrogorsky, 'Iz istorii moego uchitel'stva', *Obrazovanie*, v (1892), no. 10, p. 220.

[7] Kostomarov, 'Avtobiografiya' (n. 5), 34.

[8] See N. V. Riasanovsky, *A Parting of the Ways: Government and the Educated Public in Russia, 1801–1855* (Oxford, 1976), 119 and *supra* for a discussion of the strong interest in Russian history which developed in the reign of Nicholas I.

[9] Ibid. 119.

those historical personages whom he described. L. F. Panteleev, the publisher and critic, recalled that Kostomarov could illustrate any subject with an apt quotation from a chronicle or document.[10]

Kostomarov's popularity was also a function of the very openness of the university. In order to engage the support of the public in his reforms, as well as to make university facilities available to the general public, Shcherbatov had removed all the restrictions imposed by Nicholas I in 1848 on attendance at lectures. In the post-Crimean period, the University of St. Petersburg acquired something of the character of the Collège de France.

M. M. Stasyulevich, also a member of the Historical-Philological Faculty, readily used the opportunity provided by this situation. He had been appointed to his chair a year before Kostomarov after spending two years at German universities and at institutions of higher learning in Paris. In 1858, on returning to the university in which he had begun his academic career, he found himself able to lecture to large audiences consisting of both registered students and free auditors. Stasyulevich resumed his teaching by emulating such French professors as Guizot and Édouard Laboulaye, whom he had so recently admired. He not only adopted their style, but echoed them in emphasizing the importance of Western, and particularly French, thought and culture.[11] V. Ostrogorsky, a writer on pedagogical questions, has described Stasyulevich as a 'brilliant . . . popularizer who knew how . . . to capture the whole auditorium so that the attention of his listeners did not waver. . . . Those who had heard lectures in Paris said that . . . he reminded them of French [scholars]. . . .'[12]

The Historical-Philological Faculty was not alone in its rebirth. K. D. Kavelin, appointed to the Faculty of Law in 1857, supervised a similar revival in his department of the university.

Among professors at the University of St. Petersburg in the post-Crimean period he was unique, having held a number of influential positions in government administration. He had directed a department in the Ministry of the Interior and from 1853 to 1857 a section in the Chancellery of the Council of Ministers.[13] Kavelin could number among his friends such prominent members of the bureaucracy as the Milyutin brothers, Dmitry and Nikolay, and Konstantin and Yakov Grot, as well as A. P. Zablotsky-Desyatovsky, who had helped to initiate and implement the reforms of Alexander II.[14] Kavelin had also

---

[10] L. F. Panteleev, *Iz vospominanii proshlogo*, ed. S. A. Reiser (M.–L., 1934), 117.

[11] Stasyulevich assigned Guizot's *Histoire de la civilisation en Europe* as the textbook for his medieval history course. See Panteleev, op. cit. (n. 10), 120.

[12] Ostrogorsky, op. cit. (n. 6), 220.

[13] D. A. Korsakov, 'Zhizn' i deyatel'nost' K. D. Kavelina', *Sobranie sochinenii K. D. Kavelina*, ed. D. A. Korsakov, i (Spb., 1898), p. xxii.

[14] See W. Bruce Lincoln, 'The Genesis of an "Enlightened" Bureaucracy in Russia,

occupied a prominent position in the University of Moscow: he had been a respected lecturer in the Faculty of Law when he resigned in 1848 in protest against the educational policies of Nicholas I. A decade later, on Kavelin's appointment as law tutor to the Tsarevich, Shcherbatov invited him to accept the vacant Chair of Civil Law at St. Petersburg.[15] Once in the university Kavelin was also encouraged by Shcherbatov to create a circle of reform-minded colleagues akin to the group he had known in the bureaucracy. The familiarity with academic life that he brought with him from Moscow facilitated his efforts in St. Petersburg.

Shortly after his arrival the Chair of Criminal Law fell vacant. It was proposed that V. D. Spasovich, a young instructor, should be sent to study abroad in preparation for assuming it.[16] Kavelin had known Spasovich since 1852, and had recently been impressed by his dissertation on ancient Polish law.[17] At Kavelin's instigation and with the support of the Dean of the faculty, P. D. Kolmykov, Spasovich was appointed to the chair immediately, without any period of study abroad. As the youngest professor in the Faculty of Law, he became secretary of the faculty and was well placed to aid Kavelin in other projects.[18]

The appointment of Boris Utin was not so easily arranged. Conservative professors opposed it because as a young man Utin had befriended a member of the Petrashevsky circle. This had earned him six months in the Fortress of St. Peter and St. Paul and banishment from St. Petersburg. He took his law degree 'in exile' at Dorpat.[19] Utin enjoyed partial rehabilitation when he was permitted to study in the West in the late 1850s. Largely as a result of Kavelin's efforts, he was able to begin lecturing on comparative law at St. Petersburg University by 1860.[20]

These 'westerners', as they were known,[21] shared a commitment to new standards of teaching. Their lectures were enthusiastically attended and contrasted sharply in style, for example, with those of the professor of literature, N. V. Nikitenko, who, 'bound by no programme, plan, or syllabus', simply expatiated on Russian poetry, occasionally digressing to offer an interpretation of some Shakespearean soliloquy.[22]

1825–1856', *Jahrbücher für Geschichte Osteuropas*, xx (1972), and the same author's 'Russia's "Enlightened" Bureaucrats and the Problem of State Reform, 1846–1856', *Cahiers du monde russe et soviétique*, xii (1971), for an account of Kavelin's friendship with these and other reformers and his influence on them.

[15] V. D. Spasovich, 'K. D. Kavelin', *Vestnik Evropy* (henceforth *VE*), 1898, no. 2, p. 597.
[16] Ibid.
[17] Ibid. 594.
[18] Ibid. 597.
[19] M. S. [Stasyulevich], 'Nekrolog: Boris Isaakovich Utin', *VE*, 1872, no. 7, p. 470.
[20] M. K. Lemke (ed.), *M. M. Stasyulevich i ego sovremenniki v ikh perepiske*, i (Spb., 1911), 344: I. D. Delyanov to Stasyulevich, 18 Aug. 1859.
[21] See A. N. Pypin, 'Poslednie trudy N. I. Kostomarova', *VE*, 1890, no. 12, p. 798.
[22] Ostrogorsky, op. cit. (n. 6), 231.

Professors like Nikitenko, who taught in the traditional manner, now found their classrooms nearly empty. But it was more than popularity that gave the 'westerners' unity. As a group, they shared a commitment to the Shcherbatov reforms from which they had benefited. As a group, too, they were drawn to Kavelin's salon.

Every Sunday evening Kavelin and his wife held open house, where one might meet academics Kavelin had known in Moscow or reformers from the bureaucracy.[23] The gatherings were similar to those he had held once a week at the University of Moscow and those he had earlier attended as a member of westernist circles in the 1840s. Now, years later, the colleagues who visited Kavelin's home were precisely the progressive and popular lecturers whose appointments had coincided with Kavelin's own arrival at the University of St. Petersburg. For Spasovich those Sunday evenings were the sole recreation he allowed himself during his first years as a professor.[24] Of his colleagues who were also present he mentioned Boris Utin, Stasyulevich, and A. N. Pypin, Stasyulevich's friend from their days of travel in the West, who was just beginning his work as a professor of Western literature. Spasovich did not mention Kostomarov as one of those regularly present, although in the first months of his professorship Kostomarov saw Kavelin 'often enough'.[25] The omission was revealing. By early 1861 Kostomarov had become hostile towards those professors of Kavelin's circle, with whom he might have been expected to ally himself.

Kavelin had been one of Kostomarov's most ardent supporters in the university once Alexander II had approved his candidacy for the Chair of Russian History.[26] Not only had Kavelin regarded Kostomarov as a notable addition to the academic life of the university, but he could also assume that Kostomarov shared his commitment to progress and reform. Both men had seen their academic careers interrupted as a result of the repressive policies of Nicholas I, albeit under different circumstances. Furthermore, Kostomarov had worked with Kavelin at one stage on the preparations for the emancipation of the serfs. At Kavelin's request he had written a memorandum on the history of enserfment in the Ukraine.[27] Having first met Kavelin in 1855, Kostomarov wrote 'for a long time after [our introduction] he produced a sympathetic impression on me'. Two years after that first meeting they could still sit 'talking . . . almost till dawn'.[28] Yet, once in

[23] Spasovich, 'K. D. Kavelin' (n. 15), 605.
[24] Ibid.
[25] D. A. Korsakov, 'N. I. Kostomarov v ego otnosheniyakh k K. D. Kavelinu', *Istoricheskii vestnik*, cxlix/cl (1917), 162.
[26] N. I. Kostomarov, 'Peterburgskii universitet nachala 1860–kh godov' in: S. A. Vengerov (ed.), *Yubileinyi sbornik Literaturnogo fonda* (Spb., 1909), 123. See also Korsakov (n. 25), 160–2.
[27] Korsakov, 'N. I. Kostomarov' (n. 25), 159.
[28] Kostomarov, op. cit. (n. 26), 123.

the university, Kostomarov drew away from Kavelin and, at times, even opposed those with whom Kavelin associated most closely.

The disagreement between the two began over differing interpretations of Russia's past. As a proponent of the 'State' school of Russian history, Kavelin had disagreed with Kostomarov on many issues. A conflict developed once both of them held professorships and devoted themselves to academic work. Kavelin's nephew, the historian D. A. Korsakov, has published some of the correspondence between his uncle and Kostomarov and has given details of their disputes in 1860 and 1861.[29] Kavelin 'attacked him [Kostomarov] for giving prominence to the role of the popular masses in history, for excessive praise of the *veche* principle [which Kostomarov regarded as Ukrainian in origin], for not understanding the historical mission of the Great Russian people, the significance of the centralizing role of Moscow, or the reforming activity of Peter the Great.'[30] To Kostomarov, what began as an argument of historical interpretation and method, became an issue of personal acceptance; and his resentment of Kavelin extended also to Kavelin's associates.

The first recorded clash between Kostomarov and those who were to form the *Vestnik Evropy* circle occurred in connection with a speech which Kostomarov was to make at the University Speech Day of 8 February 1861. Russian universities, on the model of their German counterparts, inaugurated the opening of the second semester of the academic year with a day of professorial speech-making. It was an honour to be chosen to participate. The occasion was not strictly academic; the speeches were usually short and humorous. In practice, a committee within the professor's own faculty had to approve his contribution. In the case of Kostomarov, because of his immense reputation the committee of the Historical-Philological Faculty granted approval without examining the text of his proposed lecture, although it bore a title unusual for the occasion: 'On the . . . treatment of Russian history in the works of Konstantin Aksakov'.[31]

The day before Kostomarov was to read his address the government intervened and forbade him to speak, although permitting the ceremony itself to proceed as planned. In his autobiography, dictated in 1875, Kostomarov maintained that 'the lecture had stirred up against me Stasyulevich, Pypin, and Boris Utin, who saw in it a move towards Slavophilism. Kavelin was on their side and saw in my speech a deviation from the straight and narrow.'[32] Kostomarov, in fact, accused his colleagues of intervening with the authorities to prevent his speech, repeating a rumour which, as Pypin subsequently explained, had had 'sufficient refutation'.[33]

[29] Korsakov, 'N. I. Kostomarov' (n. 25), 162–5.   [30] Ibid. 164.
[31] Pypin, op. cit. (n. 21), 798.   [32] Quoted ibid. 797.   [33] Ibid. 798.

At the time of the Speech Day Kostomarov turned on Pypin with his accusations. Of those he blamed Kostomarov had known Pypin the longest, from the time when both had carried out research in the Saratov archives in the early 1850s.[34] Pypin described their exchange in the following account:

I, living then two steps from Kostomarov, went straight to him [with his letter] and asked him about the origin of the nonsense. He met me with hostile disbelief, but I . . . reminded him that he must know the decision made on his speech by the faculty committee on which I had just served . . . [and] I demanded that he tell me the source [of the rumour]. He became confused, referred to 'everyone', finally, when I persisted . . ., it turned out that 'everyone' consisted of two people, who, after the prohibition of the speech, could not explain it to themselves other than as a manœuvre of the 'westerners'.[35]

Pypin himself ascribed the cancellation to the authorities' fear of the crowds which the popular Kostomarov would attract.[36] Another possibility exists, concerning the very subject of the speech. Years before, Kostomarov had met and become friendly with Konstantin Aksakov. Aksakov's death in December 1860 prompted him to make Aksakov the subject of his Speech Day address. Those responsible for the recently completed emancipation settlement knew that Aksakov had been among the most outspoken critics of the Editing Commission which had devised the final statute.[37] Through his friend, Prince Vladimir Cherkassky, a member of the Commission, Aksakov had regularly received the reports of the Commission's various committees and responded with sharp and detailed criticisms at each stage, basing his comments on his interpretation of Russia's past.[38] From the title of his speech, it appeared that Kostomarov intended to devote himself to Aksakov's historical work and thus publicize his condemnation of the Editing Commission. The government was not altogether satisfied with the emancipation statute and, fearing open revolt amongst the peasantry once its terms became known, it forbade Kostomarov's speech.

Within the university, those whom Kostomarov had accused resented his allegations. As Pypin observed, some of them subjected Kostomarov to 'unpleasant comments'.[39] The real threat, they recognized, lay with arbitrary government interference in the affairs of the university.

To prevent such interference, Kavelin decided to act. A month

[34] A. N. Pypin, 'N. I. Kostomarov', VE, 1885, no. 5, pp. 419–22.
[35] Pypin, loc. cit. (n. 21).
[36] Ibid.
[37] E. Chmielewsky, Tribune of the Slavophiles: Konstantin Aksakov (Gainesville, 1962), 82–3.
[38] Ibid.
[39] Pypin, loc. cit. (n. 21).

after Kostomarov had been forbidden to speak on Aksakov, students in St. Petersburg had turned a memorial service for Polish students, slain by troops in Warsaw, into a large-scale demonstration. Kavelin quickly formed a committee to devise rules by which to regulate student behaviour, choosing as his co-members Stasyulevich, Spasovich, and Boris Utin.[40]

Events, unfortunately, overtook him. Even before the work of the Kavelin Committee could be formally approved by the Ministry of Education, Alexander II made two appointments which revealed his displeasure with the university. Particularly resentful and fearful of the university in the capital, where the most conspicuous changes and worst student unrest had occurred, he appointed in May Admiral E. V. Putyatin as Minister of Education and General G. I. Filipson as Superintendent of the St. Petersburg Educational District. Neither had had any experience of educational administration. Putyatin, who had been recommended by the Metropolitan of Moscow as a man of sound conservative principles, was known mainly for the trade treaties he had negotiated with Japan, China, and Persia.[41] Filipson had for years commanded troops fighting Caucasian tribesmen:[42] presumably he would know how to deal with student unrest.

Upon assuming office, Putyatin turned first to the newly arisen 'university question', and issued a statement designed to provide guidelines for new student regulations.[43] It was timed precisely to undercut the work of the Kavelin Committee, whose activities were already well known to Putyatin's ministry. The university formed a second committee to devise regulations in compliance with Putyatin's directive.[44] Among its members were Stasyulevich, Boris Utin, and Pypin, who tried to preserve as many of the proposals of the Kavelin Committee as they could.

In the end neither the university committee nor the two new officials of the Ministry of Education were able to agree on regulations to govern the university and control student behaviour. Once the university reopened in September 1861, the students who had arrived for classes began to demonstrate in the streets in protest against the rumoured imposition of a new and onerous fee, devised to reduce the large student population, which was such a striking feature of the University of St. Petersburg after 1855 and which had been the ultimate source of the

---

[40] See Spasovich, op. cit. (n. 3), 26; also Panteleev, op. cit. (n. 10), 74.

[41] 'E. V. Putyatin', *Entsiklopedicheskii slovar'*, xxv (Spb., 1898), 819. For references to Putyatin's piety, see A. V. Nikitenko, *Dnevnik*, ii (M., 1955), 198, 237: 2 Aug. and 3 Nov. 1861. See also Osborn Collection, Beineke Library, Yale University, Milyutin Correspondence, iii, 1861–4: A. V. Golovnin to N. A. Milyutin, 6/17 June 1867; Gen. D. A. Milyutin to N. A. Milyutin, 20 May 1861.

[42] 'G. I. Filipson', *Russkii biograficheskii slovar'*, [xxi] (Spb., 1901), 125–6.

[43] K. D. Kavelin, 'Zapiska o besporyadkakh', *Sobranie sochinenii* (n. 13), ii, col. 1195.

[44] Spasovich, op. cit. (n. 3), 28.

demonstrations in the previous academic year. For the next three weeks, from late September until mid October, the university ceased to function and the capital was thrown into turmoil by student demonstrations, which engaged the curious and frequently sympathetic populace.

Kostomarov and Spasovich have both described this period and its immediate aftermath. Although their descriptions do not contradict each other, they reveal very different attitudes toward Kavelin's role at the time. Spasovich described Kavelin as

the leader of a professorial circle . . ., which in decisive moments all the other professors joined . . . without any election or prior agreement. . . . In arguments with the administration . . . [he represented] the university. He resolved . . . our doubts and hesitations and it was due to him that we . . . did not deviate from the strictest legality.[45]

By the end of October Kavelin had resigned in protest at the government's policies towards the university and the students, hundreds of whom had been arrested. Spasovich wrote: 'To this decision of Kavelin, which he forced on no one, only four professors responded: M. M. Stasyulevich, A. N. Pypin, Boris Utin and I.'[46] Kostomarov, while agreeing that Kavelin represented the 'head and soul' of the professorial party, had less respect for his leadership. 'Kavelin', he wrote, 'proposed resignation *en masse*. Stasyulevich, Pypin, Boris Utin, and Spasovich . . . joined him . . .; of those [who remained] . . .[Kavelin] put more pressure on me than on any of the others. I resisted and this was the beginning of the estrangement between myself and . . . him. . . . Our former friendly intimacy was no more. I never visited his home nor he mine.' In fact, Kostomarov admitted, 'between . . . [those who resigned] and me . . . icicles hung'.[47]

Kostomarov made no secret of his estrangement from Kavelin. In a series of exchanges which appeared in the liberal newspaper *Sankt-Peterburgskie vedomosti* he opposed the advocacy by Stasyulevich of solutions for the unrest which in effect repeated the proposals made earlier by the Kavelin Committee.[48] Kostomarov even went so far as to ally himself with Nikitenko, long an opponent of the 'ultra-progressives', as he termed them.[49] It is difficult to determine whether

[45] Spasovich, 'K. D. Kavelin' (n. 15), 612. See also idem, op. cit. (n. 3), 33, 49–51 for more on his 'professorial circle'.

[46] Spasovich, 'K. D. Kavelin' (n. 15), 612.

[47] Kostomarov, op. cit. (n. 26), 124.

[48] See *Sankt-Peterburgskie vedomosti*, 1861, nos. 241, 281, and my 'Scholar and Journalist: the Career of M. M. Stasyulevich, 1850–1882' (unpublished dissertation, Yale University, 1976), 156.

[49] Nikitenko, *Dnevnik*, ii (n. 41), 237: 10 Dec. 1861.

Kostomarov sincerely objected to Stasyulevich's ideas or was motivated in part by lingering resentment at the 'strong comments' made in answer to his accusations at the time of the Speech Day.

Stasyulevich advocated extending the responsibility of the University Council, which consisted of the professors of all the faculties. He recalled the series of measures, designed to enhance the authority of the Council, by which the Kavelin Committee had hoped to create university autonomy and provide an administration both respected and responsive to the needs of the university. Kostomarov and Nikitenko proposed instead that the university should cease to function as an autonomous institution altogether and that anyone who wished to pursue higher education might do so, without examinations or degrees, as auditors at public lectures.[50] There would thus be no possibility of that corporate student identity which, they believed, was the source of unrest in the university.

Although Kostomarov intended to remain aloof from his colleagues who had resigned, he soon shared their fate. In the spring of 1862, while the University of St. Petersburg remained closed, radical students took up the Kostomarov–Nikitenko proposals and invited their erstwhile professors to give public lectures.[51] The so-called Free University was to keep alive the intellectual life of the capital and provide funds for needy students now deprived of government grants.

Despite such good intentions, the venture was short-lived. One of the professors was arrested for an inflammatory speech made at a private gathering.[52] The student organizers decided to stop the lecture programme as a protest against the authorities' action. When they informed the participants of their decision, most, seeing no connection between the arrest of one of their number and the continued activity of the Free University, refused to comply.[53] It was Kostomarov, scheduled as the next speaker, who saw his lecture turned into a riot as the result of a demonstration of the kind then commonly staged by radical students.

Kostomarov may have sustained a brief period of student disfavour, but this did not mean that he had gained the support of the Minister of Education. A. V. Golovnin, who had succeeded the discredited Putyatin in January 1862, temporarily forbade Kostomarov to lecture.[54]

---

[50] See *Sankt-Peterburgskie vedomosti*, 1861, nos. 237, 258, 261, 262, 275, 281.

[51] For an account of the Free University, see L. F. Panteleev, 'Vol'nyi universitet', *Leningradskii universitet v vospominaniyakh sovremennikov*, ed. V. V. Mavrodin, i (L., 1963); see also T. S. Vol'fson, '"Vol'nyi universitet", 1862', *Vestnik Leningradskogo universiteta*, 1947, no. 7, pp. 96–107.

[52] R. E. Zelnik, 'The Sunday School Movement in Russia, 1857–62', *Journal of Modern History*, xxxvii (1965), 158.

[53] Panteleev, op. cit. (n. 51), 103–7.

[54] Vol'fson, op. cit. (n. 51), 101.

In May 1862, isolated and demoralized, Kostomarov resigned his professorship.

Golovnin's appointment had, in fact, marked a turning-point. Though a reformer and at one time a member of the same official circle as Kavelin,[55] he had no intention of continuing Shcherbatov's policy of encouraging the appointment to university posts of scholars who were gifted but out of favour. He informed those who had resigned that 'in higher circles [they] were considered instigators and leaders of the student movement', and that for their own sake he could not advocate their reappointment.[56] He was willing nonetheless to employ all of them as advisers on various projects of educational reform under discussion within his ministry.

Even with that compromise, Golovnin proceeded cautiously. He sent Kavelin, the most prominent leader of dissent, to report on the structure of Western European universities, and thus to offer his advice from abroad. Kavelin wrote to his old friend Herzen about the assignment:

I do not know what my journey abroad means. Golovnin says that in view of my awkward position, [caught] between [the animosity of] the government which looks upon me with contempt . . . and [that of] the students who consider me a conservative, he wishes to safeguard me for the future; but other people who understand the situation say that Golovnin has politely let me down and separated himself from me.[57]

Kavelin himself contributed to his isolation. He requested an extension of his assignment and remained in the West until November 1864. While he was on a brief visit to Russia in the summer of 1863, his nephew, D. A. Korsakov, noted a profound change in the once lively Kavelin: '. . . his whole figure had somehow grown thin; he had become stooped and in general aged much'.[58] His assignment with Golovnin at an end, Kavelin entered the Ministry of Finance in late 1864, working under his old friend Konstantin Grot, director of the Department of Unassessed Taxes.[59] Kavelin had become a *chinovnik* with the state alcohol monopoly.

Kostomarov fared a little better. Supported by the sale of his books, he was able to withdraw 'into a circle of a few close acquaintances' and work diligently in the St. Petersburg Public Library on the history of Russia in the early seventeenth century.[60]

Pypin, with whom Kostomarov had once pursued research on

[55] See M. S. [M. I. Semevsky], 'A. V. Golovnin', *Russkaya starina*, liii (1887), 772–7.
[56] Spasovich, 'K. D. Kavelin' (n. 15), 613.
[57] Quoted ibid. 614.
[58] D. A. Korsakov, 'K. D. Kavelin', *VE*, 1886, no. 10, p. 745.
[59] Ibid. 757.
[60] D. A. Korsakov, 'Iz vospominanii o N. I. Kostomarove i S. M. Solov'eve', *VE*, 1906, no. 9, p. 231.

medieval chronicles, had no private means and was forced to abandon scholarship. He had grown up in Saratov, close to the family of his mother's sister, who had married a parish priest named Chernyshevsky. As a boy Pypin had revered his cousin, N. G. Chernyshevsky, who was five years his senior.[61] He never outgrew that youthful hero-worship and in the early 1850s supplemented his meagre academic salary by contributing articles on literature to *Otechestvennye zapiski*, following the example of his cousin, who was just taking up journalism himself. After Chernyshevsky's arrest in 1862, Pypin joined the editorial board of *Sovremennik* in order to earn his living and to assist the journal which his cousin had served as its most influential contributor.

Spasovich, too, entered journalism in order to support himself. He had spent the summer of 1862 in Warsaw expecting to begin teaching law there in the newly founded university.[62] Instead, he became appalled at the growing revolutionary situation and the 'rank cowardice' of the educated class when faced with it.[63] He returned to St. Petersburg and worked briefly in the Ministry of Education. By late 1864, 'forced to support myself', he wrote, 'I became a regular contributor to *Sankt-Peterburgskie vedomosti*, published then by V. F. Korsh'.[64] There Spasovich found Stasyulevich, who since the previous year had been an active participant in the work of that newspaper.[65]

By 1865 much had changed for those professors, once popular lecturers, who had grouped themselves round Kavelin in an outspoken commitment to reform. Kavelin himself had aged and lost the capacity to lead. The extended period he had spent abroad had left him out of touch with developments in Russia. Like Boris Utin, who was in the Ministry of Justice working on statutes for a new legal system, he was caught up in the questions of his official department.[66] Only Pypin, Stasyulevich, and Spasovich could claim to have maintained their former unity through their pursuit of a common occupation.

In this work a certain dissatisfaction also united them. Pypin, while gaining valuable journalistic experience, was not at home with the staff of the radical *Sovremennik*.[67] Stasyulevich and Spasovich had their frustrations working for *Sankt-Peterburgskie vedomosti*. Korsh, the paper's editor, was unreliable and extravagant, 'by nature . . . soft, a stranger to any kind of toughness, who did not express his convictions forthrightly but limited himself to hints and qualifications'.[68]

[61] For an account of Pypin's life and that of Chernyshevsky up to 1858, see A. N. Pypin, *Moi zametki* (Spb., 1910).

[62] Spasovich, 'K. D. Kavelin' (n. 15), 623.

[63] Ibid. 624.   [64] Ibid.

[65] A. [M. M. Stasyulevich], 'Nekrolog: V. F. Korsh', *VE*, 1884, no. 8, p. 874.

[66] Stasyulevich, op. cit. (n. 19), 471.

[67] See V. Evgen'ev-Maksimov, *Poslednie gody 'Sovremennika', 1863–1866* (L., 1939), 17–23, for an account of Pypin's disagreements with other members of the editorial board.

[68] 'V. F. Korsh', *Russkii biograficheskii slovar'*, [ix] (Spb., 1903), 295.

It was Spasovich who proposed a solution. He turned to Stasyulevich in August 1865 suggesting that he should establish his own journal.[69] Stasyulevich had, in fact, been contemplating such a venture for months.[70] Spasovich's encouragement decided the issue. Not only had Stasyulevich experience of journalism, but, unlike the others in their circle to whom Spasovich might have turned, he had the capital to initiate a publication. His father-in-law, the banker and First Guild merchant, Isaak Utin, could provide money or at least guarantee the loans needed for entry into publishing.[71]

On 9 November 1865 Stasyulevich petitioned the press authorities for permission 'to begin in 1866 the publication of a journal devoted to historical-political scholarship' to be called *Vestnik Evropy*.[72] The very title, that of the journal once edited by Karamzin, conjured up an association with historical scholarship. The title also recalled the 'westernizing' activity of Stasyulevich and the members of his circle in the university who now joined him on the editorial staff.[73] Not only was Stasyulevich intending to make the best use of those whose talent he could rely on, but, as he admitted to P. A. Pletnev, the former Rector of St. Petersburg University, he saw the scholarly nature of the journal as a form of self-protection: '. . . a failure will not be so ignominious for me as [it would] if I were to fail with a political journal'.[74]

But not all those who had lectured well could necessarily provide readable copy for a journal which depended on subscriptions to survive. Stasyulevich himself, while able to crowd a lecture hall with the 'fluency and beauty of his speech', produced work that was derivative and unimaginative. Pisarev bluntly accused him of plagiarism;[75] and when, after leaving the university, Stasyulevich produced a three-volume collection of medieval sources, consisting of hundreds of pages

---

[69] *Stasyulevich i ego sovremenniki* (n. 20), ii, 27: Stasyulevich to his wife, 23 Sept. 1889.

[70] Ibid. i, 197: P. A. Pletnev to Stasyulevich, 24 May/5 June 1865.

[71] Although no specific evidence of financial aid granted to Stasyulevich by his father-in-law in 1865–6 appears to be available in the West, Stasyulevich had substantial income at this time and assumed all financial responsibility for *Vestnik Evropy*. See letter of Kostomarov, 7 Dec. 1865, *Stasyulevich i ego sovremenniki* (n. 20), ii, 1–2. Moreover, Utin subsequently made his son-in-law the executor of his estate. See ibid. i, 53.

[72] Ibid. i, 228: Stasyulevich to Pletnev, 10/22 Nov. 1865.

[73] Pypin did not actually join *Vestnik Evropy* until 1867. He may have been delayed in 1866 by his responsibilities with *Sovremennik*, of which he was editor-in-chief; cf. Kostomarov's doubtful explanation for the delay in 'Peterburgskii universitet' (n. 26), 132. It should also be noted that B. Utin, since 1859 Stasyulevich's brother-in-law, was also to bring another member of the family, his brother Evgeny, into close association with the journal.

[74] *Stasyulevich i ego sovremenniki* (n. 20), i, 228: Stasyulevich to Pletnev, 10/22 Nov. 1865. Pletnev, himself a past editor of a 'thick' journal (*Sovremennik* in the 1840s), in addition to his role as Stasyulevich's confidant at this time, was instrumental through various connections in extracting permission from the Minister of the Interior, V. A. Valuev, for Stasyulevich to publish. See K. K. Arsen'ev, 'Vzglyad na proshloe', *VE*, 1909, no. 1, p. 219.

[75] See D. I. Pisarev, 'Nasha universitetskaya nauka', *Izbrannye sochineniya*, ed. V. Ya. Kirpotin *et al.*, i (M., 1934), 343–4 and my discussion of the incident in 'Scholar and Journalist' (n. 48), 87–9.

of translated documents, Golovnin went back on his promise to publish the second and third volumes under the auspices of the Ministry of Education, because the first volume would not sell.[76] In contrast, Kostomarov's work sold in proportion to the excitement his lectures generated. His studies on Bogdan Khmel'nitsky and Sten'ka Razin had caused a sensation when they had first appeared in *Otechestvennye zapiski* in the late 1850s. Stasyulevich could hardly do better than engage him for the new journal.

In a move which was bound to flatter Kostomarov as well as to ensure the prominence of his name, Stasyulevich proposed that he become co-editor of the new journal. He would be responsible for reading all contributions on the subject of Russian history and would receive 15 per cent of the profits if the journal succeeded.[77] With equal astuteness, he deputed Spasovich to convey the offer.

Kostomarov had always had a special fondness for Spasovich, who had assisted him in his research by putting his extensive knowledge of Polish literature at his disposal.[78] Even after the university troubles, during the summer of 1862, the two had travelled together in Poland.[79] Spasovich also managed to persuade Kostomarov that he approved of the efforts of the Marquis Wielopolski 'to reconcile the Poles with the Russians on the principles of Slavonic unity'.[80] Unsympathetic towards the Poles, the Ukrainian patriot found Spasovich's attitude all the more significant: 'It is not surprising', he wrote, 'that I loved [Spasovich] . . . and respected him greatly.'[81]

While flattering Kostomarov by the substance of his message and the choice of his messenger, Stasyulevich also protected himself. Kostomarov had to agree not to publish in any journal other than *Vestnik Evropy*. To Pletnev he confided the real nature of their relationship: 'Kostomarov will be my secretary in Russian history, but I alone will be the publisher and responsible editor.'[82]

In part, owing to Kostomarov's essays on the *Smuta*, *Vestnik Evropy* did well enough in its first two years for Stasyulevich to expand the journal by including belles-lettres and publishing more frequently. Kostomarov maintained that as a result he was no longer necessary, and Stasyulevich soon found an excuse to break with him. When Kostomarov accepted an article by an old friend, the Ukrainian historian Kulish, and Stasyulevich refused to print it, Kostomarov resigned as co-editor.[83]

[76] *Stasyulevich i ego sovremenniki* (n. 20), i, 130–1: Stasyulevich to Pletnev, 18/30 Dec. 1863.

[77] Ibid. ii, 2: Stasyulevich to Kostomarov, 7 Dec. 1865; cf. Kostomarov's account of the terms, Kostomarov, op. cit. (n. 26), 138.

[78] Ibid. 127.   [79] Ibid.

[80] Ibid. 128.   [81] Ibid.

[82] *Stasyulevich i ego sovremenniki* (n. 20), i, 228: Stasyulevich to Pletnev, 10/22 Nov. 1865.

[83] Kostomarov, op. cit. (n. 26), 138.

It is unlikely that Stasyulevich chose deliberately to break with Kostomarov. Their relationship had never been a real partnership, and when Kostomarov sensed his diminished importance at the time that Stasyulevich decided on expansion, it may have been Kostomarov who sought an excuse to dissolve their artificial arrangement. He did, however, continue to publish in *Vestnik Evropy* for several more years.

Kostomarov's importance to the journal, at least initially, cannot be denied. In 1875, when S. N. Shubinsky founded a popular historical monthly *Drevnyaya i novaya Rossiya*, he ensured its success by enlisting Kostomarov as a collaborator.[84] Korsakov described how he sat in Shubinsky's office 'while a considerable number of people came in who wanted to subscribe'. One of them gave voice to a general misgiving by asking: 'And in the coming year will there be articles by Kostomarov?' Shubinsky hastened to assure them that there would be. All present subscribed forthwith.

For Stasyulevich, Kostomarov's importance was evident from the effort he made to woo him. Despite their estrangement, even long-standing hostility, he went so far as to make Kostomarov co-editor. Kostomarov's name attracted attention, as Turgenev's error in his letter to Fet revealed.[85] Stasyulevich's success in engaging Kostomarov was an early indication of that skill in acquiring important contributors and keeping them within the journal's fold which he was subsequently to demonstrate in the case of Turgenev himself.[86] His success with Kostomarov was also symbolic of his new-found role among those who had once looked to Kavelin's leadership.

Kavelin was an organizer and adept at forging a group, but he lacked Stasyulevich's ability to reconcile himself and others to diverse opinions, which is so necessary for success in journalism. Korsakov has written of his uncle that if he 'noted a disrespectful attitude towards his views, [he could become] implacable . . . and would often [break off] all relations with an individual. . . .'[87] Kavelin had tried to win Kostomarov over to his cause in October 1861, but could not close the breach which had earlier begun to divide them. Unable to endow his protest with the *cachet* Kostomarov would have supplied, he saw his position deteriorate and went into self-imposed exile abroad.

Other issues connected with the origins of *Vestnik Evropy* can be explained by reference to the University of St. Petersburg in the post-Crimean period. Kostomarov did not remain with the journal, except as an irregular contributor, after 1869. His sensitivity, volatility, and the obsession with the past which made him such an exciting lecturer affected other areas of his life. He did not fit into groups, fearing that

[84] Korsakov, op. cit. (n. 60), 261.   [85] See *supra*, p. 84.
[86] See their correspondence, *Stasyulevich i ego sovremenniki* (n. 20), iii, 1–236.
[87] Korsakov, 'K. D. Kavelin' (n. 58), 741–2.

their members might collectively undermine him. A connection may be seen between his panic and accusations against the Kavelin circle at the time of the Speech Day and the isolation he maintained even when nominally an editor of *Vestnik Evropy*. In the summer of 1867 Stasyulevich asked Korsh if he knew of Kostomarov's whereabouts, noting that 'it is difficult to find out about [him]'.[88]

Nor did Kostomarov share a commitment to that particular kind of reform which Kavelin and his circle had begun to espouse when the 'university' question first arose. Then, and later in the pages of *Vestnik Evropy*, they advocated autonomous institutions, responsive to those dependent on them, and providing some local control within the framework of the autocracy. Kostomarov was concerned more with Ukrainian autonomy than with the autonomy of any particular institution, as both his political difficulties and his position on the university question revealed. By the same token he was not a Westernizer in the sense that Kavelin, Stasyulevich, Spasovich, Pypin, and Boris Utin were. Unlike Kostomarov, who had never ventured west of Poland, they had all travelled in Western European countries and studied in the major universities of the West. All of them contributed essays to *Vestnik Evropy*, extolling as a model for Russia one aspect or another of Western Europe. Kostomarov was interested solely in history and that of the Slavs in particular, and, once his association with *Vestnik Evropy* had confirmed his importance for the subscription rate of a new journal, he could find any number of outlets for his work—and did.

Kostomarov, therefore, was the exception among those former professors who first joined Stasyulevich as collaborators on *Vestnik Evropy*. The others remained with the journal, maintaining a unity they had begun to develop first at Kavelin's Sunday evening gatherings and then strengthened in the political turmoil which afflicted the university in 1861. The regrouping under Stasyulevich's leadership four years later marked a termination of self-doubt and financial uncertainty which again they had all shared.

This account of the origins of one journalistic circle in nineteenth-century Russia contrasts with Noel Annan's portrait of English reformers 'able to move between the worlds of speculation and government' or, through ties of school and family, into 'the Victorian intellectual periodicals'. It reveals nonetheless that there were sources of unity and reasons for stability within the circle of those most closely associated with *Vestnik Evropy*.

<hr />

[88] *Stasyulevich i ego sovremenniki* (n. 20), ii, 478: Stasyulevich to Korsh, 6/18 July 1867.

The Tree-stump and the Horse:
The Poetry of Alexander Kusikov

By GORDON McVAY

I

By early 1922, at the age of twenty-five, Alexander Kusikov seemed to stand on the threshold of literary fame. Today, half a century later, he is seldom remembered. This article examines Kusikov's evolution as a poet, and considers some aspects of his complex personality.

In 1922 the poet wrote a brief autobiography, which provides an exotic evocation of his early years:

> . . . I was born in a cow-shed
> To the September neighing of a horse
in the Northern Caucasus in 1896. . . .
> At first I had near me the wise Circassian Chech', a serf of my father's, and then a Russian nanny, Anis'ya:
> And I was told
> That God has a beloved Son,
> That there is none but Allah in the clouds.
> When I was old enough to ride a horse I again had near me a Circassian, Pit, the son of Chech'. . . . I went with him from village to village, to Cossack settlements, watered the horses in the river, drove my mother's buffalo to the common pasture, and in the evening, when I was alone, I sat on a tree-stump . . . and looked up at the sky. . . .[1]

In 1974 Kusikov expanded on these remarks.[2] He was born on 17 September (Old Style) 1896, in Vol'nyi Aul (Free Village), where he spent his childhood. The nearest large town was Armavir. Alexander's parents, both Circassians, had (he claimed) no fewer than seventeen children. His father, Boris Karpovich Kusikov, was a rich landowner; his mother, Ol'ga, was beautiful and the person closest to him in childhood. Young Alexander used to attend the local mosque and say Moslem prayers; in contrast, his sisters were of Orthodox (or Catholic) faith. Kusikov insisted that he himself was a Circassian, contrary to recent assertions that he was an Armenian, Kusikyan.

[1] From Kusikov's autobiography, dated 2 April 1922, in *Novaya russkaya kniga* (Berlin), 1922, no. 3, pp. 43–5. The lines of verse quoted in this passage are from Sections 5 and 3 of Kusikov's poem *Koevangelieran*, written in 1918–20. His favourite tree-stump figures in his poem *Al'-Kadr*, as well as in *Dzhul'fikar* and *Iskandar Name*, all written in 1921; it is also recalled in 'Pochemu v Berline vorob'i ne chirikayut' and *Pesochnye chasy*, both of 1922.

[2] In a conversation with the present writer, Paris, 25 September 1974.

His 1922 autobiography continues with a lively account of his mischievous schooldays. He took to chasing after women, he drank, caused scandals, and was expelled from one school after another. He also 'started to "compose" verse in the second form, and developed a passion for hunting ever since the fourth form'. His schooldays drew to a close in the large Cossack village of Batalpashinsk. Young Alexander went to Moscow to receive his school leaving certificate. The First World War had begun, and Kusikov's 1922 autobiography alludes to a six-month period as a student before he donned the uniform of 'cavalryman in the King of Denmark's Seversky Dragoon Regiment'.

In 1917 he welcomed the news of the February Revolution. His autobiography states: 'I had long awaited the storm, ever since I was a schoolboy. And one memorable day it happened. . . .' Several months passed. 'At that time I was military commissar (at first, assistant) in the port of Anapa [on the Black Sea].' Conflicting telegrams kept on arriving, alternately from Kornilov and Kerensky, and Kusikov abruptly moved to Moscow. It was in 1918, shortly after the Revolution, that the Circassian in Moscow published his first book of verse.

Kusikov's first volume, *Zerkalo Allakha* ('The Mirror of Allah'), was dedicated to 'my dear good *mamochka*, with whom I passed the best minutes of my radiant childhood'.[3] The blue front cover by Zyakin is attractively oriental, depicting a man squatting on a prayer rug, with his hands raised to his turban in supplication. The first part of the book contains many elements of local colour—Arabic or Persian words, the voice of the *muezzin* calling the Circassians to the mosque. There are descriptions of Caucasian scenery, and Kusikov romantically calls himself a 'Caucasian eaglet'. The imagery tends to be verbosely colourful and conventionally exotic.

The verse in this opening section, where dated, stems from the years 1914–16, but the last seven poems are marked 1917 and 1918. These later poems confirm Kusikov's 1922 declaration: 'For a long time I shunned [the] October [Revolution]. I submerged myself completely in poetry and withdrew into myself. I used to sit in the "Poets' Café" and in the "Chekas", but felt that I was the proud observer of a most interesting epoch. . . .' These poems do reflect the violence and bloodshed of 1917–18, but seem politically neutral—the Bolsheviks are never mentioned, either in praise or condemnation. Yet Kusikov is not indifferent to what is occurring—he is saddened that there is a 'shadow over the earth'.[4] In his 1922 autobiography he specifically linked *Zerkalo Allakha* with his growing affection for Russia:

For the first time, still vaguely and dimly, somehow agonisingly and strangely, I began to feel love for Russia.

I published my first book of verse, which to me is important because of the lines:

I prayed for Russia,
For the Russian people. . . .[5]

As the volume progresses, the duality of Kusikov's position, as a southerner in the northern city, becomes increasingly apparent. In an early poem, there is the Moslem faith; later, he assumes a Christian aspect. In the more timeless 'Caucasian' poems, a warrior's weapons are the *yataghan* (sword), pistol, and lasso; whereas machine-guns, cannon, and searchlights figure in the warfare of 1917–18. A distinct 'anti-urban' note pervades the book, but it is Kusikov's inner loneliness which is the more revealing psychological trait. 'It's as if I'm cut off from life . . . . / In this northern and alien / City, / I am friendless. . . .'[6]

In 1974 Kusikov dismissed much of his early verse as 'schoolboyish', while recalling that several poems had become extremely popular 'romances' when set to music at the time.[7]

The Moslem prayer rug on the front cover of *Zerkalo Allakha* forms a link with the title of the collective volume *Zhemchuzhnyi kovrik* ('The Pearl Prayer Rug'), issued, it seems, in 1918.[8] This was evidently the first book published under the All-Russian Union of Poets' imprint, 'Chikhi-Pikhi' ('Sneezy-Wheezy'). Kusikov is the dominant figure in this volume, which consists of oriental evocations and stylizations. The other two poets—Konstantin Bal'mont and Antony Sluchanovsky —both include poems dedicated to him, and the book's title clearly derives from Kusikov's first poem ('. . . My Prayer Rug is embroidered with pearls, with the tears of my Heart . . .').[9]

The section by Kusikov (pp. 25–45) bears the general heading 'From

---

[4] 'Strastnaya subbota (1918 g.).'

[5] Lines from the poem 'Strastnaya subbota (1918 g.)'. Kusikov knelt before the icon of the Mother of God: '. . . And in ecstasy, in delirious despair / I sobbed and prayed about something . . . / I prayed for Russia, / For the Russian people.'

[6] From the poem 'Nine Kirsanovoi'. In 1974 Kusikov claimed that he and the dancer Nina Kirsanova lived together as man and wife; she was beautiful, and died young.

[7] At the end of *Zerkalo Allakha* there is a list of Kusikov's poems which had been set to music by A. R. and M. R. Bakaleinikov, and by S. N. Vasilenko.

[8] Alexander Kusikov, Konstantin Bal'mont, Antony Sluchanovsky, *Zhemchuzhnyi kovrik*, published by 'Chikhi-Pikhi'. Front cover by Boris Erdman. There is no printed date on two copies of this book in the Lenin Library, Moscow—but in several of Kusikov's 1920 volumes *Zhemchuzhnyi kovrik* is explicitly listed as 'Moscow, 1918'.

[9] *Zhemchuzhnyi kovrik* (n. 8), 27.

the Minaret of my Heart'. The overall mood is warmly exotic, but without any strong individual stamp. Some poems are republished from *Zerkalo Allakha*; there are translations from Saadi's *Gulistan* and of chapters from the Koran; there is verse about an aged wise shepherd with 'Allah in his soul', and a nicely expressed acrostic to E. Shershenevich (where the initial letters of the lines spell out the name 'Evgeniya'). In the most 'autobiographical' poem Kusikov emphasizes his remote origins—'I was born amidst the white visions' of the mountains; 'I love / The eagle's cry . . .'; 'Mount Elbrus, the white-humped camel, / Caressed me with its icy heart'.[10]

As yet Kusikov had largely followed Bal'mont's exhortation: 'You have known since childhood the soaring of eagles / And the lengthy chatter of the cranes. / So keep to your predestined path— / Be faithful to your Native Land.'[11] In 1919, however, a change was to come, a temporary aberration.

This 'aberration' was Kusikov's next volume, *Sumerki* ('Twilight'), a poorly printed book with many misprints, and containing thirty-three poems.[12] Here he departed from his previous orientalism, and lost himself in effete anonymity. The Moslem and exotic elements of his former verse are almost completely absent, as are virtually all topical allusions to the political situation. Instead, the 'Caucasian eaglet' lies inert; there is the twilight of gloom in his soul, and the literal twilight of evening. In no other volume, before or after, does the usually masculine Kusikov appear so listless: 'I rock my body to sleep in weary languor'; 'The day passed so uselessly, so feebly . . . / Again morning will come, again I'll be discontented . . .'; 'I am empty, limp and superfluous . . . / I feel rather disgusted / At myself / And everyone else.'[13]

In some poems Kusikov seeks 'oblivion' in Christian prayer. In sharp contrast, others have a blatantly erotic content, telling how as an adolescent he slept with a housemaid (poem 24), or found 'love' in the bed of a coquettish woman (poem 29). In one poem he describes 'sick love', as he departs 'with a cold kiss' after a night of 'the delirium of love, the acute moment of pleasure' (poem 28). Yet neither religion nor eroticism appears to satisfy him: he remains tired, depressed, and essentially alone. Typically, the volume ends with a reference to his 'autumnal grief'.

Kusikov himself quickly recognized the failure of *Sumerki*. His 1922 autobiography bluntly remarks: 'Apart from *Zerkalo Allakha* I published:

[10] *Zhemchuzhnyi kovrik* (n. 8), 28.

[11] The closing lines of Bal'mont's first poem dedicated to Kusikov, ibid. 5.

[12] There seem to have been 'four editions' of *Sumerki* (M., 1919), published by 'Chikhi-Pikhi'. One poem, 'Gorod', is reprinted from *Zerkalo Allakha*.

[13] From, respectively, poems 7, 25 and 23 of *Sumerki*.

in 1919 *Sumerki*, a very bad and hopeless book which I now reject and disown. . . .' And at the back of a volume of his verse in 1922 he listed among his publications: '*Sumerki*—really atrocious and accidental poems.'[14]

Despite this brief descent into 'twilight', Kusikov's poetic maturity was near. His next major work, *Poema poem* ('The Poem of Poems'), written in 1918–19, is distinguished by a note of elevated agitation. The poem evokes a passionate love-affair against a background of the alien town. It is dedicated to Nina Kirsanova (whose early death Kusikov had lamented in *Zerkalo Allakha*), and the sexual explicitness of some passages in Chapter 3 apparently offended certain people at the time: 'All the same I squashed / The cherries of your breasts, / These cherries / Of sick revelations . . . / And I wanted your body, / Yet again / And again. . . .'[15] These lines do not, however, justify the assertion that eroticism is characteristic of Kusikov's verse.[16] Furthermore, both the title and the tone of *Poema poem* clearly owe something to Solomon's *Song of Songs*.

Poema poem marks a distinct advance in Kusikov's writing. The largely traditional style of his earlier books is here replaced by a kind of rhythmical 'free verse', often with only one word or syllable in a line, and approximate rhymes. Even more significant is the condensed imagery. Chapter 2 includes the following clusters: 'The tiny fish / Of your / Smile / Swam / Into the backwaters / Of your cheeks'; 'I was the first to carry my grief / Across the sky into the clouds / In a wheelbarrow of stars'; 'I am the first enamoured / Silver swan / Who wants to swim / To this dark-blue / Grief'; 'The chimneys / Limped / Boldly / Across the roofs.'

Poema poem evidently first appeared in 1919 or—more probably—1920 under the trade-mark 'Sandro' (Kusikov's nickname); in 1920 a second edition came out under the imprint 'Imazhinisty' ('The Imaginists'). The artist Boris Erdman provided drawings in the text, of a top-hatted man and bare-breasted woman.[17] The 'Imazhinisty' label and the collaboration of the Imaginist Erdman are not fortuitous. The peak years of Kusikov's fame had now begun.

[14] See Alexander Kusikov, *Ptitsa bezymyannaya* (Berlin, 1922), 63.

[15] In 1974 Kusikov recalled that proletarian poets and critics like Friche condemned these lines as 'erotic' and 'anti-Marxist'.

[16] See *Kratkaya literaturnaya entsiklopediya*, iii (M., 1966), 928; also *Literaturnaya entsiklopediya*, v (M., 1931), col. 773.

[17] Alexander Kusikov, *Poema poem*, 2 ed. (M., 1920), published by 'Imazhinisty'. This is the text discussed in the present article. A list of Kusikov's works there includes: '*Poema poem*, "Sandro", Moscow, 1919. Numbered edition. Cover and drawings by hand (*ot ruki*) by B. Erdman (sold out).' In other books by Kusikov, the date 'Moscow, 1920' is given for this numbered 'Sandro' edition. See the manuscript copy of *Poema poem* in the Institute of World Literature, Moscow, *fond* 298, *opis'* 1, no. 1. The text here is handwritten in black ink, and the illustrations are coloured by hand.

2

In 1922 Kusikov wrote a lively article, 'Mapa i Pama imazhinizma' ('The Mapa and Pama of Imaginism'), in which he acknowledged 10 February 1919 as the birth of the New Day called Imaginism.[18] On that day the first *Deklaratsiya* ('Declaration') of the Imaginists was published in Moscow, bearing the names of the poets Sergey Esenin, Ryurik Ivnev, Anatoly Mariengof and Vadim Shershenevich, and the artists Boris Erdman and Georgy Yakulov.[19] Kusikov's name is notably absent here, although by this time he probably knew most or all of the four above-mentioned poets. The 1919 *Deklaratsiya* derided the Futurists and emphasized the primacy of the 'image' in poetry. Kusikov —who was now entering a phase of intensive literary activity—evidently found the outlook of his new companions congenial. In the search for publicity, he joined Esenin and Mariengof in daubing verse on the walls of the Convent of the Passion (*Strastnoy monastyr'*) in Moscow on the night of 27–8 May 1919.

In his 1922 autobiography, after remarking how 'for a long time' he 'shunned October', he claimed:

But in 1919 there began my Holy Communion, in wine and blood, partaking of the Great Russian Revolution. . . .

And in that same year, 1919, in the Petrovsky Park [near Moscow] I formed, together with Colonel Ts., the first Soviet mounted regiment and was appointed commander of a [small] separate cavalry division. . . .

From the end of 1920, or rather from the beginning of 1921, I gave up military service once and for all. . . .

Yet, despite this professed 'communion' with the Russian Revolution, Kusikov was allying himself with the essentially anarchistic Imaginists. In April–May 1919 he contributed some poems to the Moscow journal *Zhizn' i tvorchestvo russkoi molodezhi* ('The Life and Works of Russian Youth'), which had as its sub-title 'The Organ of the All-Russian Federation of Anarchist Youth'. On 13 April 1919 Shershenevich published there a defiant article, 'Art and the State'. On the same page as this article (which mentioned that Kusikov had now joined the Imaginists) Kusikov's poem *Belyi kon'* ('The White Steed') was printed. It seems to be a lightly veiled plea for anarchism: 'The white steed has taken the bit between its teeth— / It is a cloud galloping across the sky. / White steed! Demand / That in the sky brocade should be spread out

[18] See 'Mapa i Pama imazhinizma', dated 'Berlin, 1922'. Published in the 'international review of modern art', *Veshch'. Objet. Gegenstand* (Berlin), March–April 1922, no. 1–2, pp. 10–11.

[19] The Imaginist *Deklaratsiya* had also appeared in the Voronezh journal *Sirena*, dated 30 January 1919. See, e.g. Sergey Esenin, *Sobranie sochinenii v pyati tomakh*, iv (M., 1967), 251–6 (and notes, ibid. 320–2).

before you. / Today you are free and unfettered: / Your rider has been thrown, / So throw off your bridle too. . . .'[20]

Although he did not share Shershenevich's extreme attitude to the role of the 'image' in poetry (a disagreement which became increasingly open in 1921–2), Kusikov felt a greater personal liking for Shershenevich than for any of the other Imaginists. While Esenin and Mariengof served in the bookshop, the *Artel' khudozhnikov slova* ('The Artel of Artists of the Word'), on Bol'shaya Nikitskaya, Shershenevich and Kusikov worked together in 1920–1 in the bookshop of the All-Russian Union of Poets, in Kamergersky pereuloii.

Shershenevich was a contributor to the anthology *My* ('We'), in which Kusikov published a cycle of seven poems dated between April and October 1919, and dedicated 'to the silver memory of my beloved brother Georgy, who died on 14 March 1919'.[21] This cycle is rich in images derived from the realm of nature. Occasionally, the imagery is explicitly exotic—the sky is the 'holy Koran', a cloud grazes, 'a sheep beloved of Allah'—but more often there is a general tenderness and warmth, which makes Kusikov closer to Esenin than to the urbanistic dissonances of Shershenevich and Mariengof. Personifications abound. The moon yawns and is also a shepherd who has thrown back his red hood, the clouds are like a blue herd of buffaloes, the day has palms and also departs on tiptoe, the breeze turns a somersault before falling silent. An underlying melancholy (*toska*) pervades the cycle. The poet expresses a longing to 'dissolve', and to find oblivion:

> Затеряться, забиться мне где бы,
> Как в плетне черепок кувшина.
> Я люблю предвечернее небо,
> Когда лапу сосет тишина.
>
> Я люблю, когда вымытой шерстью
> Уплывают в затон облака,
> Когда выронит ветер свой перстень
> И опустит туман рукава.
>
> Быть неслышным, никем незамеченным,
> На луну заронить свою тень . . .
> Если б мог я рябиновым вечером
> Черепком затаиться в плетень.[22]

---

[20] This is also poem 13 in Kusikov's volume *Sumerki*—but the anarchistic implications are more evident in the context of the journal.

[21] See the anthology *My* (M., 1920), published by 'Chikhi-Pikhi'. Kusikov's seven poems are ibid. 20–7. In 1974 Kusikov explained that his eldest brother, Georgy, went mad after being struck by rifle-butts and died in a lunatic asylum in 1919. Other contributors to *My* include Bal'mont, Vyacheslav Ivanov, Ivnev, Pasternak, Sergey Tret'yakov, Khlebnikov, and Shershenevich.

[22] Poem 4, in *My*: 'Where can I lose and conceal myself, / Like a broken jug in a fence? / I love the sky before evening, / When silence sucks its paw. // I love it when, like washed wool, / The clouds sail away into the backwater, / When the wind drops its ring, / And the mist

A *leitmotif* of Kusikov's life recurs: he feels alone and surrounded by strangers. The cycle ends: 'Melancholy on the fence like a horse's skull / Bares its teeth through the blue into the autumnal distance. . . . / Could I but return to my native village [*aul*], to the humped peaks. . . . / O my thought in an alien land—a winged steed.'

Kusikov's gloom contrasts with the title of the 1920 volume issued jointly by himself and Shershenevich: *Korobeiniki schast'ya* ('Pedlars of Happiness'). The title, in fact, derives from Shershenevich,[23] and originally the book was planned to include verse by a third poet, the Futurist Sergey Tret'yakov.

The volume opens with one of Kusikov's best-known works, *Koevangelieran*, written in 1918–20. The title is composed of the Koran cut in two by the Gospel ('Kogospelran')—a verbal indication of Kusikov's inner division. The poem begins: 'The Crescent and the Cross, / Two Prayers, / Two Hearts, / (Only to me / —given to nobody else) / In my soul of a Christian infidel / Are two Suns, / And but one in the sky. . . .'[24] In Section 6 menace appears—the obsolete world shall not avoid anguish: 'Until everyone flies beyond the boundaries, / Beyond the impossible on a winged horse, / There will be the dying of the centuries, / And al-Huṭma [Hell-fire] shall glow. . . .' The poem ends with Kusikov's characteristic assertion that he himself has 'penetrated invisibly into the nowhere . . .'.

His otherworldly and prophetic aspirations are continued in the following poem, *Al'-Barrak*, dated 14 April 1920. Al-Burāḵ is the name of the winged horse on which Mohammed visited paradise, and Kusikov himself claims: '. . . I have hastened on a winged horse / To the impossible, beyond the boundaries, into nowhere. . . . // In conscious delirium I carry / This world into another land. . . . // There is no God but God in the sky / And I am His Third Prophet. . . .'[25]

unrolls its sleeves. // To be inaudible, noticed by no one, / To cast my shadow on to the moon. . . . / If only one rowan-tree [red] evening / I could hide like a broken pot in the fence.' The present article reproduces the text from the volume *V Nikuda* (Berlin, 1922), 57, as the most satisfactory in punctuation and spelling.

[23] 'We are the last in our caste / And our life shall not be long! / We are pedlars of happiness, / Artisans of heartfelt lines! . . .' (Vadim Shershenevich, in *My* (n. 21), 62). Also in Shershenevich's book of verse, *Loshad' kak loshad'* (M., 1920).

[24] Section 1 of *Koevangelieran*—sub-titled 'Poema prichashcheniya' ('A Poem of Communion')—in the book *Korobeiniki schast'ya. Imazhinisty. Aleksandr Kusikov, Vadim Shershenevich* (Kiev (M.?), 1920).

[25] In *Al'-Barrak*, Kusikov unequivocally declared himself to be the 'Third Prophet'. In *Koevangelieran*—after the lines 'There has been the Nazareth Carpenter, / There has been the Cameleer'—he wrote: 'And then one Unskilled Labourer / Did not believe,—and howled with his hammer.' Some contemporary critics implied that Kusikov's 'two faiths' (Christian and Moslem) were here joined by a 'third', 'Communist', faith. On 2 April 1976 Kusikov himself interpreted the Nazareth Carpenter, the Cameleer, and the Unskilled Labourer as, respectively, Jesus Christ, Mohammed, and the Revolution.

In the remaining four short poems, Kusikov's eyes are drawn 'to beyond the clouds'. His poetry in *Korobeiniki schast'ya* contains many concise images, as befits a newly-fledged Imaginist, but his imagery continues to be warm, gentle, and derived from the world of nature, and closer to Esenin than to Mariengof or Shershenevich: 'Rainbow comb of my hopes, / Comb the grey hair of the clouds' (from *Koevangelieran*, Section 4); 'When the dawn places into the palms of the leaves / The red copecks of its bounty.'[26]

After Kusikov's contributions, *Korobeiniki schast'ya* is concluded by Shershenevich's *Pesnya pesnei* ('Song of Songs'), dedicated 'to Solomon— the first Imaginist'. The contrast with Kusikov's verse is considerable. Shershenevich devises machine-age and rather coarse images to describe parts of the woman's body. Furthermore, he endeavours to break up grammar by avoiding all finite verbs (only the infinitive form is occasionally employed).

Shershenevich was fully conscious of the gulf between his poetry and Kusikov's. On a copy of *Korobeiniki schast'ya* Shershenevich wrote the following inscription to the theatre director Alexander Tairov:

Милому Александру Яковлевичу —
В этом содружестве я отвечаю только за свои стихи.
Попытка безглагольной грамматики.
Театральный жест — не есть жест житейский.
Поэтическая грамматика — не есть грамматика разговорная.
С любовью
Вад. Шерш.[27]

Koevangelieran, Al'-Barrak, and three of the four shorter poems from *Korobeiniki schast'ya* are reprinted in Kusikov's next volume, entitled *Koevangelieran.*[28] They are flanked by ten new poems, ranging in length from four to twenty-four lines, and written between May 1919 and May 1920. Most of these new poems are dated December 1919.

The volume *Koevangelieran* finds Kusikov increasingly engaged in

---

[26] In the poem 'Tak nichego ne delaya, kak mnogo delal ya' (1919).

[27] Shershenevich's inscription to A. Ya. Tairov, inside the front cover of a copy of *Korobeiniki schast'ya* (TsGALI (Central State Archive of Literature and Art), Moscow, *fond* 2328, *opis'* 1, ed. *khran*. 1169): 'To dear Alexander Yakovlevich—In this collaboration I accept responsibility only for my own verse. An attempt at verbless grammar. Theatrical gesture is not the same as everyday gesture. Poetic grammar is not the same as conversational grammar. With love. Vad. Shersh.'

Kusikov for his part inscribed an unspecified book to Shershenevich: 'My living buffalo and your iron one will get along together in the same yard. After all, I shall drive my buffalo across all the pits and bumps in the literary field' (quoted in V. Shershenevich, *Komu ya zhmu ruku* (1921), 23).

[28] Alexander Kusikov, *Koevangelieran* (M., 1920), published by 'Pleyada'. Cover and drawings in the text by B. Erdman. Elsewhere, *Koevangelieran* is described as an 'Imazhinisty' edition—'Pleyada' seems rather like a variant of 'Imazhinisty' at this time.

self-examination, a kind of probing into his prophetic powers and intuition. The works of December 1919 are much concerned with his own knowledge or lack of knowledge—three of the first seven poems have lines ending in an incantatory refrain of either 'I know' or 'I don't know'. Yet Kusikov's underlying sorrow and melancholy remain, as well as his religious and cultural duality: 'On my breast is a cross, / At my thigh is a sword . . .'; 'All I want is to return to my native *aul*.'

Some favourite creatures recur in Kusikov's imagery. There is the exotic camel, whose ginger-red hair is echoed in the sun, sunset, or autumn (and whose hump is outlined in the mountains of Kusikov's native land); the dog (*pes*), which, like the poet, howls desolately at the absent moon; and there is the 'hour of the owl'. Most prominent of all is the horse (*kon'*), which undergoes many metamorphoses. Kusikov was born 'to the September neighing of a horse'; his thoughts are a herd of horses; the horse is central in *Al'-Barrak*; 'the horse of the storm flashes its hoofs'; a cloud is 'a white horse in a golden harness'.[29] The Imaginists in general took the horse as their emblem—but Kusikov, who had loved and ridden horses since childhood, had a special right to claim, as he did in his 1922 autobiography: 'My only and faithful friend is the horse. . . .'

The year 1920 saw the appearance of yet another book by Kusikov— *V Nikuda* ('Into Nowhere').[30] The volume is prefaced by an apt quotation from Tyutchev: 'O my prophetic soul! / O heart filled with alarm, / How you tremble on the threshold / As it were, of a twofold reality! . . .' *V Nikuda* represents a kind of poetic stock-taking—of its thirty-six works at least three-quarters are repeated from earlier publications.

The title of the first section, 'Asfal'tovyi kovrik' ('The Asphalt Prayer Rug'), highlights the contrast between the Moslem south and the northern city. A poem affectionately dedicated to Sergey Esenin— from a poet of the mountains to a poet of the plains—shows their common bond in rural sorrow.[31]

After the second section, 'Koevangelieran', which contains no new works, the third and final part, 'V Nikuda', begins with a short poem dedicated to Vadim Shershenevich. Kusikov seems to have adapted his imagery here to suit his dedicatee: in the opening lines the cloud weeps 'like a shaggy mongrel' (p. 55)—an image much 'lower' than elsewhere

---

[29] Subsequent horse-images include: 'The white horses of my hands / Meekly slumber in the [horse's] collar of prayer' (*Iskandar Name*, Section 3). In 1920 Kusikov entitled a poem 'Koni beznogie'—' . . . Legless horses sailed in the distance . . .' (in *V Nikuda* (Berlin, 1922), 55). In 1922 he wrote 'Koni vetvistye', where trees seen from a moving train are 'branched horses' speeding towards Russia.

[30] Alexander Kusikov, *V Nikuda. Vtoraya kniga strok* (M., 1920), published by 'Imazhinisty'. Portrait of Kusikov and cover by Georgy Yakulov. The whole volume is 'dedicated to the memory of my late brother Georgy Borisovich Kusikov' (see n. 21).

[31] Ibid. 24. Poem written in 1919.

in the volume, where a cloud is 'like Allah's satin slipper' (p. 37), 'a sheep beloved of Allah' (p. 58), or 'a white horse in a golden harness' (p. 61), and clouds are 'like a blue herd of buffaloes' (p. 27), 'a white forest' (p. 38), 'like washed wool' (p. 63), or 'a white flock of sheep' (p. 68). In another 'new' poem (p. 62) Kusikov again acknowledged: 'I shan't overcome the torment of my melancholy soul....' Significantly, the word *toska* occurs ten times in *V Nikuda*, and *grust'* ('sorrow') five times.

The volume *V Nikuda* bears the sub-title 'Vtoraya kniga strok' ('A Second Book of Verse'). During these extremely productive months— when in quick succession *Poema poem*, *Korobeiniki schast'ya* and *Koevangelieran* were issued—Kusikov had provisionally announced a 'first book of verse', *Al'-Barrak*, to precede *V Nikuda*. Yet no book entitled *Al'-Barrak* was published in 1920, and thus the 'second book of verse' appeared alone, without its predecessor. This was not the only occasion when projected books evidently failed to materialize—other instances include a second edition of *Zerkalo Allakha* (1918–19, also contemplated in 1921); a volume in collaboration with Esenin, to be entitled *Dvuryaditsa* (1919); and a 'book of quatrains', *Rubaiyat* (1920).[32]

Kusikov's books of 1919–20 contain few direct political references. His preoccupations at this time were personal, prophetic, and mystical, rather than political. Nevertheless, he was no 'counter-revolutionary'. In a poem of December 1919 he proclaimed: 'The Red Hurricane will pass through all the lands—I know.'[33]

Yet Kusikov's encounters with political authority were not untroubled. His 1922 autobiography, while stating that in 1919–20 he was commander of a small Soviet cavalry division, also hinted at spells of arrest and imprisonment: 'I used to sit in the "Poets' Café" and in the "Chekas" [offices or prisons of the secret police]. . . .' In January 1968 he maintained that, for reasons unknown, Sergey Esenin once spent thirty days in the 'Cheka', and he himself thirty-three days.[34] Shortly after his release, on this or another occasion, Kusikov inscribed a photograph of himself to his sister, Lyusi Kusikova, and her husband, Anton (Tosya) Trumm: 'To Tosya and Lyusi. On the first day after the liberation of the arrested commander. Yours, A. Kusikov. Moscow 1920.'[35]

[32] In *V Nikuda* (pp. 78–9), Kusikov's participation is also announced in two forthcoming Imaginist anthologies, *Imazhinisty* ('The Imaginists') and *Lapta zvezdy* ('The Ball-Game of the Star'). In fact, *Imazhinisty* appeared in 1921 without any contribution from Kusikov—while *Lapta zvezdy* was never issued, although it was advertised again in 1921 at the back of *Zvezdnyi byk*, with only Esenin and Mariengof as its proposed contributors.

[33] Last line of the poem 'Tosku zastyvshuyu beskrylykh gor — ya znayu', dated 19 December 1919. Published in *Koevangelieran* and *V Nikuda*.

[34] Kusikov agreed that this was perhaps the incident referred to in Esenin's letter to Ivanov-Razumnik on 4 December 1920—see, for example, S. Esenin, *Sobranie sochinenii* (n. 19), v, 89, 276. It seems unlikely that Esenin actually spent 'thirty days' under arrest.

[35] Photograph in Kusikov's personal collection.

In 1921 Kusikov and Esenin were joint authors of a slim volume, *Zvezdnyi byk* ('The Starry Ox'), which Esenin allegedly printed on the press in Trotsky's train.[36] The book opens with Esenin's *Pesn' o khlebe* ('Song about Grain'), funereal in its imagery of slaughter and suffering. Then comes Kusikov's contribution, *Al'-Kadr*, sub-titled 'Poema prozreniya' ('A Poem of Insight'), and dedicated 'to a fine Circassian —my father'. *Al'-Kadr* is dated 6–10 January 1921, and prefaced by some lines from the Koran. In a note at the end Kusikov explains the title: 'Al-Ḳadr means immutable decisions, the night of decisions. In this night—when the Koran was sent down to Mohammed via the angel Dzhabriel' (Gabriel), and which is reckoned to be the 23rd or 24th day of Ramadan—all the affairs of the universe are decided for the coming year.'

The title seems, however, to bear little direct relevance to the poem, except perhaps in its mood of wise meditation and nostalgic fairy-tale. *Al'-Kadr* begins with a spellbound scene. An aged tree-stump frowns and thinks; on the nearby fence is an aurochs skull containing truth . . .

1

У меня на Кубани есть любимый пень
С кольцами лет на сморщенной лысине.
Время-мох наклонило к нему плетень,
На плетне турий череп,
А в черепе истина.

Есть потеря у всех,
И у пня есть потеря.
Снится ль хруст ему в пальцах веток,
Иль как лист,
Каждый лист,
Умывал он в росе —
Вспоминает теперь безответно?..
Знает пень шепелявую радость в лесу.

Так в глубокую тайну корнями засев,
Молча, молча он думу супит.

2

Чвик-чивикнет рассвет на плетне воробьем,
Каркнет вечер на черепе вороном,
Пень и я,

[36] The title-page gives the details: Alexander Kusikov, Sergey Esenin, *Zvezdnyi byk*, 'Imazhinisty', 1921. (The front cover merely says: Esenin, Kusikov, 'Imazhinisty', 1921). Page 14 lists as 'ready' ('gotovo') a forthcoming book by Kusikov entitled *Al'-Kadr*, but no such book was issued. That *Zvezdnyi byk* was printed in Trotsky's train is claimed by V. Shershenevich, in *Esenin: Zhizn', lichnost', tvorchestvo* (M., 1926), 56.

Мы вдвоем,
Будто думу одну затая,
Ловим каждой звезды оторванность . . .[37]

Kusikov too is acquainted with loss; missing him, his horse neighs
alone. Without rancour he alludes in Section 3 to 'trenchant October'
(*khlestkii oktyabr'*), and affectionately addresses, first his horse, and then
the tree-stump. Characteristically, the poem is almost devoid of references to other human beings. 'Old friend, / My tree-stump, / Bench
of my childhood, / It is you, / It is you who nursed me, / On your
lopped-off shoulders. / Nurturing my delirium, / I learnt silence from
you, / But my silence is not like yours, / But different' (Section 4). The
fifth and final section, which provides the title-phrase for the whole
volume, is warm and nostalgic: '. . . I loved this golden rain, / Whistling
with two fingers in my mouth, and the sob of the owl . . . // The starry
ox butted the cradle of my thoughts / As it lulled me to sleep by
night. . . .'

Al'-Kadr is a work of considerable mastery—rich in rhyme and
rhythm, harmoniously unified in its central images, and with a purity
and monumental simplicity of tone. By comparison—for all their
distinctiveness—*Koevangelieran* and *Al'-Barrak* seem rather remote, and
Koevangelieran is also somewhat diffuse.

From 1 to 15 March 1921 Kusikov wrote his next long poem,
Dzhul'fikar. A note at the end explains the typically exotic title: 'Dhu'l-
Faḳar is one of the nine wonderful swords of Mohammed, on the blade
of which there were two divergent lines.'[38]

More than any of his previous long poems, *Dzhul'fikar* is a reaction to
external pressures, to the situation in Russia at large. The opening
stanzas (Sections 1–6) introduce several motifs: the 'piercing' of first
love, the sob of a wounded hare, addresses to the motherland (*rodina*),

[37] 'I have in the Kuban' a favourite tree-stump / With rings of the years on its wrinkled
bald patch. / The moss of time has tilted the wattle fence towards it, / On the fence is an
aurochs skull, / And in the skull there is truth. // Everyone meets bereavement, / And the
tree-stump is bereaved. / Does it dream of the cracking in the fingers of its branches, / Or
remember now unrequited / How a leaf, / Every leaf, / It bathed in the dew? . . . / The tree-
stump knows a lisping gladness in the forest. // So sinking its roots deep in mystery, / Silently,
silently it frowns and thinks. // Chirrup-chirp goes the dawn like a sparrow on the fence, /
The evening croaks like a raven on the skull, / The tree-stump and I, / The two of us together, /
As if cherishing one thought, / Grasp the isolation of every star. . . .' Cf. Kusikov's childhood
recollections in his 1922 autobiography (n. 1): '. . . And in the evening, when I was alone,
I sat on a tree-stump . . . and looked up at the sky. . . .' L'vov-Rogachevsky interpreted the
tree-stump with its losses as an image of the 'old world' (*Imazhinizm i ego obrazonostsy. Esenin,
Kusikov, Mariengof, Shershenevich* (1921), 62).

[38] See the slim book of the same name: Alexander Kusikov, *Dzhul'fikar. Neizbezhnaya poema*
(M., 1921), published by 'Imazhinisty'. The poem is undated in this edition; the date is provided in Kusikov's book, *Al'-Barrak. Poemy* (Berlin, 1922), 28.

allusions to fear and to various weapons (gun, dagger, knife), a degree
of self-hyperbolization. These seemingly disparate elements gradually
crystallize into an opposition of pity and cruelty. Kusikov wants 'the
moon to kiss the dawn', and the earth to abandon its intoxicated drink-
ing of blood. His preference for harmony and peace is demonstrated in
Section 7, with its ingenious dactylic rhymes and its crescendo of gentle
lyricism:

О, знал я как тандыкает
Перед дождем гигикалка,
И белой песней никнет как
В лесу черешня дикая.

Я знал как терен красными
Царапается пальцами,
И как подсолнух заспанный
На солнце просыпается...

Все разгадал, все выслушал,
Весь мир познал в навозе я,
Намокший облак высушил
На камышовом озере...[39]

In Section 8, the longest of the poem, Kusikov's tone becomes increasingly agitated. 'Melon-field and mountains, / How can I forget
you? / O, I went away in order to return anew.' His fist clenches as he
anxiously tries to reassure himself, and to preserve and reinforce his
link with his native region: 'Not return, / No, / I have not departed, /
O no, no, / O, I am not in a foreign land . . . / My old tree-stump, /
My cow-shed, / My melon-field and mountains . . . .' A note of doom
enters, and the 'bullets' of his thoughts whistle. After mentioning grief
(grust'), Section 8 ends: 'I have a motherland—the Kuban', / I have
too a fatherland—upturned Rus'.'

In Section 9 he alludes to someone 'writhing, burdened by fear', and
calls out in warning: 'Comrades, the world is collapsing, collapsing,[40] /
Look around you, arise, it is time!' 'But there is no reply . . . / I hear
only myself. . . .' Dzhul'fikar ends with a quatrain close to, but not quite
identical with, its opening lines. In the course of the poem, the images
have become poignantly meaningful: 'O, no one can ever forget / The
piercing of first love. / I heard the weeping of the wounded hare, / In
which the pale-blue evening trembled.'

[39] 'O, I understood how before the rain / The gigikalka [bird that announces the rain]
chimes and hoots, / And how the wild cherry in the wood / Fades away like a white song. //
I understood how the thorn scratches / With its red fingers, / And how the sleepy sunflower /
Wakes up in the sunlight. . . . // I unriddled everything, I sounded everything, / I perceived
the whole world in a piece of dung, / I dried out a drenched cloud / By a reedy lake. . . .'
[40] The Russian here is: 'Tovarishchi, rushitsya, rushitsya.' In 1974 Kusikov interpreted
this as signifying 'mir rushitsya' ('the world is collapsing').

Dzhul'fikar is an impressive work, with many of the features now characteristic of Kusikov's longer poems. It is lyrically intense, and inventive in image, rhythm, and rhyme. Perhaps its sub-title—'Neizbezhnaya poema' ('An Unavoidable Poem')—implies that this was Kusikov's 'inevitable' reaction to the surrounding violence and bloodshed. It possibly also indicates his conviction that the poem is historically necessary and enduring.[41]

The title of Kusikov's next long poem, *Iskandar Name*, literally means 'Alexander Book', 'A Book about Alexander'.[42] It was written between 2 August and 2 September 1921, and published in a large-format 'Imazhinisty' edition, with a portrait of the poet and several full-page illustrations, all in colour, by the artist Vera Alexandrova.[43]

Iskandar Name has several points of interest. One is the unaccustomed vulgarity of the opening line, which flaunts the word *svoloch'* ('swine', 'scum'): 'People say of me that I'm a *svoloch'*, / That I'm a cunning and malicious Circassian, / That there is the meekness of an eagle and a wolf / In my bashed face and sharp profile. . . .' Kusikov evidently relished the first line for a while, until its growing notoriety made him regret that it had ever been written.[44]

The poem contains topical allusions. Kusikov sees blood everywhere—in a tree, a beetroot, the rain (Section 5). Section 6 impressionistically evokes the Revolution and Civil War—horses, gunfire, the double-headed Imperial eagle. The poet repeats in bewilderment: 'What is it? / Where am I? / What is it?' The sense of loss, so prominent in *Al'-Kadr*, recurs in Section 9: 'I'd like to sit down / Again on the bald tree-stump . . . / . . . Whose voice is not distorted in losses? / Who does not feel the fear of death?' The poem ends with Kusikov on the Arbat in Moscow, sensing the creaking of a bullock-cart—'Moscow, Moscow, / You are like Mecca to me, Moscow, / And your Kremlin is the black sweetness of the Kaaba.'[45]

Iskandar Name leaves an indistinct impression. True, it incorporates

[41] In 1921 N. Ya. Abramovich (op. cit. (n. 51), 19) named *Al'-Kadr* and *Dzhul'fikar* as Kusikov's 'best two works' to date. In 1974 Kusikov agreed with this judgement.

[42] Kusikov's own explanation in 1974. He stated also that the stress is on the last syllable in both words: 'Iskandár Namé'. The poem is sub-titled 'Poema menya'—'Poem (of) Me'.

[43] Alexander Kusikov, *Iskandar Name* (M., 1921-2), published by 'Imazhinisty'. There are two editions, both dated '1921-22' on their title-page—although at the back of both editions the date '1921' is given for the first appearance of *Iskandar Name*. The IDC microfiche copy of the first edition has the handwritten date '24 December 1921' on its title-page, which suggests that the book was printed by that time.

[44] The opening line rebounded on Kusikov—people began to quote it to denigrate his entire work (see, for example, Il'ya Erenburg, *Lyudi, gody, zhizn'*, iii–iv (M., 1963), 39).

[45] This closing tribute to Moscow is perhaps somewhat deflated by the words chosen for the inverted rhymes—*kvasom* ('rye-beer') is shown as an anagram of *Moskva* ('Moscow'), and *byka* ('ox') is paired with *Kaaby*.

many features typical of Kusikov's work—the eagle and the owl, the horse and the aurochs, the prayer rug and the tree-stump—and it includes lines of tender lyricism: 'No, you don't know how the owly twilight / Rocks the dawn to sleep with its speckled feather'; 'And I remembered how the creak of my wicket-gate / Aroused the night slumber of the wild roses'; 'O, if only you knew how sweet it is to halloo / Favourite words in the cavern of one's thoughts . . . .'[46] Yet too often the images seem esoterically Imaginistic, disconnected, and obscured by exclusive personal associations. Kusikov's inner loneliness can tend towards egoism, and this can keep the reader at a distance. Furthermore, *Iskandar Name* appears unduly artificial in its construction, with the natural flow of images too often subordinate to the demands of the rhymes. In Section 2, for instance, all the rhymes are palindromic (*bol'* / *lob*, *rog* / *gor*, *berech'* / *cherep*) or with the rhyming syllables inverted (*ko-soi* / *soi-ku*). Many other examples of palindromic or inverted rhymes are found throughout the poem, bearing witness to Kusikov's virtuosity rather than his spontaneity.

Iskandar Name remains, nonetheless, a significant work. At the end of Section 9 Kusikov suddenly pleads: 'O, motherland, forgive my treachery, / Forgive me, motherland, this treachery.' In 1974 he interpreted the nature of this 'treason'—that he was about to leave both the Caucasus, and Russia in general.[47] A list of Kusikov's publications at the back of both editions of *Iskandar Name* indicates that his forthcoming book *Al'-Barrak* was already being printed in Berlin.[48]

3

During his productive years (1920–1), Kusikov had attracted a considerable amount of largely favourable critical attention. Thus I. Aksenov in 1920 noted his essential 'discord' and '*toska*', his 'unprecedented words about the horse', and the 'feeling for the East' which is his 'forte', and declared: 'We are entitled to expect from him much further work and greater achievements.'[49] Another critic remarked upon the lyrical nature of Kusikov's poems, and their power of imagery:

---

[46] Bal'mont singled out these last two lines ('O, esli b znali vy, kak sladostno aukat' / V peshchere dum lyubimye slova') as 'captivating', when writing to Kusikov on 27 February 1922 (see n. 74).

[47] In the context of the poem, however, this 'treachery' could consist in his abandonment of his 'motherland' (the Kuban') when he moved to Moscow. That is how V. Sh. understood these lines, in *Nakanune* (Berlin), 9 August 1922, no. 102, p. 6.

[48] At the back of *Dzhul'fikar*, earlier in 1921, an edition of *Al'-Barrak* was said to be 'in preparation' by 'Imazhinisty', Moscow. The switch of place and publisher evidently occurred in the second half of 1921.

[49] I. Aksenov, reviewing Kusikov's 1920 books, *Poema poem*, *Koevangelieran*, and *V Nikuda*, in *Khudozhestvennoe slovo*, 1920, no. 2, pp. 63–4.

'The author's talent is beyond doubt. . . . It would appear that this poet has by no means said his last word, and it is possible that he is destined to be one of the first harbingers of the new poetic classics of the future.'[50]

Kusikov received high praise from N. Ya. Abramovich, a critic sympathetic to the 'mystical' and 'prophetic' notes in his verse, his 'child-like wisdom', and his 'desert soul of a bedouin-poet-dreamer'. Abramovich concluded with a prediction: 'Kusikov will smash the witchcraft and black magic of Imaginism, and emerge free and independent into the open oceanic space in his truly brilliant "I". . . .'[51]

In 1921 Valery Bryusov named Kusikov as one of the 'most interesting young poets in Moscow',[52] and in the following year again mentioned Kusikov, this time in connection with Imaginism. Bryusov felt cool towards Shershenevich and Mariengof, but much warmer towards Esenin. He continued: 'Of the other Imaginists one may note A. Kusikov . . ., also [like Esenin] weakly linked with the school and interesting when he speaks of his native Caucasus. . . .'[53]

Kusikov was usually discussed at this time in the context of Imaginism. Many critics were hostile to the Imaginist school or movement, and some merely identified Kusikov with what they regarded as its general excesses.[54] More often, however, he was amnestied alongside Esenin, and these two were then urged to break away from the reviled Mariengof and Shershenevich. This is the underlying theme of L'vov-Rogachevsky's book, *Imazhinizm i ego obrazonostsy. Esenin, Kusikov, Mariengof, Shershenevich* ('Imaginism and its Image-bearers. Esenin, Kusikov, Mariengof, Shershenevich').[55] A similar approach was taken by other critics,[56] although in everyday life Esenin continued to

[50] (Kii), reviewing *Poema poem, Koevangelieran*, and *V Nikuda*, in *Kniga i revolyutsiya*, 1921, no. 8–9, February–March, pp. 82–3.

[51] N. Ya. Abramovich, *Sovremennaya lirika. Klyuev, Kusikov, Ivnev, Shershenevich* ('Segodnya', 1921), 24. The section on Kusikov is on pp. 15–24. See n. 41.

[52] In *Pechat' i revolyutsiya*, 1921, no. 3, November–December, p. 270. Bryusov named as the 'most interesting young poets in Moscow' V. Mayakovsky, B. Pasternak, K. Bol'shakov, S. Esenin, A. Kusikov, and Adalis.

[53] 'Vchera, segodnya i zavtra russkoi poezii', in *Pechat' i revolyutsiya*, 1922, no. 7, September–October, p. 59.

[54] See, for example, A. Gornfel'd's onslaught on the work of the Futurists, Imaginists, Vorticists 'and so on', when reviewing L'vov-Rogachevsky's *Imazhinizm i ego obrazonostsy* (n. 37), in *Letopis' Doma literatorov*, 1921, no. 2, 15 November, p. 7. Another Petrograd journal, reporting Kusikov's recital of 13 January 1922 at the *Dom literatorov*, remarked: 'Of Kusikov as a poet one can say only one thing: he . . . is an Imaginist like all Imaginists . . .' (Unsigned report, 'Aleksandr Kusikov i Boris Pil'nyak v Dome literatorov', in *Vestnik literatury*, 1922, no. 2–3 (38–9), pp. 36–7).

[55] L'vov-Rogachevsky's 68-page book (see nn. 37 and 54) was published under the imprint 'Ordnas' in 1921. 'Ordnas' is 'Sandro'—the nickname of Kusikov—spelt backwards. Kusikov is mentioned on pp. 7, 10–12, 16–17, 30, 46, 55, 57–64, 67.

[56] See, for example, A. Evgen'ev, 'Perly i adamanty imazhinizma', in *Vestnik literatury*, 1921, no. 10 (34), pp. 6–7, and no. 11 (35), p. 7; Il'ya Gruzdev, in *Kniga i revolyutsiya*, 1922, no. 8 (20), p. 41; also ibid. 1923, no. 3 (27), pp. 36–7.

befriend Mariengof and was evidently unwilling to be 'married off'
to Kusikov.[57]

Kusikov's relationship with his Imaginist colleagues was now coming to a head. In 1920–1 many theoretical and critical booklets were
published by the Imaginists and their supporters. Kusikov figured
prominently in two booklets by Sergey Grigor'ev,[58] and was mentioned
by Ivan Gruzinov[59] and Ippolit Sokolov.[60]

In 1921 Ryurik Ivnev aimed four revealing 'shots' at his Imaginist
friends, Esenin, Kusikov, Mariengof, and Shershenevich. His second
'shot' was directed at Kusikov, whom Ivnev regarded as 'the most
striking and typical representative of our transitional era', an era of
'incredible contradictions'. Ivnev refused to believe that Kusikov could
be meek:

I see your face quite differently: stonily warlike, with sharp steely eyes in
which oriental cunning is blended with fiery tenacity. . . . I am struck,
amazed, in part entranced, in part outraged by this crying contradiction
between what you are and what you write. When you say: 'On my breast is
a cross, At my thigh is a sword', then I feel the sword, very keenly, but not
the cross. . . .[61]

Differences of opinion on theoretical matters increasingly divided
the Imaginists. As early as 1920, in his booklet $2 \times 2 = 5$, Shershenevich had insisted that 'the combining of individual images into a poem
is mechanical work, and not organic, as Esenin and Kusikov suppose.
A poem is not an organism, but a multitude of images. . . .'[62]

In 1921 Shershenevich 'shook hands' with his Imaginist colleagues
Mariengof, Kusikov, Ivnev, and Esenin, by means of four open letters.
The second letter was addressed: 'To the cow-shed—near the old tree-
stump. To Alexander Borisovich Kusikov.' After noting that Bal'mont,
Vyacheslav Ivanov, and Bryusov were all enchanted by Kusikov's
'Orient', Shershenevich maintained that Kusikov was in fact 'overcoming nationality' and evolving 'towards the supranational'. Shershenevich approved of this, since 'love for one's motherland is poor
sentimentality'. '. . . In the orchestra of Russian Imaginism, where
Esenin plays the trumpet part, Anatoly [Mariengof] the cello, I (but
why the devil should I talk about myself!), Ryurik Ivnev the triangle,

[57] See Ivan Rozanov, *Esenin o sebe i drugikh* (M., 1926), 4; also in the volume *Pamyati
Esenina* (M., 1926), 39.
[58] See Sergey Grigor'ev, *Proroki i predtechi poslednego zaveta. Imazhinisty. Esenin, Kusikov,
Mariengof* ('SAAV', 1921), 6, 12–13, 23–39, 44–6; also *Obraz Konenkova* (M., 'SAAV', 1921).
[59] Ivan Gruzinov, *Imazhinizma osnovnoe* (M., 'Imazhinisty', 1921), 6, 8, 9, 10, 18, 19.
[60] Ippolit Sokolov, *Imazhinistika* ('Ordnas', 1921), 8, 9, 12, 14.
[61] Ryurik Ivnev, *Chetyre vystrela v Esenina, Kusikova, Mariengofa, Shershenevicha* ('Imazhinisty',
1921). Kusikov is mentioned on pp. 5, 8, 12–17.
[62] Vadim Shershenevich, $2 \times 2 = 5$. *Listy imazhinista* (M., 'Imazhinisty', 1920), 15. Dated
February 1920.

you have taken upon yourself the profession of violin. . . . Esenin's images are always more powerful than yours, Mariengof's images are always more exact and profound, but you possess that lyrical quality in which we are all deficient. . . .'[63]

In May 1921 Esenin published an article dissociating himself in part from his Imaginist 'brothers',[64] and in 1921–2 it was announced that Alexander Kusikov was preparing a book of theoretical articles, *Imazhinizm* ('Imaginism').[65]

Although this 'theory' was never issued, Kusikov did make a declaration of principle on 13 January 1922, at a recital in the Petrograd *Dom literatorov*. He told the meeting that the four main Imaginists had split into two directions in their attitude to the image—the 'right wing' (Kusikov and Esenin), and the 'left wing' (Shershenevich and Mariengof). The 'right wing', said Kusikov, regarded the image as a means, whereas the 'left wing' saw the image as an end in itself and were not interested in content. A contemporary journal report claimed—perhaps somewhat ironically—that this statement was of 'historico-literary importance'[66]—and yet Kusikov seems mainly to have confirmed the differences mentioned two years earlier by Shershenevich in $2 \times 2 = 5$.

Nevertheless, the turning-point was near. The latest Imaginist projects involving Kusikov were never to be realized—the poem *Alif-Lyam-Mim*, advertised as if already published; an 'Imazhinisty' edition, stated to be in preparation, of his first book, *Zerkalo Allakha*; at least one collective Imaginist volume in which he was to participate.[67]

Kusikov did contribute one poem to the Imaginist anthology, *Konskii sad. Vsya banda* ('The Horse Garden. All the Band'), published in early 1922. The poem, dated July 1921, is a manifestation of spiritual

[63] Vadim Shershenevich, *Komu ya zhmu ruku* (also entitled: *Shershenevich zhmet ruku komu*) ('Imazhinisty', 1921). The open letter to Kusikov is on pp. 19–28; he is also mentioned on p. 32. See also A. Marchenko, *Poeticheskii mir Esenina* (M., 1972), 196.

[64] See 'Byt i iskusstvo', in e.g. S. Esenin, *Sobranie sochinenii* (n. 19), iv, 202–8, 299–303. See also my *Esenin. A Life* (Ann Arbor and London, 1976), 153–4, 305. Despite these disagreements, in June 1921 Kusikov and Esenin were among the Imaginists who signed the call for a 'general mobilization' in defence of the 'new art'—see *Esenin. A Life*, 157–9.

[65] In *Dzhul'fikar*, only the title and description are given: '*Imazhinizm* — teoriya imazhinizma' ('*Imaginism*—a theory of Imaginism'). In *Iskandar Name*, and in *Al'-Barrak* (1922), the work is also said to be 'in preparation'. In Ivnev's *Chetyre vystrela* . . . (n. 61), p. 30, Kusikov's book is described as '*Imazhinizm. Stat'i*' ('Imaginism. Articles'). According to *Novaya russkaya kniga* (Berlin), 1922, no. 2, p. 38, Kusikov had 'ready a work about Imaginism'. No such book appeared.   [66] See *Vestnik literatury* (n. 54), 36–7.

[67] On p. 31 of Ivnev's *Chetyre vystrela* . . . (n. 61) the volumes listed include '*Stoilo Pegasa*. R. Ivnev, A. Kusikov, V. Shershenevich', and '*I v khvost i v grivu*. With the participation of all the Imaginists'. Both titles have characteristically equine connotations. Neither volume was published, although perhaps *I v khvost i v grivu* became *Konskii sad* (see n. 68). Shershenevich later entitled one of his articles 'V khvost i v grivu', in *Gostinitsa dlya puteshestvuyushchikh v prekrasnom*, no. 1 (3), 1924. The book-review section in *Gostinitsa* . . . was usually entitled '[I] v khvost i v grivu'.

anxiety. Millions of hens seem to be cackling in his ears, and Kusikov declares: 'I only know that soon on the bonfire of my thoughts / I shall burn to ashes both the Koran and the Gospel. / That is why I am afraid, so terribly afraid. . . .'[68]

Kusikov had reached the parting of the ways. Many years later, when asked about his 'meetings' with his fellow-Imaginists, Sergey Esenin, Anatoly Mariengof, and Vadim Shershenevich, he replied: 'I did not have "meetings" with my Imaginist friends—Serezha, Tolya, and Vadim—but a huge segment of literary life with its tragedies and joys, with its delights and disappointments, and with its fatal and final break. *In 1922.*'[69]

Shershenevich had sensed in him the 'inclinations of an adventurer'.[70] Ivnev had predicted that Kusikov's horse would break loose from the *Stoilo Pegasa* (Pegasus Stall—the name of the Imaginists' café-tavern) and whisk him away from Moscow to the cliffs of his romantic motherland: '. . . Or perhaps, in a sudden change of direction, it will take you off into your cosmic, universal "NOWHERE".' Ivnev raised his paper revolver and fired an imaginary bullet at Kusikov: 'But you are already far away. Understand then, rider, that you were saved by your faithful al-Burāk.'[71]

Ivnev's words proved remarkably prophetic. Al-Burāk, it seems, had flown to Berlin ahead of Kusikov.

4

Kusikov's book entitled *Al'-Barrak*, described in late 1921 as being printed in Berlin, was duly published there by about January 1922.[72] It is devoted exclusively to the five long poems which had first appeared in Russia in 1920–1, here arranged in the sequence: *Al'-Barrak, Ko-evangelieran, Al'-Kadr, Dzhul'fikar, Iskandar Name.* These poems, grouped together, vividly convey Kusikov's idiosyncratic talent.

In February 1922 Alexander Kusikov himself arrived in Berlin, where he took up residence in Martin-Lutherstrasse.[73] Konstantin

---

[68] From Kusikov's poem 'Kvochki', in *Konskii sad. Vsya banda* (M., 1922), published by 'Imazhinisty'. The contributors to the anthology were Gruzinov, Esenin, Ivnev, Kusikov, Mariengof, Roizman, Shershenevich, and Erdman.

Kusikov also wrote a foreword, dated Moscow, 1921, to a book of love poems by the Estonian poet Henrik Visnapuu. See pp. 7–11 of Genrik Visnapu, *Amores. Pervaya kniga stikhov,* tr. from the Estonian by Igor' Severyanin (M., 1922).

[69] Letter from A. Kusikov to the present writer, Paris, 11 December [1967].

[70] *Komu ya zhmu ruku* (n. 63), 28.   [71] *Chetyre vystrela . . .* (n. 61), 17.

[72] Alexander Kusikov, *Al'-Barrak. Poemy* (Berlin, 1922), published by 'Skify'. Opposite the Russian title-page is a title-page in German: Alexander Kussikoff, *All-Barrack. Poemen.* See also n. 48. I. E. [Il'ya Erenburg] reviewed both *Iskandar Name* and *Al'-Barrak,* in *Novaya russkaya kniga* (Berlin), January 1922, no. 1, p. 24.

[73] Kusikov's Soviet passport, authorizing his visit to Germany, was issued in Moscow on 5 December 1921, and was at first valid for six months. The passport (from his personal collection) has Tallinn (Estonia) stamps of 20 and 31 January, and 3 February 1922, and various visas for Latvia, Lithuania, and Poland dated February 1922.

Bal'mont, who had left Russia in June 1920, was overjoyed to hear of his arrival: 'Dearest Sandro, but this is fabulous, just what I wanted most! . . . You should realize that I care more for you than for anyone else. Yours, Bal'mont. . . .'[74]

On 2 April Kusikov wrote his brief autobiography. He clearly did not regard himself as an '*émigré*', and planned to return soon to Russia:

> . . . Now I am only a poet, revolutionary, and Alexander Kusikov. I despise anything connected with the White Guards,—I'm not a member of the R.K.P. [Russian Communist Party].
> . . . At present I'm in Berlin, but I'll soon go back. I'm fed up here—and I want to return to Russia. People perish there, but I can't shed crocodile tears from a thousand miles away. The *émigrés* haven't managed to teach me that. . . .
> What do I love most of all?
> Upturned Rus', my mother and my poetry—my father is another matter, he is God to me, and I don't talk about God. I love the epoch because of myself, and myself because of the epoch. . . .[75]

While Kusikov in Berlin was describing 'The Mapa and Pama of Imaginism',[76] he himself was remembered by the Imaginists in Moscow. In a conciliatory letter on 27 March—evidently in reply to some friendly words from Kusikov—Mariengof admitted that previously he had felt hostility and even malice towards him. Mariengof was depressed by the disunity in the Imaginist ranks: 'Things are sad in Moscow. Everyone goes his own way. We're not a band, but a discord. . . .' Mariengof urged Kusikov to return: '. . . You know, people have already started talking about us in the past tense. . . .'[77]

There were many reasons for the growing disintegration of Imaginism. In 1974 Kusikov claimed a central role, maintaining that the group virtually collapsed when he left Russia in 1922. Yet Kusikov was not the only Imaginist who ventured abroad in that year. Mariengof had written on 27 March: 'Sergey is planning to go to Berlin. . . .' Esenin married Isadora Duncan on 2 May and arrived with her in Berlin on 11 May. He had drafted some instructions to Kusikov: 'Sandro! . . . Announce in the newspapers in both languages our forthcoming recital. Esenin.'[78]

[74] Postcard from K. Bal'mont to Kusikov, dated '27 February 1922, morning'. Bal'mont gives as his address St-Brévin-les-Pins, L. Inf. [Loire-Inférieure], villa Ferdinand [Brittany]. In Kusikov's personal collection, which also contains letters from Bal'mont dated 6 March, 15 April, and 17 May 1922.

[75] From Kusikov's autobiography (n. 1).

[76] Quoted earlier (see n. 18).

[77] Letter from A. Mariengof to Kusikov, dated [Moscow], 27 March 1922. In Kusikov's personal collection.

[78] Draft, probably of a telegram, published e.g. in S. Esenin, *Sobranie sochinenii* (n. 19), v, 104, 285.

According to Kusikov's 1974 recollections, the relationship between himself and Esenin had been decidedly cool. This may be so, but it did not prevent the two Russian Imaginists from immediately making common cause in Berlin. They had both been 'guests' or outsiders in Moscow, and now felt even more disorientated when abroad. Their behaviour in Berlin tended to be provocative and seemed born of desperation.

In memoirs of this period Kusikov cuts an unsympathetic figure. Maxim Gor'ky saw him with Esenin and Isadora at Aleksey Tolstoy's flat: 'Alongside Esenin, Kusikov—a very impudent young man— seemed out of place. He was armed with a guitar, the favourite instrument of barbers, but he evidently didn't know how to play it. . . .'[79] Alexey Tolstoy's wife recalled: 'The poet Kusikov came later, a coarse man wearing a Circassian coat, and with a guitar. Nobody had invited him, but in Berlin he followed Esenin everywhere, like a shadow. . . .'[80] Il'ya Erenburg writes dismissively: 'Esenin spent several months in Berlin, languishing and of course brawling. He was invariably accompanied by the Imaginist Kusikov, who played the guitar and declaimed: "People say about me that I'm a *svoloch'*, that I'm a cunning and malicious Circassian". They drank and sang. . . .'[81]

While Esenin and Isadora set off on their travels across Europe, Kusikov, it seems, remained in Berlin. He contributed poems to Russian-language periodicals, above all to the newspaper *Nakanune*. Moreover, he had plans for further volumes of his verse. His autobiography of 2 April 1922 had already stated: 'I am preparing *Kniga izbrannykh stikhov* ("A Book of Selected Verse") for the publishing-house "Skify" ("The Scythians"), and *To, chego net v Korane* ("What is not in the Koran")[82]—new poems—for the publishing-house "Gelikon" ("Helicon"). . . .'

The first project was realized by August 1922 with the publication of *Ptitsa bezymyannaya* ('The Nameless Bird'). The sub-title 'Izbrannye stikhi 1917–1921' ('Selected Verse 1917–1921') indicates the volume's retrospective nature.[83] Only one poem falls outside this time-scheme—

---

[79] M. Gor'ky, *Sobranie sochinenii v tridtsati tomakh*, xvii (M., 1952), 60. From the sketch 'Sergey Esenin', first published in 1927.

[80] N. V. Tolstaya-Krandievskaya, in *Vospominaniya o Sergee Esenine* (M., 1965), 328.

[81] Il'ya Erenburg, *Lyudi, gody, zhizn'* (n. 44), 39—Erenburg slightly misquotes two lines from *Iskandar Name*.

[82] No book of that name was issued. The words come from the fifth stanza of the poem 'Sizyi venik': 'Wasn't it I who cast the lassos / Of my hopes onto the sullen sleep of the mountain peaks, / In order to experience what is not in the Koran, / And what is born in the roar of machines?' (quoted from A. Kusikov, *Ptitsa bezymyannaya* (Berlin, 1922), 53). The journal *Russkaya kniga* (Berlin), July–August 1921, no. 7–8, p. 25, had already reported that Kusikov was preparing a book of 'revelations' entitled *Chego net v Korane*.

[83] Alexander Kusikov, *Ptitsa bezymyannaya. Izbrannye stikhi 1917–1921* (Berlin, 1922), published by 'Skify'. Opposite the Russian title-page is a title-page in German: Alexander

the initial title-poem, dated 'Berlin, 17 June 1922'. Surveying his past
work had proved a disturbing experience for the uprooted poet. 'Today
I turn over the pages / Lived through long ago and now so distant. //
It's as if a nameless grey bird / Had flown out of the mist / And fallen
near / Me. // . . . My verse, you are no longer the same, / Yet I myself
don't know why. . . .' Only some six other poems are 'new'—that is,
not found in previous volumes containing his verse. For the most part
they express a spiritual intensity which at times may border on mental
unbalance. In the evocation of how blind eyes 'see', one senses that
Kusikov, too, possesses 'these eyes of a blind man / Gazing restlessly
into nowhere'.[84] A poet's fate is depicted as one of torment and
insomnia.

In Berlin in 1922 Kusikov wrote a poem which, half a century later,
he still treasured as one of his very best works. It occupied first place in
a new—1922—edition of *V Nikuda* ('Into Nowhere').[85] The twenty-
five-year-old poet, September-born and in autumnal mood, hesitated
to 'indict' the revolution:

О, нет, то не сентябрьский лес редеет,
Не гуси к лету оголяют грудь.
Лысею я, и взор мой холодеет,
И рифме хочется закованно вздохнуть.

Где ты расседланная юность на Кубани,
Где годы чрезвычайные в Москве?
Так пропадают коршуны в тумане,
Так прометётся ветерок в траве.

Все так давно и так еще недавно,
Прошли недели, месяцы, года,
И я быть может навсегда бесславный
С одной уздечкой сгину в никуда.

Порой мне кажется, что сердце молодеет,
Порой мне кажется, что стынет в жилах кровь.
Но то не лес сентябрьский редеет —
Лысею я, и взор мой холодеет.
А где-то бьется первая любовь.

Kussikoff, *Der ungenannte Vogel. Gedichte.* The front cover was designed by El Lissitzky (as
p. 62 reveals).

[84] From the poem 'Glaza slepye', dated 1920, ibid. 46.

[85] Alexander Kusikov, *V Nikuda* (Berlin, 1922), published by 'Epokha'. The whole book is
'dedicated to the memory of my late brother Georgy Borisovich Kusikov' (see nn. 21 and 30).

Осенняя весна. Да разве так бывает?
Мне дятел выстукал вот только двадцать пять.
Кто виноват в моей весне — я знаю,
Но никого не буду обвинять.

Нет больше не могу я мерными стихами:

О, революция,
Тебя ли обвинять
Смиренной ковкой рифм в отчаяньи?
О, революция,
(Она теперь растерзанно стихает)
Тебя ли обвинять?
Ведь сам я ждал кровавую усладу,
Тебя ли, революция?
Тебя? . . .

А разве ветер с ветром не встречается?

Я так устал от самого себя,
Я так устал от песен неразгаданных.[86]

Spiritual and perhaps also creative exhaustion had become increasingly characteristic of Kusikov. The 1922 *V Nikuda* contains little else that is 'new'—only five four-line poems, and one of eight lines, all dating from 1920. The final poem of the 1920 books *Koevangelieran* and *V Nikuda* recurs here in penultimate position, still threatening an abrupt cessation of his literary activity: '. . . On some heap of ruins / I shall renounce everything. // I shall stop loving my small volume / Of songs. . . .'[87]

[86] The opening poem in *V Nikuda* (n. 85), pp. 9–10, dated '1922, Berlin' (ibid. 77). In *V Nikuda*, the first word in line 8 is *Kak*, which seems mistaken. In 1974 Kusikov recited this first word as *Tak*—and indeed it is printed as *Tak* in his book *Ryabka* (Berlin, 1923), 45. Accordingly, line 8 has been corrected above.
'O, no, it's not the September forest thinning, / Nor geese that bare their breast to [greet] the summer. / I am growing bald, and now my gaze is chilling, / And in their chains my rhymes wish to draw breath. // Where are you, my unsaddled youth in the Kuban', / Where are the extraordinary years in Moscow? / So kites vanish in the mist, / So the breeze sweeps by in the grass. // Everything is so distant and still so recent, / The weeks, months, and years have passed, / And I perhaps for evermore inglorious / Shall be lost in the nowhere with only a bridle. // At times I think my heart is growing younger, / At times I think my blood freezes in my veins. / But it is not the September forest thinning— / I am growing bald, and now my gaze is chilling. / And somewhere first love quivers. // Autumn in spring. Do such things ever happen? / The woodpecker has tapped out only twenty-five of my years. / I know who is to blame for my springtime, / But I shall not indict anyone. // No, I can't continue in regular metre: [*Up to this point, the poem is in five-foot or six-foot iambic lines*] // O, revolution, / Am I to indict you / In the meek forging of rhymes in despair? / O, revolution, / (Which now subsides, tormented) / Am I to indict you? / For I too awaited the sanguinary delight, / [Am I to indict] you, revolution? / You? . . . // Does not the wind encounter the wind? // I am so tired of myself, / I am so tired of undiscovered songs.'
[87] From the poem 'Kakie-to smutnye dali', dated 9 May 1920 in the 1920 books *Koevangelieran* and *V Nikuda*. The poem was also included in *Ptitsa bezymyannaya* (1922), 47; *V Nikuda* (1922), 71–2; and *Ryabka* (1923), 7–8.

Several women at this time were fascinated by the poet. During 1922 Asya Turgeneva (Andrey Bely's first wife) sent many candid letters from Dornach, Switzerland to Kusikov in Berlin. Half a century later, Kusikov linked with Asya a quatrain he prized:

Про не воспетую, про нашу, про любовь...
(Ах не придумать новых слов любовью...
Неволю стих... но вот сочится кровь
И обливается четверостишие кровью...)[88]

On 26 September 1922 a woman called Aniko warned him: 'You will ruin your talent and your life by drink. . . . Sandro, can't you understand that you are on the edge of a huge yawning abyss from which there is no return. . . .'[89]

In February 1923 Sergey Esenin completed his ill-fated, four-month tour of America. On 7 February, in the 'Atlantic Ocean', he wrote a revealing letter to Kusikov, expressing disillusionment with both America and the October Revolution.[90] Later in February Esenin revisited Berlin, where Kusikov continued to live at No. 8 Martin-Lutherstrasse. The two poets often appeared together in March 1923. Roman Gul' recalls evenings spent at Kusikov's: 'There people drank and sang, Kusikov—gipsy songs to a guitar accompaniment, Esenin—*chastushki* to a balalaika. . . .'[91]

It is evidently Kusikov's guitar that features in one of Esenin's most desperate tavern-poems of this time: 'Sing then, sing. On the accursed guitar / Your fingers dance in a semi-circle. / I'd like to choke in this intoxication, / My last and only friend. . . .'[92] Indeed, Esenin dedicated 'to A. Kusikov' the section of poems entitled 'Moskva kabatskaya' ('Moscow of the Taverns'), in his 1923 Berlin volume *Stikhi skandalista* ('A Brawler's Poems'). By August 1923 Esenin was back in Russia, for ever.

The year 1923 saw the publication of an impressive volume by Kusikov, entitled *Ryabka* ('The Partridge'). Although many of its works are not 'new', they are well chosen, showing Kusikov's oriental imagery

---

[88] Manuscript in Kusikov's personal collection. 'About the unsung, our, love . . . / (Oh, one can't devise new words for love . . . / I force my verse . . . yet now the blood trickles / And the quatrain is covered in blood . . .).'

[89] Letter from Aniko to Kusikov (in his personal collection), 26 September [1922]. Aniko had first met Kusikov in Moscow, apparently in late 1921.

[90] Letter from Esenin to Kusikov, 7 February 1923. Published in *The Slavonic and East European Review*, xlvi (1968), 479–80, reprinted in *Le Contrat social*, xii (Paris, 1968), 249–51, and by Roman Gul' (Goul) in *Novyi zhurnal*, xcv (New York, 1969), 227–30.

[91] Roman Gul', *Zhizn' na fuksa* (M.-L., 1927), 224; see also ibid. 220–1.

[92] The first four lines of Esenin's 'Poi zhe, poi. Na proklyatoi gitare'. In the first publication of this poem, line 13 mentioned Kusikov by name: 'Sing, Sandro! . . .'—see Sergey Esenin, *Stikhi skandalista* (Berlin, 1923), 56.

and mystical wisdom in full maturity. Eight of the poems had not appeared previously in any of his volumes.[93] The most outstanding is 'Kogda vishnya v tsvetu' ('When the cherry-tree is in bloom'). Its first lines are haunting:

> Никогда так не чувствуешь смерть,
> Как весной, когда вишня в цвету.
> Никогда так не хочется верить,
> Как под страх, когда чуешь беду.[94]

Kusikov is acutely conscious of hanging, and bayonets, and blood. The poem ends: 'Everywhere one seems to see death and death, / Only death when the cherry-tree is in bloom. / But I so want to believe, / Even if gropingly, even if in delirium.'

There is a certain 'circular' quality to *Ryabka*. It begins with the poem found at the end of earlier books, threatening: 'On some heap of ruins / I shall renounce everything . . .'[95]—and ends with the opening title-poem of *Ptitsa bezymyannaya*, expressing puzzled estrangement from his past verse.[96]

Kusikov published another volume in 1923—a second, expanded, edition of *Al'-Barrak*, here sub-titled 'Oktyabr'skie poemy' ('October Poems'). This edition incorporated, in the same order, all five works of the 1922 *Al'-Barrak* (*Al'-Barrak*, *Koevangelieran*, *Al'-Kadr*, *Dzhul'-fikar*, *Iskandar Name*)—followed by two 'new' poems, dated 'Berlin, 1922': *Pesochnye chasy* and *Vasil'kovyi marsh*. This volume of longer works was completed by the 36–line 'Okhlyab'', which is also found in *Ryabka*.[97]

Pesochnye chasy ('The Sand-glass') is sub-titled 'Poema trekh nochei' ('A Poem of Three Nights'). It is a confessional poem, showing intoxication (emotional and, apparently, literal). To the refrain of 'the hours flow—the amber juice dwindles', Kusikov passes three nights in anguished recollection. His initial mood mirrors his spiritual and creative exhaustion—as the first night ends, sobriety returns and his

---

[93] See Alexander Kusikov, *Ryabka* (Berlin, 1923), published by I. T. Blagov. The 'new' poems are on pp. 39–44, 48–58, although some of these had already been published in *Nakanune*.

[94] *Ryabka* (n. 93), 54. 'One is never so aware of death / As in spring when the cherry-tree is in bloom. / One is never so in need of faith / As when frightened and sensing doom.' The poem was first published in *Nakanune*, 27 August 1922. *Novaya russkaya kniga* (Berlin), August 1922, no. 8, p. 36, reported that Kusikov had 'sold to the Moscow Gosizdat [State Publishers] a book of verse written in Berlin, *Kogda vishnya v tsvetu*'. No such book was issued.

[95] *Ryabka* (n. 93), 7–8; see also n. 87.

[96] *Ryabka* (n. 93), 59–60; as in *Ptitsa bezymyannaya* (n. 83), 7–8.

[97] See Alexander Kusikov, *Al'-Barrak. Oktyabr'skie poemy* (Berlin–Moscow, 1923), 2 enlarged ed., published by 'Nakanune'.

verse fades, disconsolate. The next night sees him intoxicated once more, and haunted by memories. His recent Imaginist colleagues— Esenin, Mariengof, Shershenevich—are mentioned first, only to be promptly dismissed: 'What do I care about Serezha, Tolya, and Vadim / (The love of friends is concealed treason)!' More lingering are his thoughts of childhood: 'I want to go home as soon as possible, / Back to the smile of Chech' and to the wrinkles of my nanny.' He recalls the twenty years he spent in the Kuban': 'But my past life lives in my poems / Down to the root of the tree-stump, and the bald patch of the tree-stump, / Down to my first joy and my first sorrow. . . .' Towards the end of the second night, Kusikov declares: 'I know I have not long to live.' The third night opens with references to recent history: 'The shadow of my brothers fell upon October. . . . // One went mad, the other was killed in battle— / Two Red Decorations remain as souvenirs. . . .'[98] Yet Kusikov, who is acquainted with delirium and loss, also knows that 'everything grows calm, and everything subsides . . .': 'And the Revolution, tired, licks its paw.' The poem culminates in his poignant desire to live simply and to be like other people — to join, as it were, the 'collective', the mainstream of mankind.

Pesochnye chasy—though somewhat diffuse—is a powerful and moving work, which held a special place in Kusikov's affection. In January 1968 he called it his 'credo', and in 1974 described it as his 'very best and most mature long poem'. He derived satisfaction from the fact that, in late 1924, it was handsomely printed in a French translation.[99]

The next poem in the 1923 *Al'-Barrak*—*Vasil'kovyi marsh*—seems to be prompted by polemic with Mayakovsky, whom Kusikov met in Berlin in October–November 1922. Its terse epigraph states: 'Mayakovsky—it's time you sensed the epoch.' So Kusikov, declaring 'In October my heart began to sing like a bird', offers this 'Cornflower [-blue] march', sub-titled 'Poema pobednogo zatish'ya' ('A Poem of Triumphal Calm')—evidently as an alternative to Mayakovsky's strident, full-throated *Nash marsh* ('Our march', 1917) and *Levyi marsh* ('Left march', 1918). Instead of the tramp of feet, ringing voices, drums, and loud exhortations, Kusikov sings a 'new march with a hidden rhythm'. The poem ends: 'Quietly, quietly—our rhythm is secret — / The hoar-frost has not yet melted from the roofs. // There are millions of us, / Our / March / Is stillness.'

Vasil'kovyi marsh is an unusually optimistic poem, reflecting, it seems, not only the lull after the revolutionary storm, but also a temporary

98 'One went mad'—Georgy (n. 21); 'the other was killed in battle'— Nikolay, at the battle by the Borisoglebsk tower (*Ryabka* (n. 93), 42).

99 Alexandre Koussikoff, *Le Sablier. Poème en trois nuits* ([Paris], 'Au Sans Pareil'). Translation by Y. Sidersky, drawings by V. Barthe. 500 copies, printing completed on 20 November 1924.

calm in Kusikov's troubled emotional life. As at the end of *Pesochnye chasy*, he appears to be trying to re-establish his common link with humanity, after being so alone and self-absorbed.

In late 1923 and early 1924 Kusikov published several pieces in the newspaper *Nakanune*. For Bryusov's fiftieth birthday he wrote an affectionate verse tribute to his 'old friend', the 'stern, strict master' in a tightly buttoned frock-coat, and also a lively prose memoir acknowledging Bryusov's mastery, poetic form and literary judgment.[100] A few days later saw the publication of the long poem *Moskva* ('Moscow'), a rambling work which again reveals Kusikov's 'split personality' and his mixed attitude to Russia and the Revolution.[101]

Kusikov's hypersensitivity and his alienation (from himself as well as from others) seem to have led him to recurrent insomnia and the point of breakdown. His poem *Bessonnitsa* ('Insomnia'), published on 13 January 1924, is a frightening pathological document. He is aware of someone very like him, who writes with his hand and yet not with his hand, who with him listens to the silence—'But it is not myself!— It is someone else, a chance stranger!' The poem ends: 'Can I really have dried up my own soul? / It's terrifying, terrifying for me to contemplate this.'[102]

Although Kusikov hoped that *Moskva* and other works would be accepted for publication in far-off Moscow, Vera Alexandrova informed him that the journal *Krasnaya nov'* had rejected the poem (and others), ostensibly because of the poet's split personality, but really because of the hostility of 'Klychkov and Co.'. V. Pravdukhin, the editor of *Krasnaya niva*, had also felt unable to publish the poems, because of their 'decadent' mood, near-mysticism, and 'abstract [revolutionary] enthusiasm'. Vera Alexandrova candidly asked Kusikov: '. . . Who knows you in Russia, who is aware of your entire creative evolution? Here people remember (if anybody does remember you) Kusikov of the cross and crescent, Kusikov's small-scale lyrical revelations, but who has had the chance of seeing your full stature as shown in your recent works? . . .'[103]

By late 1923 Kusikov, restless and evidently homesick, resolved to

---

[100] See the poem 'Valery Bryusov', in *Nakanune*, no. 507 (16 December 1923), 3, and the prose memoir 'Dve vstrechi s Valeriem Bryusovym', ibid. 6–7. See also G. Nivat, 'Trois correspondants d'Aleksandr Kusikov', in *Cahiers du monde russe et soviétique*, xv (1974), 201–19 (two letters from Bryusov to Kusikov, two letters from S. Budantsev, three letters from Shershenevich, also an article by the latter—all in Kusikov's personal collection).

[101] See *Moskva*—described as 'Otryvok iz poemy'—in *Nakanune*, no. 514 (late December 1923), 1–3. In the copy in Kusikov's personal collection the claim that the rest of the poem would appear in a subsequent number of *Nakanune* has been crossed out.

[102] *Nakanune*, no. 11 (528) (13 January 1924), 1.

[103] Letter to Kusikov, dated Moscow, 8 April 1924 (in Kusikov's personal collection). *Moskva*—'otryvok iz poemy'—eventually appeared in *Nedra* (Moscow), 1925, no. 7, pp. 73–80.

visit Russia the following spring. His Imaginist colleague Vadim
Shershenevich was delighted at the prospect: 'Three months isn't long
to wait after two years. . . . The day you come to Moscow and we sit
over a bottle of wine will be one of the happiest days for me. . . .'[104]
Bryusov, however, advised otherwise: 'Why do you want to come to
Moscow? You have a job to do, and a serious one, in Berlin. . . . In
Moscow at present you're unlikely to find a more worthwhile task. . . .'[105]

Presumably the projected visit to Russia fell through.[106] Soon Kusikov abandoned Berlin too, for by March 1924 he moved to France and
took up permanent residence in Paris.

In Paris, at 10 p.m. on 21 October 1924, he began to keep a kind of
diary, for the first time since his childhood. Earlier that day he had
bought the exercise book in a trance, to begin this 'confession of an
October poet'. '. . . My soul is fading away, my heart is slowing down,
and there is such black loneliness, such terrible loneliness. I'd never
previously contemplated suicide, but of late this thought never leaves
me. The day before yesterday I nearly brought myself to it, yet . . .
I am very afraid. . . .'[107] The next day he noted: '. . . In the course of
this year I've not written a single poem, and at present I'm in absolutely
no condition to write. . . . Death is terrifying, but living has become
even more terrifying for me. . . .'[108]

Mariengof and his wife Anna Nikritina met Kusikov in Paris in 1924
(and also in 1927). Kusikov included a damning indictment of Mariengof in his 'confession' of 21 October 1924.[109]

In 1925 Kusikov overcame his silence of 1924 and wrote several
poems. In the most memorable of these he imagines the future scholar
who will discern his 'Asiatic profile' and 'frowning brows'. The poem
begins and ends with the meditation:

> Когда умрут мои и недруги и други,
> И современники мои когда умрут,
> Чья беспристрастная рука перелистает на досуге
> Всей моей жизни полупраздный труд?[110]

104 Letter from Shershenevich, Moscow, 4 January 1924 (in Kusikov's personal collection).
Shershenevich sent Kusikov a copy of the Imaginist journal *Gostinitsa dlya puteshestvuyushchikh
v prekrasnom* (M., 1924), no. 1 (3), with the inscription: 'To the dear good-for-nothing Sandro
from his constant friend. Vad. Shersh. 21/II 24. (*Milomu shalopayu Sandro ot vsegdashnego druga.
Vad. Shersh. 21/II 24.*)'—in Kusikov's personal collection.

105 Letter from Bryusov, Moscow, 3 February 1924.

106 Although he remained outside Russia, Kusikov continued to renew his Soviet passport
until June 1929.

107 See the notebook, 'Posleoktyabr'skaya letopis' poeta. Kniga 1-aya' ('The Post-October
Chronicle of a Poet. Book 1'), in Kusikov's personal collection.   108 Ibid.

109 Kusikov wrote: '. . . My attitude to Mariengof is one of friendly indifference. At one
time I was even ready to feel genuine affection for him. But he is empty, uninspired, without
intrinsic culture . . .; a would-be "aesthete" shop-assistant from some fancy-goods store. . . .'
(as n. 107).

110 'When my enemies and my friends all die, / And when my contemporaries die, / Whose
dispassionate hand shall turn over at leisure / The near-idle labour of my entire life?' A

In 1974 Kusikov named this as his favourite short poem; a French translation was published in 1925.[111]

There are a few other manuscripts and typescripts of poems dated 1925, and Kusikov continued to hope that his verse might be published by Moscow journals. Yet it seems that his artistic inspiration had dried up; his poetic career was virtually at an end. He did not, however, imitate his colleague Sergey Esenin, who on 28 December 1925 found the solution to life's problems in suicide. Kusikov was shocked by Esenin's action, and noted: 'I've never met a person who loved life as much as Esenin did. And I've never seen anyone who feared death so much. . . .'[112]

5

Kusikov's activities and whereabouts after 1925 remain to a considerable extent shrouded in obscurity. The present writer first met the poet in Paris on 6–8 January 1968, and then spent several days at his house in Touraine in the second half of August 1968. On 2 August Kusikov had remarked of his country house and garden: 'Everything is overgrown with weeds and neglected, yet in all this there is a kind of sadness, a kind of reflection of my tragedy of recent years. . . . Lyrical disorder and bohemian romanticism—a millionaire with no money.'[113]

Kusikov's last years were clouded by ill health and disappointment. I met him again in Paris, 24–7 September 1974. On 27 September he observed: 'All my life I've been alone, always alone. . . . That's the way I'm made. . . .' He named as his favourite poet Pushkin, followed by Tyutchev and Blok; he expressed a great liking for Pasternak's verse, and respect for Mandel'shtam and Akhmatova, and said: 'I don't recognize any of the Imaginists. . . .'

I visited Kusikov for the last time on 1–3 April 1976, near Paris. It was evident that this complex, difficult, proud, egoistic, mistrustful, sensitive, lonely man had not long to live. On 1 April 1976 he broke down when reciting 'O, net, to ne sentyabr'skii les redeet'.[114] After saying the words 'Ya tak ustal . . .' ('I am so tired . . .') in the penultimate line, he was unable to finish the poem.

typescript with Kusikov's pencilled corrections (in his personal collection) is dated Paris, 23 March 1925.

[111] Alexandre Koussikoff, 'Lorsque vous serez morts, ennemis ou amis . . .', tr. Maurice, in *La Tour de Babel* (Paris), November 1925, no. 1, pp. 46–7. Here the poem is dated 'Paris, 1924'.

[112] From Kusikov's notebook (n. 107), which contains the rough draft of his article '"Tol'ko raz ved' zhivem my, tol'ko raz . . ." Pamyati Esenina', published in *Parizhskii vestnik*, 1926, no. 207.

[113] Letter from Kusikov to the present writer, Paris, 2 August 1968.

[114] See n. 86.

Alexander Borisovich Kusikov died at 2 a.m. on Monday, 20 June 1977, and was buried on 22 June near Paris. He was a genuine (if somewhat esoteric) poet whose best works—*Al'-Kadr*, *Dzhul'fikar*, 'O, net, to ne sentyabr'skii les redeet', and others—are of abiding literary and historical value.

Sixteenth-century Croatian Glagolitic Books in the Bodleian Library

By ROBERT AUTY

In recent years increasing interest has been shown by scholars in the books printed in the glagolitic character at Venice, Senj, Rijeka (Fiume), and elsewhere in the fifteenth and sixteenth centuries. All these books are very rare, and many of the extant copies are more or less seriously defective as a result of long use or careless treatment. It is therefore a matter of importance for the further investigation of these works that the whereabouts and condition of all surviving copies should be established. The listings of them in existing bibliographies are incomplete: in particular, they fail to record many of the copies held by libraries in the United Kingdom. The purpose of the present article is to rectify this situation as far as the sixteenth-century holdings of the Bodleian Library, Oxford, are concerned.[1]

Four books printed in the glagolitic character in the sixteenth century are held by the Bodleian. We briefly characterize them below in chronological order of their publication.[2]

1. [INTRODUCTORIUM CROATICE]. Venice (Andreas Torresanus), 1527. ff. 6. 4°. Badalić 29, Kruming 8, Schmitz 37 (with the wrong date). Pages reproduced in Breyer (plate VII) and Schmitz (plate IV). This small book (also referred to as *Bukvar*, *Psaltir*, or *Azbukvidarium Croaticum*) is a spelling primer incorporating some essential prayers and psalms. It was described by Petar Kolendić in 1934;[3] and in the same year J. D. A. Barnicot published a brief article

---

[1] I should like to express thanks, for help, advice, and information given me in connection with the present article, to Professor R. Filipović, Mr. R. J. Roberts, and Mr. J. S. G. Simmons. I am also particularly indebted to Dr. Anica Nazor for making available to me the as yet unpublished text of her lecture 'Glagoljsko tiskarstvo na području Hrvatske' delivered at Varna in 1975.

[2] The following bibliographical works are referred to by their authors' surnames: I. Kukuljević Sakcinski, *Bibliografija hrvatska. Dio prvi* (= *Bibliografija jugoslavenska*, i) (Zagreb, 1860); M. Breyer, *O starim i rijetkim jugoslavenskim knjigama. Bibliografsko-bibliofilski prikaz* (Zagreb, 1952); T. Blažeković, *Fluminensia croatica. Bibliografija knjiga, časopisa i novina izdanih na hrvatskom ili srpskom jeziku na Rijeci* (Zagreb, 1953); J. Badalić, *Jugoslavica usque ad MDC. Bibliographie der südslawischen Frühdrucke*, 2 ed. (Baden-Baden, 1966; 1 ed. 1959); A. A. Kruming, 'Slavyanskie staropechatnye knigi glagolicheskogo shrifta v bibliotekakh SSSR', *Problemy rukopisnoi i pechatnoi knigi*, ed. A. A. Sidorov *et al.* (M., 1976); W. Schmitz, *Südslawischer Buchdruck in Venedig (16.–18. Jahrhundert). Untersuchungen und Bibliographie.* (Marburger Abhandlungen zur Geschichte und Kultur Osteuropas, 15) (Giessen, 1977).

[3] P. Kolendić, 'Najstariji naš bukvar', *Južni pregled*, ix (Skopje, 1934), 198–201.

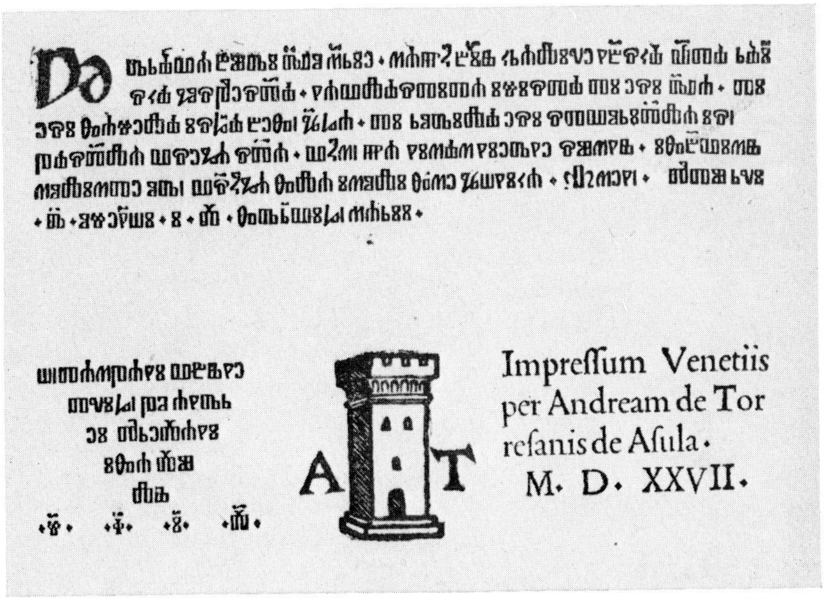
Impreſſum Venetiis
per Andream de Tor
reſanis de Aſula.
M. D. XXVII.
A T

I. Colophon (f. 6v) of *Introductorium croatice* (actual size).
Reproduced by permission of the Bodleian Library

II. Colophon (f. 248ᵛ) of Bishop Kožičić's Missal (actual size).
Reproduced by permission of the Bodleian Library

about it.[4] As a result of these publications the Oxford copy does figure in the second edition of Badalić and in some recent articles. Four copies of the *Introductorium* are known to exist, in the following places: (1) Vienna, Österreichische Nationalbibliothek; (2) Leningrad, Saltykov-Shchedrin State Public Library; (3) New York, Pierpont Morgan Library; (4) Oxford, Bodleian Library (4° C 51 Th. Seld.). In addition, Kolendić stated in 1934 that the bookseller Karl Hiersemann of Leipzig had offered a copy for sale in the previous year; it is not clear where that copy now is.

The Bodleian copy is the third item in a volume containing seven other short works of Anglo-Saxon, Aramaic, Greek, and Hebrew interest. The latest of these is dated 1610, and they are all recorded in the Bodleian printed catalogue of 1620. This catalogue does not, however, mention the *Introductorium*—though, in view of its placing in the early seventeenth-century limp vellum binding of the volume, it must have been present (if not comprehended). It is first recorded in the 1674 catalogue, where its designation as *Aliquot preces lingua serviana* continued to mislead bibliographers and to father a number of bibliographical ghosts until Mr. Barnicot set matters straight in the article referred to above. The *Introductorium* must be distinguished from another *Bukvar/Psaltir* printed by Bishop Šimun Kožičić in 1530 or 1531, as was conclusively shown by Anica Nazor in 1964.[5] Copies of both works are held by the Saltykov-Shchedrin Library in Leningrad.

2. MISALI PO ZAKON' RIMSKOGA DVORA . . . Venice (Francesco Bindoni and Maffeo Pasini), 1528. ff. viii, 224. 4°. Kukuljević 40, Badalić 34, Kruming 9, Schmitz 38. Title-page reproduced by Breyer (plate VI). This book, the third printed edition of the glagolitic Missal, was produced by the Franciscan, Pavao Modruški. Eight copies are known to exist: (1–2) two copies in the Nacionalna i sveučilišna knjižnica, Zagreb; (3–4) two copies in the Saltykov-Shchedrin State Public Library, Leningrad; (5) in the Gor'ky State Library, Odessa; (6) in the Österreichische Nationalbibliothek, Vienna; (7) in the British Library (Reference Division), London; (8) in the Bodleian Library, Oxford (Slav. 3. 45). In addition J. Vajs stated that three copies were held by Bohemian libraries, one each in Prague University Library, the Czech National Museum in Prague, and the monastery of Teplá.[6] Breyer also mentioned a copy offered for sale by the Munich bookseller Jacques Rosenthal, but the fate of this is unknown. The

[4] J. D. A. B[arnicot], 'Introductorium Croatice, 1527', *Bodleian Quarterly Record*, vii (1932–4), 464–6.

[5] A. Nazor, 'Kožičićev Bukvar', *Slovo*, xiv (1964), 121–8.

[6] J. Vajs, *Najstariji hrvatskoglagoļski misal* (Djela Jugoslavenske akademije znanosti i umjetnosti, 38) (Zagreb, 1948), 167.

Bodleian copy lacks the title-page and f. 182.[7] Many pages have been repaired and the leaves have been cropped at the head. Three leaves bound in before the beginning of the text contain manuscript notes in glagolitic, as do fifteen others bound in at the end after the colophon. The verso of the first front flyleaf bears the bookplate of Frederick North, fifth Earl of Guilford (1766–1827).[8] It is not known when and where Guilford acquired this book. We know that he learned Church Slavonic, that he travelled widely in the Adriatic area, that he was a secret convert to the Orthodox Church, and that he bought Slavonic books. These were destined to go, after his death, to the University of the Ionian Islands in Corfu, which had been founded by Guilford and of which he was the first Rector. In fact, however, they were sold, and it seems probable that this copy was bought by H. W. Chandler (1828–89), Waynflete Professor of Moral and Metaphysical Philosophy at Oxford, whose name appears on the inside cover above Guilford's bookplate. Chandler, described in the *Dictionary of National Biography*[9] as 'an enthusiastic bibliophile', was a Curator of the Bodleian. His library went after his death to Pembroke College, and so we may perhaps assume that the Bodleian acquired the glagolitic missal from him during his lifetime.

3. MISAL HRVACKI PO RIMSKI OBIČAI I ČIN . . . Rijeka (Fiume), 1531. ff. viii, 248. 4°. Kukuljević 41, Blažeković 2, Badalić 38, Kruming 11. Title-page reproduced by Breyer (plate IX) and Blažeković (plate III). This is one of the six books which Šimun Kožičić (Begna), Bishop of Modruš, had printed on his press in Rijeka in 1530 and 1531.[10] It is a missal in Croatian Church Slavonic. E. Hercigonja,[11] following A. Nazor,[12] stated that six copies of this work are extant. These must, however, be supplemented by the copies in Soviet libraries, identified by Kruming, by a copy in the Vatican Library, and by two copies in the United Kingdom. The locations of the known copies are therefore as follows: (1) Zagreb, Nacionalna i sveučilišna knjižnica; (2) Ljubljana, Narodna in univerzitetna knjižnica; (3) Dubrovnik, Narodna biblioteka; (4) Punat (on the island of Krk); (5) Wrocław; (6–7) two copies in the Saltykov-Shchedrin State Public Library, Leningrad; (8) Odessa, Gor'ky State Library; (9) Rome, Vatican

---

[7] Between ff. 178 and 179 there is a stub with fragments of unidentifiable text which is probably all that remains of the missing f. 182.

[8] For an account of his life and, in particular, of his concern with Slavonic languages, see M. Partridge, 'An English Eccentric and some Slavs and Slavists', *Wiener Slavistisches Jahrbuch*, xxi (1975), 202–13; also K. Ware, 'The Fifth Earl of Guilford (1766–1827) and his Secret Conversion to the Orthodox Church', *Studies in Church History*, xiii (1976), 247–56.

[9] xxii (1909), 410–11.

[10] For an account of Bishop Kožičić and his press, see P. Kolendić, 'Zadranin Šimun Kožičić i njegova štamparija na Reci', *Južni pregled*, ix (1934), 61–71, and Nazor, op. cit. (n. 5).

[11] E. Hercigonja, *Srednjovjekovna književnost (Povijest hrvatske književnosti)* (Zagreb, 1975), 426–7.   [12] In the Varna lecture (n. 1).

Library;[13] (10) London, British Library (Reference Division); (11) Oxford, Bodleian Library (4° Th. BS L 12). Of the eleven copies listed above nos. 1, 2, 3, 6, and 7 are stated to be defective. The condition of nos. 4, 5, and 8 is not stated in the works that list them. The Vatican copy and the two British copies are complete and in good condition. The provenance of the Bodleian copy is not known. The binding is of the mid nineteenth century, and the press-mark is one that was used up to that period. It is therefore possible that Bishop Kožičić's missal, like the Venetian one, came to the Bodleian in the last century. It would seem from its excellent condition that this copy had seen little use; and this makes it probable that it was removed from Croatia early in its existence.

4. [BREVIARIUM CROATICE]. Venice (Joannes Franciscus Torresanus), 1561. ff. viii, 494, 31. 8°. Kukuljević 54, Badalić 76, Kruming 16, Schmitz 71. This is the new edition, made by Nikola Brozić, parish priest of Omišalj, of the Croatian Church Slavonic breviary of Baromić (Venice 1494). The locations of known copies are: (1) Zagreb, Library of the Jugoslavenska akademija znanosti i umjetnosti; (2) Košljun, Franciscan monastery library; (3) Leningrad, Saltykov-Shchedrin State Public Library; (4–5) two copies in the Vatican Library, Rome;[14] (6) London, British Library (Reference Division); (7) Oxford, Bodleian Library (8° A 27 Th. BS). Another copy was offered for sale by Messrs. Ellis of 29 New Bond Street, London, as no. 749 of their catalogue no. 262 (undated but probably c. 1928), which contains an illustration of f. 1; nothing is known of the present whereabouts of this copy. The Bodleian copy is recorded in the second edition of Badalić. It is in an early seventeenth-century English binding, and the present press-mark has superseded an earlier one (Arch. B 56) which is thought to date from the same period. There is no further evidence as to its provenance.

[13] This copy is mentioned by Vajs, loc. cit. The present press-mark is Riserva V 89, which has replaced that given by Vajs.
[14] It seems unlikely that either of these copies (whose press-marks are Stamp Barb C I 34 and Aldine A III 238) was among the three described by K. Horvat in 'Glagolitica Vaticana. Nekoliko prinosa glagolskim spomenicima, što se čuvaju u Rimu', *Starine Jugoslavenske akademije znanosti i umjetnosti*, xxxiii (1911), 529–31. The question of the Vatican copies of Brozić's breviary requires further investigation.